T0336903

Privacy, Intrusion Detection, and Response:

Technologies for Protecting Networks

Peyman Kabiri
Iran University of Science and Technology, Iran

Managing Director:	Lindsay Johnston
Senior Editorial Director:	Heather Probst
Book Production Manager:	Sean Woznicki
Development Manager:	Joel Gamon
Development Editor:	Michael Killian
Acquisitions Editor:	Erika Gallagher
Typesetters:	Mackenzie Snader
Print Coordinator:	Jamie Snavely
Cover Design:	Nick Newcomer

Published in the United States of America by
    Information Science Reference (an imprint of IGI Global)
    701 E. Chocolate Avenue
    Hershey PA 17033
    Tel: 717-533-8845
    Fax: 717-533-8661
    E-mail: cust@igi-global.com
    Web site: http://www.igi-global.com

Copyright © 2012 by IGI Global. All rights reserved. No part of this publication may be reproduced, stored or distributed in any form or by any means, electronic or mechanical, including photocopying, without written permission from the publisher.
Product or company names used in this set are for identification purposes only. Inclusion of the names of the products or companies does not indicate a claim of ownership by IGI Global of the trademark or registered trademark.

Library of Congress Cataloging-in-Publication Data
Privacy, intrusion detection, and response: technologies for protecting networks / Peyman Kabiri, editor.
    p. cm.
  Includes bibliographical references and index.
  Summary: " This book discusses the latest trends and developments in network security and privacy, and serves as a vital reference for researchers, academics, and practitioners working in the field of privacy, intrusion detection, and response"--Provided by publisher.
  ISBN 978-1-60960-836-1 (hardcover) -- ISBN 978-1-60960-837-8 (ebook) -- ISBN 978-1-60960-838-5 (print & perpetual access) 1. Computer networks--Security measures. I. Kabiri, Peyman, 1968-
  TK5105.59.P757 2012
  005.8--dc23
                   2011019909
British Cataloguing in Publication Data
A Cataloguing in Publication record for this book is available from the British Library.

All work contributed to this book is new, previously-unpublished material. The views expressed in this book are those of the authors, but not necessarily of the publisher.

List of Reviewers

Ahmad Akbari, *Iran University of Science and Technology, Iran*
Hassan Asgharian, *Iran University of Science and Technology, Iran*
Mohammad Abdollahi Azgomi, *Iran University of Science and Technology, Iran*
Sebastián García, *UNICEN University, Argentine*
Ali A. Ghorbani, *University of New Brunswick, Canada*
Peyman Kabiri, *Iran University of Science and Technology, Iran*
Mohsen Moshki, *Iran University of Science and Technology, Iran*
Bijan Raahemi, *Iran University of Science and Technology, Iran*
Govindaraju Radhamani, *Al Musanna College of Technology, Sultanate of Oman*
Ciza Thomas, *College of Engineering, India*
Pablo Velarde-Alvarado, *Autonomous University of Nayarit, Mexico*
Ji Zhang, *University of Southern Queensland, Australia*

Table of Contents

Section 1

*Ulf E. Larson, Chalmers University of Technology, Sweden &
    Omegapoint, Sweden*
Erland Jonsson, Chalmers University of Technology, Sweden
*Stefan Lindskog, Norwegian University of Science and Technology, Sweden
    & Norway and Karlstad University, Sweden*

Nana K. Ampah, Jacobs Engineering Group, USA
Cajetan M. Akujuobi, Alabama State University, USA

Zoltán Czirkos, Budapest University of Technology and Economics, Hungary
Gábor Hosszú, Budapest University of Technology and Economics, Hungary

Section 2

Chapter 9
Applying Weighted PCA on Multiclass Classification for

Mohsen Moshki, Iran University of Science and Technology, Iran
Mehran Garmehi, Iran University of Science and Technology, Iran
Peyman Kabiri, Iran University of Science and Technology, Iran

Preface

With the recent advances in communication and computer networks, network-based applications are rapidly growing. New Internet or network-based applications are constantly introduced and quickly accepted by the society. Internet or network-based systems are used in many areas such as communications, data transfer or sharing, equipment control or monitoring, remote control or remote presence, entertainment media and military operations.

Many business sectors are dependent on the services provided by computer networks. The financial sector shows an increasing demand for reliable and secure network-based services. The growing demand for e-banking, e-business and online trading in stock markets are some examples of this high demand.

The industrial sector is using a computer network for the distributed networking and applications where coordination between sophisticated systems is needed to run a plant or a service in a coordinated way. Here, systems operating separately and located in remote locations can be controlled to operate as one plant.

Network security has been known to be mainly about encryption/decryption for a long time. In the past decade network security has gradually but surely moved towards securing the network environment rather than the transferred data. In the past decade research interest in intrusion detection experienced a rapid growth.

The increased interest on the intrusion detection together with prevention and response proves that protecting the data either in storage or during transfer is necessary but not sufficient for the security of a network. It should be noted that encryption technologies consume a large portion of the available processing power.

With the wide spread Internet usage and the ever growing dependency of every aspect of our life on the Internet, malicious activities on the Internet have increased significantly. Security of the networks and the Internet affects the industrial and economical growth of any society and ignoring this issue will have a significant negative impact on all aspects of the society. To make the situation even worse, the privacy issue has made the use of the networks, especially the Internet something to worry about.

Introduction and the wide spread of the wireless networks in different types made the situation even worse. The concern is due to the fact that sending the information via waves through the air leaves the data with no protection. In the wired network, communication environment is a closed environment where the service provider is responsible for its protection. However, in the wireless environment the service provider has no responsibility in this regard. Problem with wireless communication security can be even tougher than the wired network.

The introduction of the wireless network and free Wi-Fi or wireless Internet access zones in some cities may ease hit and run scenarios for the attackers such as Wardriving and may become a source for new problems. Therefore, wireless network security is one of the greatest concerns.

Privacy of the network users is also an important concern. Many researchers have focused their research on improving privacy on the Net. Nevertheless, this issue is still unsolved and data collection from the network users and in particular Internet users is an ongoing problem.

Threats on data and privacy in computer networks force network security officers to look for prevention and response methods. Response can be found in two forms; one in cyberspace and the other in the form of legal responses. Both aspects are research areas where researchers are looking for ways to make a malicious act difficult to do or to make it lose its attractiveness by the legal consequences that it may bring. Here it would be nice to mention that the legal system in many countries still suffer from the lack of clear laws and legal procedures for cyber crime.

Some technologies are driven by the need for them even though the scientific society does not show enough interest in them. Honey pots are one example of these technologies. One guess is that, since this area has no theoretical concept and justification for publication can be difficult, researchers might not find it interesting enough to invest in.

Honey pots use deception techniques and they are merely a deception, tracking and data collection system. Nevertheless, in the past few years the number of papers published in this area has increased. Honey pots have proven to be effective and implemented technologies in them are getting more and more sophisticated. Intruders are concerned and anti-honey pot technology is gaining momentum as well.

Viruses and worms are also a serious concern for the people responsible for the security of the networks. Execution of these codes can disrupt the operation of the targeted systems and is the first step to gain control over a computer or a network.

Nowadays, Botnets are attracting much attention, and recruiting Bots and gaining access to other computers can be a valuable asset. Selling the collected information, processing power, and the power to coordinate DDoS attacks can be worth millions of dollars.

Finally, it would feel nice to work in a cyberspace where user feels safe and protected instead of being secured by different types of safes and locks e.g. Encryption/Decryption technologies. To reach there, researchers are working hard finding new ways to detect the malicious acts over the Internet and computer networks, but so are the hackers. Only the future will prove which one will be winner. For the time being, no real end can be imagined for this conflict.

The audience for this book will include but not be limited to scholars and industry experts. Network administrators and security officers may also find the book interesting. The intension was to select chapter reporting research in the area of interest of the audience of the book.

Selected chapters mainly present works reporting experimental results as proof for the effectiveness of the proposed method of approach. There is one chapter explaining the data collection method for intrusion detection where it presents a survey on the methods applied in this area.

Chapters are sorted in such a way that they address data collection methods for intrusion detection followed by several reported works in the area of intrusion detection. One of the major problems in intrusion detection is the size of the problem and the time constraint for it. The Intrusion Detection System (IDS) should be designed in such a way that the calculations needed for detection of the intrusion attempts can be performed in a timely manner.

If IDS cannot meet the time constraints set by the bandwidth of the network it is operating on, its operation in real time will not be possible. Once the network traffic is not processed fast enough, the IDS will have two options, one is to slow down the traffic and two is to start sampling the traffic (packet dropping), neither one is desired. Improving the efficiency of the calculations for the IDS monitored network parameters should be selected carefully and implemented methods should be optimized. Large number of parameters may improve the accuracy of the detection and reduce the detection speed. There should be a balance between the accuracy required and the computation cost for the detection. Using feature selection methods makes it possible to reach to such a balance. This issue is addressed in the second part of the book where curse of dimensionality is a major concern.

Chapters in the first section are as follows:

Chapter 1 talks about data collection methods for intrusion detection and provides detailed explanations about data collection mechanism components. It provides useful hints and guidelines for mechanism selection and deployment.

Chapter 2 uses an auto-reclosing technique applied on long rural power lines together with multi-resolution techniques to develop an IDS that helps to keep IPS up to date. The proposed method can block SYN-flood attacks, distributed denial of service attacks (DDoS) based on SYN-flood attacks, and helps to improve the limitations of existing IDSs and IPSs.

Chapter 3 introduces a peer-to-peer based intrusion detection system called Komondor and it is based on the Kademlia system. The proposed system is composed of independent software instances running on different hosts organized into a peer-to-peer network. The goal of the chapter is to explain modifications and enhancements made on the Kademlia.

Chapter 4 reports a work where entropy-based behavioral traffic profiles are used for anomaly-based intrusion detection. The proposed method is based on the Method of Remaining Elements (MRE) as its core.

Chapter 5 targets one of the important security concerns in the world, i.e. Botnets. It reports an analysis of botnets detecting intrusion attempts more effectively and without relying on any specific protocol, characteristics of bots such as synchronism and network load within specific time windows are analyzed.

Chapter 6 aims on the NGN and addresses the security issue in SIP protocol. The main security concern in the reported work is the DoS attack on SIP. It proposes a combination of the specification- and anomaly-based intrusion detection techniques to detect the attack.

The main concern in the chapters in the second section is to improve the performance of the detection by increasing its speed while keeping its accuracy around the same value.

Chapter 7 presents a work where the Principal Component Analysis (PCA) is applied on the DARPA'99 dataset for feature selection and to reduce the dimensionality of the sampled dataset. Here, the intension is to increase the speed of the detection process by reducing the complexity and dimensionality of the problem without significant decrease in the detection accuracy.

Chapter 8 reports a case study of anomaly detection in large and high-dimensional network connection data streams using Stream Projected Outlier deTector (SPOT) to detect anomalies from data streams using subspace analysis. The dataset used in this work is the 1999 KDD CUP dataset.

Chapter 9 reports a work where Weighted PCA (WPCA) is applied on the DARPA99 dataset for feature extraction. A difference is reported in the accuracy of the result when the number of features is limited, the number of classes is large, and population of classes is unbalanced.

Peyman Kabiri
Iran University of Science and Technology, Iran

Acknowledgment

I would like to thank my wife Mahak for her support in preparing this book. Without her help I could not succeed. I would also like to thank the IGI Global editorial department and their staff for their support and interest in working with me.

Peyman Kabiri
Iran University of Science and Technology, Iran

Section 1

Chapter 1

A Structured Approach to Selecting Data Collection Mechanisms for Intrusion Detection

Ulf E. Larson
Chalmers University of Technology, Sweden & Omegapoint, Sweden

Erland Jonsson
Chalmers University of Technology, Sweden

Stefan Lindskog
Norwegian University of Science and Technology, Sweden & Norway and Karlstad University, Sweden

ABSTRACT

This chapter aims at providing a clear and concise picture of data collection for intrusion detection. It provides a detailed explanation of generic data collection mechanism components and the interaction with the environment, from initial triggering to output of log data records. Taxonomies of mechanism characteristics and deployment considerations are provided and discussed. Furthermore, guidelines and hints for mechanism selection and deployment are provided. The guidelines are aimed to assist intrusion detection system developers, designers, and operators in selecting mechanisms for resource efficient data collection.

DOI: 10.4018/978-1-60960-836-1.ch001

Copyright ©2012, IGI Global. Copying or distributing in print or electronic forms without written permission of IGI Global is prohibited.

INTRODUCTION

Collection and analysis of audit data is a critical component for intrusion detection. Previous research efforts (Almgren et al., 2007; Axelsson et al., 1998; Kuperman, 2004; Lundin Barse & Jonsson, 2004; Price, 1997; Zamboni, 2001) have concluded that by carefully selecting and configuring data collection mechanisms, it is possible to obtain better and more accurate analysis results. However, data is required to be correct and to be delivered in a timely fashion. The data should also be sparse to reduce the amount of resources used to collect and store it. Since production of audit data directly depends on the deployed data collection mechanisms, adequate mechanism knowledge is thus a critical asset for intrusion detection system (IDS) developers, designers, and operators.

This chapter consists of a theoretical part which introduces the basic concepts of data collection, and a practical part where guidelines and hints for mechanism selection are discussed. The theoretical part discusses the basics of data collection from several perspectives. The components and operation of a generic IDS is described, followed by an in-depth discussion of the components and operation of a generic data collection mechanism. Then, two taxonomies are presented, discussing mechanism characteristics and deployment considerations, respectively. Thereafter, the practical part discusses operational considerations and outlines a deployment strategy. Finally, future challenges are discussed, followed by some concluding remarks and an appendix providing a classification of 50 studied data collection mechanisms and techniques.

Both the appendix and the guidelines can be used when selecting mechanisms. They can also assist when a specific type of data collection is desired. For example, it is easy to find out what mechanisms collect samples for execution profiling, and what mechanisms that can be reconfigured without the need for restart. This is a valuable source of information which removes the need to browse multiple manual pages and white papers to find the desired mechanism. Furthermore, by using the selection guidelines, we can obtain a more resource efficient data collection and obtain a more accurate data analysis.

RELATED WORK

Anderson (Anderson, 1980) proposed to use data collection and analysis as a means of monitoring computer systems for detection of different types of intruders. Denning (Denning, 1986) proposed *An Intrusion-Detection Model* and pointed out specific log information that is useful for intrusion detection. Price (Price, 1997) then derived the audit data needs of a number of misuse detection systems and investigated how well conventional operating systems (OSs) collection mechanisms met these needs. It was clear from her report that the collection mechanisms lacked useful content. Axelsson et al. (Axelsson et al., 1998) investigated the impact on detection by carefully selecting a set of system calls as input to the detector. Their paper showed that the detection rate improved when a selected set of data was collected. Wagner and Soto (Wagner & Soto, 2002) further showed that if insufficient data is recorded, an attack may well be treated as normal behavior.

Kuperman (Kuperman, 2004) investigated in his PhD thesis the log data needs of four different types of computer monitoring systems and showed that when log data was carefully selected, the detection rate was improved. Killourhy et al. (Killourhy et al., 2004) discussed the impact of attack manifestations on the ability to detect attacks. Attack manifestations are information items that are not present during normal execution and can thus be the key to reveal attacks. Furthermore, Almgren et al. (Almgren et al., 2007) investigated what impact the use of different log sources had on detection of web server attacks. It was concluded that the properties of the log sources affect the detection capability. Finally, taxonomies regarding data collection mechanisms in general have also been proposed (Albari, 2008; Delgado et al., 2004; Larus, 1993; Schroeder, 1995). Fessi et al. (Fessi et al., 2010), discusses a network based IDS, and also provides a comparison of different types of IDS.

Log data requirements for security logging have also been proposed in several whitepapers and reports from renowned industry-centered research institutes. The SANS consensus project (SANS, 2006) proposes several log sources, such as network data, OS data and applications. In (NIST, 2006), a set of guidelines for security log management was released. The guidelines discuss infrastructure, planning, and operations management. They also discuss various log sources, including security software, OSs, and applications.

In the most recent years, application logging has become more important since more applications are published on the Internet. As such, they are exposed to a wider range of threats and must thus be properly protected. Chuvakin and Peterson (Chuvakin & Peterson, 2010) discuss logging strategies and what should be collected for web connected applications. Maggi et al(Maggi et al., 2009) has addressed the need of carefully selecting log items due to the concept drift often found in dynamic applications. Furthermore, web applications normally communicate with databases, which in turn have received more focus in the latter years (Jin et al., 2007; Mathew et al., 2010). The industry has focused much attention on COTS-products for solving data collection, analysis, and intrusion detection. This type of systems is known as SIEM (Security Information and Event Management Systems). Gartner group (Gartner group, 2010) publishes an annual survey and evaluation of important stakeholders in the SIEM field.

DATA COLLECTION FOR INTRUSION DETECTION

IDSs play a vital role in the protection of computer systems. Intrusion detection is also a field where data collection is of utmost importance and the foundation for all subsequent analysis and response activity. In this section, we first present the purpose of data collection. Then, we provide a general model of an IDS, a general data collection scenario, and a description of a log record.

Purpose of Data Collection

Collection of data is critical for intrusion detection, but its use is by no means limited to intrusion detection. Rather, it has a significantly wider applicability in the field of computer security, as noted by Bishop (Bishop, 1989) and Price (Price, 1997):

- **Maintaining Individual Accountability**: The activity of individual users or processes can be monitored. The sense of being monitored may deter potential insiders from attempting to circumvent policy controls.
- **Reconstructing Events:** Event reconstruction is an activity that is heavily used in the area of computer forensics to backtrack criminal activity and collect evidence. It is also used to identify and remove system vulnerabilities.
- **Problem Monitoring:** Monitoring is used to uncover software and hardware problems. It is used for debugging and optimization, and to discover disk and network failures.

IDSs are heavily dependent on data collection since detection decisions are based on and guided by the collected data. Using general terms, data collection means to decide what data to collect, how to collect it, and when to collect it (Lundin Barse, 2004).

Components of a Generic IDS

A model of a generic IDS inspired by Lundin Barse (Lundin Barse, 2004) is shown in Figure 1. The *data collection mechanism* collects statistics or events related to system use and performance from the *target system*, e.g., a host or a network. The data collection mechanism uses its *data collection configuration* to decide what data should be collected. The data collection configuration may for example be a configuration rule for, e.g., *tcpdump* (tcpdump, 2010), or an entry in the *httpd.conf* file for, e.g., the Apache web server.

When the data collection mechanism has collected the data, it is then sent to an output device, e.g., a log data storage such as a disk drive. The data it then

Figure 1. Components of a generic IDS, including the data collection mechanism and a response mechanism. (Adapted from Lundin Barse (Lundin Barse, 2004)).

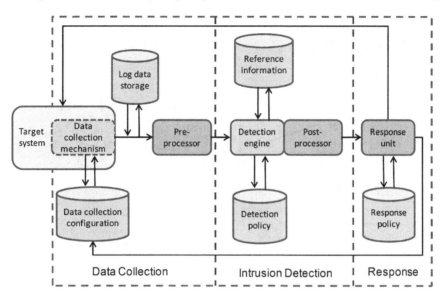

converted by the *pre-processor* from the native format to the format expected by the *detection engine*. The detection engine uses a detection algorithm to perform intrusion detection. It also uses one or more databases containing *reference information*, e.g., signatures. The analysis engine also uses a detection policy that determines how data should be interpreted by the detection engine. For example, the *detection policy* can state that connections made from IP-address 192.168.0.1 are malicious.

After processing, the detection engine outputs the results. The *post-processor* formats the output data and may also perform correlation of data from different detection engines. Finally, if a *response unit* is attached to the IDS it decides how to act on the output from the post-processor based on the *response policy*.

A General Data Collection Scenario

This section outlines a typical data collection scenario and describes the components involved. An operational scenario for a data collection mechanism can be illustrated as in Figure 2.

In the figure, there are six components which are described as follows: The *executing process* is a running application or system program which executes a sequence of machine instructions. The *log trigger* is a set of machine instructions contained within the executing process. These instructions are also known as instrumentation code, i.e., machine instructions which are not necessary for execution,

Figure 2. The interaction between a data collection mechanism and its environment (Larson et al., 2008a). (© 2008, IEEE. Used with permission.).

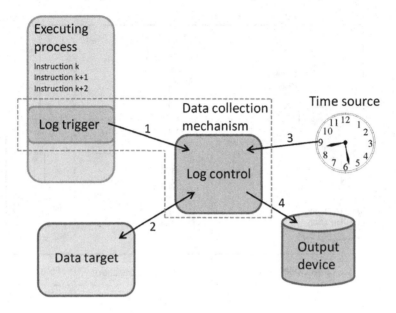

but rather for notification. The *log control* is a set of machine instructions that are located in the executing process, or as a separate process. The latter case is shown in Figure 2. The combination of the log trigger and log control is denoted as the *data collection mechanism*. The *data target* is an addressable memory area within the system, and either internal or external to the executing process. The *time source* is the entity providing time. Finally, the *output device* is a device to which the collected data is sent for display, storage, or further processing. Referring to Figure 1, the output device is located between the data collection mechanism and the preprocessing entities.

During execution, the CPU executes the machine instructions located inside the executing process. When the instruction flow reaches the Log trigger, the log control is notified (arrow 1). The log control collects the content of one or more data target memory areas (arrow 2), and appends a time stamp from the time source (arrow 3). The combination of the collected data and the time stamp now constitutes a log data record, which is sent to the output device (arrow 4). When the log control has concluded its operation, it awaits the next alert from the log trigger.

Figure 3. A log record consists of a set of attributes (A) and a time stamp (T)

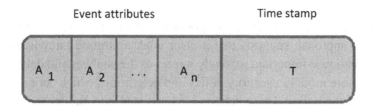

The Log Record

The log record is the result of a data collection operation. A conceptual model of a log record is illustrated in Figure 3.

The log record contains one or more *attributes* (A_i) for describing the event that caused the triggering of the data collection. It also contains a *time stamp* (T). Some mechanisms also provide statistics regarding the total number of occurred events of a certain type over a predefined time.

DETERMINING WHAT DATA TO COLLECT

Before collecting data, it must be determined what data should be collected. The rates at which events are produced in modern computer systems readily yield all exhaustive data collection strategies infeasible. Thus, disks would rapidly be filled with log data and IDS pre-processors and data collection mechanisms would consume all the available computing resources. Therefore, several more elaborate strategies have been proposed, notably based on established criteria, on the goal of the attacker, on identified threats, and on information theory.

Established Criteria

The Common Criteria (Common Criteria, 2005) states several audit requirements that must be met by a system. It states that each audit record should contain date and time of an event, the type of event, the identity of the subject responsible for generating event, and finally, the outcome, i.e., success or failure. A similar criterion includes *A Guide to Understanding Audit in Trusted Systems* (National Computer Security Center, 1988). This guide contains several important security goals that an audit mechanism should fulfill and an in-depth discussion regarding auditable events and auditable information.

Goal-Oriented Logging

Bishop et al. (Bishop et al., 1996) proposes a goal-oriented approach to data collection. This approach suggests that a clear goal, and good knowledge of what target information is important, strongly improves the analysis and data collection. Bishop therefore models a security policy and determines which actions can cause a violation of the policy. These actions are translated into auditable events which can be observed. Bishop's goal oriented approach to logging was further explored by Peisert (Peisert, 2007) in his PhD thesis.

Threat Modeling

Denning (Denning, 1986) took possible threats into consideration and attempted to identify data that could reveal these threats. Furthermore, threat and attack analyses can reveal events, or manifestations that must be collected. This method has been further explored by, e.g., Axelsson et al. (Axelsson et al.,1998). Along the same line, Kuperman (Kuperman, 2004) investigated and determined the log data needs of four types of computer monitoring systems. The log data was then represented as subsets of system calls and used as templates for data collection for the four systems.

Information-Theoretic Approaches

Lee et al. (Lee et al., 1997) and Lee and Xiang (Lee & Xiang, 2001) applied an information-theoretic approach to anomaly detection. Several measures was used to estimate, e.g., information gain and information cost from using different combinations of information. They used for example different combinations of system calls and the system object accessed by the system call and estimated which combination was the most accurate and least costly.

A TAXONOMY OF MECHANISM CHARACTERISTICS

The taxonomy presented in this section is derived from previously published work by Larson et al. (Larson et al., 2008a). The taxonomy uses the following two dimensions: *realization* and *behavior* to describe mechanism characteristics. The following subsections are structured in a manner where a description of the term is provided, followed by a brief discussion regarding the relation to and usefulness for intrusion detection. Figure 4 shows the taxonomy tree.

Figure 4. A taxonomy of mechanism characteristics. The two dimensions realization and behavior are illustrated as branches in the tree.

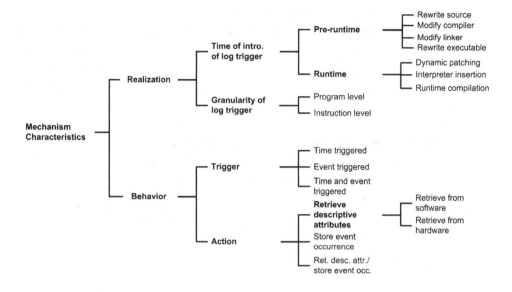

Realization

The realization of a data collection mechanism consists of two parts: the point in time the log trigger is inserted and the level of granularity of the log trigger. The two main categories in this dimension are thus: *time of introduction of log trigger* and *granularity of log trigger*.

Time of Introduction of Log Trigger

Time of introduction of the log trigger represents the time at which the log trigger is introduced into the executing process. The log control is assumed to be introduced either before or at the same time as the log trigger. This category consists of two possible times of introduction: *pre-runtime* and *runtime*.

Pre-Runtime

The log trigger is inserted into the executing process at any time before the corresponding program is loaded into the main memory by the loader. This can be accomplished in one of the following ways: *rewrite source program, modify compiler, modify linker,* or *rewrite executable*. These methods are described below.

- **Rewrite source:** Rewriting source programs means that an existing source file is modified by either manual or application based insertion of program language statements. Manual insertion is the most versatile way of inserting code. This approach allows for insertion of arbitrary statements and constructs conforming to the rules of the used programming language. It is used for inserting arbitrary log messages. An application based insertion depends on a preprocessing entity to perform a source-to-source transformation technique. The source rewriting approach only allows additions to the affected source file.
- **Modify compiler:** Modification of the compiler means that the compiler itself is enhanced with an ability to insert log triggering into the source file during compile or assembly time. This requires access to the compiler source.
- **Modify linker:** Since the linker is responsible for combining multiple object files including files residing in libraries, access to all code in the final linked executable is granted during this step. This also removes the need for having pre-configured libraries, either compiled or assembled with a modified compiler/assembler.
- **Rewrite executable:** Rewriting executables is done by inserting the log triggering directly into the complete executable binary file. This technique is also known as patching or static instrumentation of binary code. The rewriting takes place before the execution starts.

Discussion: A mechanism that is inserted before runtime requires that the monitored asset is permanently rewritten. This inevitably introduces a delay and possible downtime for the asset or the system. Thus, a busy web server should not use pre-runtime insertion of mechanisms. Pre-runtime can be useful for reflecting a long-term constant monitoring policy. It provides a deterministic processing overhead, e.g., the same code is executed each time. It is useful for policies stating, e.g., that each login attempt should be recorded. An example of a pre-runtime inserted mechanism is the UNIX *syslog* (Garfinkel & Spafford, 1996) facility which consists of function calls for transmitting data to the *syslog* daemon.

Runtime

Inserting the log trigger at runtime means that the executing process is modified in its running state. This can be accomplished either by a runtime linker or loader process or by a dedicated log process which is external to the executing process. Runtime insertion of a log trigger can be performed by *dynamic patching, interpreter insertion*, or *runtime compilation* as further described below.

- **Dynamic patching:** Dynamic patching can be performed with two different methods. One method is runtime patching which means that the logging control starts the instrumentation target as a child process and then immediately suspends it. Then, the logging control uses the symbol table of the executing process to map addresses against function names and source line numbers. The more information the symbol table provides, the more detailed the patching. The logging control inserts log triggering by introducing illegal instructions that causes interrupts and transfers control to the logging control when encountered. In this way, the logging control gathers information based on the illegal instruction interrupts.

Another method is for the logging control to attach itself to an already running process. In this way, the logging control can register itself as the parent of the executing process at runtime. By being the parent, the logging control can use the same mechanisms as in runtime patching and in addition it can detach from the executing process at any time.

- **Interpreter insertion:** An interpreter reads the contents of an executable file and translates the contents into proper instructions when the executable is in running state. Contents, for instance unresolved symbols that cannot directly be translated must be appropriately handled to enable translation. The translation process is the basis for dynamic linking of files. Whenever an unresolved symbol is encountered, the appropriate mapping is done and the execution can progress. This method allows for dynamic linking of library functions at load time and it also allows for dynamic loading of library procedures and system modules into a running executable.

An interpreter can be instructed to link or load special libraries containing log triggering instead of the normal libraries. The technique of placing a special library between the running executable call and the normal library is called interposition.

- **Runtime compilation:** Compilation of code is performed at runtime, either from source code or from an intermediate, partially compiled, representation of the source code. Runtime compilation can be done by using one of two methods. The first method is called byte-code compilation and means that the code is compiled when it is needed, i.e., when execution reaches the next instruction, this instruction is compiled and executed. The second method consists of programs that generate source code and both compile the code and run the compiled code at runtime. Both these methods can be used to insert log triggering during compilation.

Discussion: A mechanism that is inserted during runtime, e.g., *strace* (strace, 2010), rewrites the asset during execution. The mechanism can thus be enabled and disabled at will and provides an execution overhead only when it is enabled. Runtime inserted mechanisms can be used to enforce a dynamic or adaptive detection policy where monitoring is enabled on-demand. For example, if a network-based IDS indicates the presence of buffer overflow packets, monitoring that is not normally enabled, can be enabled for the web server for a shorter period of time without the need of recompiling and restarting the web server.

Granularity of Log Trigger

The granularity of the log trigger represents the level on which the log trigger is inserted. Two levels of granularity are used: *program level* and *instruction level*.

Program Level

A program level trigger is inserted as one or more program level statements in the used programming language. The trigger can operate on the granularity of the used language, e.g., statements, variables, and structures. The developer can benefit from the semantic meaning of higher-level statements which normally is easier to comprehend than a lower counterpart.

Discussion: A log trigger that is inserted on the program level can be used to collect data on program-level events, e.g., the return value of a function or system call. A typical example of a program level trigger is the *syslog* function call. A program level log trigger allows the designer to create tailored log messages and can be used to express events in terms of natural language, e.g., login attempt failed.

Instruction Level

An instruction level trigger has the resolution of the hardware architecture. Architecture level constructs such as hardware registers or single instructions and register data items can thus be resolved. While presenting a more fine-grained resolution, the semantic meaning of the constructs are harder to comprehend. Often, a mapping construct, such as a symbol table, is required to resolve the individual instructions to procedure names, source level line numbers, and variables. An example of a mechanism that inserts instruction level triggers is *Dtrace* (Cantrill et al., 2004).

Discussion: When the log trigger is inserted on instruction level, finer-grained traces or profiles of execution can be performed. Instruction level insertion is needed to gain the sufficient granularity for host-based detection of polymorphic attacks. However, instruction traces tend to grow rapidly and the space required to store the traces is significant. Using instruction traces is recommended only for critical applications and should be combined with an adaptive strategy for collecting data.

Behavior

The behavior dimension categorizes possible methods for the log trigger to activate the log control, and what actions the log control performs when it is activated. This dimension has two categories denoted *trigger* and *action*.

Trigger

The log trigger causes the log control to initiate a data collection operation. Data collection may be initiated either by the expiration of a timer or the occurrence of an event. In this context we distinguish between three sub-categories: *time triggered*, *event triggered*, and *time and event triggered*.

Time Triggered

A time trigger requires a log trigger which is invoked at regular intervals by, e.g., a hardware clock pulse, or a software timer set by the system.

Discussion: Time triggered (sampling-based) data collection is useful to create execution profiles of many applications without consuming too many resources for collection. This collection can be performed to measure the CPU consumption by different processes. A mechanism supporting time triggered collection is *OProfile* (Levon & Elie, 2009).

Event Triggered

An event trigger requires log trigger instructions that either wrap a specific event or that are placed before or after the event. Every time the specific event is reached, the log trigger is also invoked.

Discussion: Event triggered collection is most commonly used in practice for intrusion detection. Several detection engines operate on event data, e.g., Forrest et al. (Forrest et al., 1996) and Tan et al. (Tan et al., 2002). Event triggering denotes that each time a specific event occurs, corresponding data is recorded. Event triggering is used for misuse-based detection for monitoring access to specific resources, e.g., recording every occurrence of write() to the /etc/passwd file in UNIX or every login attempt. It can also be used for anomaly detection by, e.g., collecting all occurrences of system calls issued by a process or all user commands issued during a login session. An example of an event-based data collection mechanism is *strace*.

Time and Event Triggered

Some data collection mechanisms allow for both time and event triggered invocation of the log control. This category is included for completeness.

Action

The action is the response from the log control when it receives a trigger alert. There are two possible actions. Either to store data for describing the event, or to note that the event has taken place, e.g., storing the occurrence of the event. These two types are denoted *retrieve descriptive attributes* and *store event occurrence*. The retrieve descriptive attributes and store event occurrence categories denote a combination of the other two and are included for completeness.

Retrieve Descriptive Attributes

Retrieving descriptive attributes is the process of reading the contents of (1) a software construct residing in main memory, including buffers and variables, or (2) hardware-based storage mechanisms, such as on-chip CPU general purpose registers, debug registers, and performance counters. If the desired data is not confined to a specific location, several locations might need to be visited by the log control.

- **Retrieve from software:** Data retrieved from software is contents of one or more software constructs residing in main memory. This includes program buffers, OS structures, and variables.
- **Retrieve from hardware:** Data retrieved from hardware is contents of one or more hardware constructs. This includes on-chip general purpose registers, debug registers, and performance counters.

Discussion: Retrieving descriptive attributes is performed when information that describes an event or a state is required. In this case, the mechanism denotes each event with one or more <attribute:value> sets that describe the occurred events. This is useful for detection engine for determining that a user accessed the /etc/passwd file, or that the payload of a network packet contained the string /bin/sh.

Store Event Occurrence

Storing event occurrence refers to the process of storing information regarding the occurrence of a specific event. This can be done by, e.g., incrementing a counter for each time the event is observed. An example is *OProfile*.

Discussion: Storing the occurrence of events is used when constructing histogram charts of issued commands during a login session. This in turn can be used to calculate the correspondence between a known distribution and an unknown user session to reveal masquerading users.

Retrieve Descriptive Attributes and Store Event Occurrence

Some data collection mechanisms allows for the log control to retrieve data regarding both descriptive attributes and event occurrence information. This category is included in the taxonomy for completeness.

A TAXONOMY OF DEPLOYMENT CONSIDERATIONS

The taxonomy of deployment considerations presented in this section is inspired from previously published work (Larson et al., 2008a; Lundin Barse, 2004; Zamboni, 2001). This taxonomy uses the following five dimensions: *collection structure, collection strategy, location relative environment, location relative monitored asset,* and *log data*. The taxonomy of deployment considerations is illustrated in Figure 5. Each of the five dimensions is further described below.

Collection Structure

When considering deploying an IDS and data collection infrastructure, this can be done in a *centralized, decentralized*, or *distributed* manner (Hedbom et al., 1999; Lundin Barse, 2004).

Centralized

A centralized strategy means that the data collection is performed by the same entity that performs the intrusion detection.

Discussion: Since both detection and data collection is performed by the same entity, data and detection policies can be well protected against tampering. However, the system becomes a single point of failure, and correlation becomes difficult.

Decentralized

In the decentralized approach, data is collected on several locations, and is thereafter sent to a central location for analysis and detection.

Figure 5. A taxonomy of deployment considerations containing five dimensions

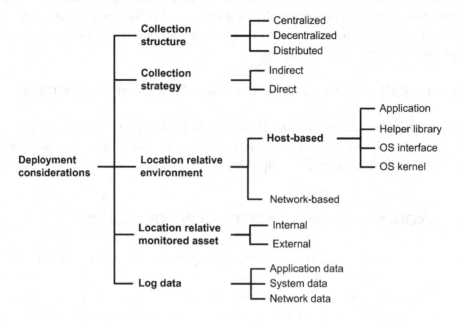

Discussion: With a decentralized strategy, the collected data can be readily correlated at the central location. However, since the collection policy must be transmitted to each node, an attacker can attack the communication channel and modify the policy and the collected data.

Distributed

Finally, with the distributed strategy, both data collection and all or parts of the intrusion detection are distributed.

Discussion: Since data is collected and analyzed at the same location, this strategy has the advantages of the strictly centralized approach, but without being a single point of failure. Data can also be readily correlated. However, the detection and data collection policies must be transmitted and may thus be subject to modification in transit.

Collection Strategy

Collection strategy denotes whether data collection is *indirect* or *direct* with respect to a monitored component.

Indirect

When data is collected from an intermediate storage in which the monitored component previously has stored data, the term *indirect* monitoring is used. An example is when the collection mechanism reads from a log file.

Discussion: Indirect collection is more convenient than direct collection since mechanisms that generate audit trails are readily available. Thus, they must not be produced before they can be used. Moreover, popular mechanisms normally have well developed interfaces and numerous configuration options which provide a diverse operation. However, an attacker may modify the contents of the log file before it is passed to the IDS. Indirect collection mechanisms may also cause mismatches between collected and required data since they do not know what the requirements of the IDS are (Crosbie & Spafford, 1995).

Direct

When data is collected directly from the monitored component, the term *direct* data collection is used. An example is to read data from a network subsystem data structure.

Discussion: A direct collection strategy means that data can be transported directly to the IDS from the monitored component. The time available to an attacker for modifying the data is thus short. Furthermore, direct data collection can be better tailored to the requirements of the IDS and thus provide exactly the required data. On the downside, direct collection mechanisms must often be specifically developed for each purpose. They must also be carefully implemented to not disturb the operation of the monitored component.

Location Relative Environment

The location of the data collector can be roughly divided into *host-based* and *network-based* collectors. These two categories and their subcategories are discussed in this section.

Host-Based

Host-based data collection takes place on a host computer and can be on *application, helper library, OS interface*, or *OS kernel* level.

Application

Applications are defined as user programs and system utilities running at user level. Applications are, for example, software based firewalls, database systems and web server and web browser software. Application instrumentation captures execution inside the application's memory space. Each application that needs to be monitored must be individually instrumented.

Discussion: An application level log trigger is tailored to a specific application and can thus be constructed with the specifics of that application in mind. Using an application level trigger, only the relevant behavior can be monitored and thus, irrelevant actions can be left out by simply not inserting triggers for them. An attacker who wants to affect the monitoring also has to affect each application, which makes it more elaborate to disguise attacker actions. However, correlation of events between applications may be somewhat problematic, especially if different designers have been involved. Then, the format of the messages may differ and extensive pre- or post-processing may be required. Furthermore, this requires the presence of a highly accurate time source.

Helper Library

Helper libraries are collections of object files that perform standard operations and provide an easier-to-use interface against the system services. The libraries are linked into the program object file at link time, and the result is the final executable. Helper libraries provide a more general point of instrumentation insertion. They are shared by all applications running on the system and instrumentation inserted into helper libraries is thus common to all applications that use the specific library.

Discussion: Helper libraries are collections of general programming functions. Thus, by inserting log triggers in helper libraries, all programs that use the libraries can be monitored. This allows for constructing complete traces of function calls, even between different helper libraries. This has been used by Kuperman and Spafford (Kuperman & Spafford, 1999). This approach also supports dynamic monitoring through dynamic linking.

OS Interface

The OS interface handles input to and output from the OS kernel. Inserting a data collection mechanism at the OS interface provides a highly general log triggering location and requests from all applications can be captured. The OS interface is implemented through interrupts. Two locations are generally used for interrupt handling: the data structures containing the interrupt descriptors and the system call descriptors. Usually, the interrupt descriptor structure is more general and routes a subset of its calls to the system call structure.

Discussion: All activities that require higher privileges must be issued through the use of well-defined system calls. Thus, this is a good place to monitor security-critical events, such as file read()s, and the use of the network. Many host-based IDS, e.g., *snare* (Intersect Alliance, 2003) operate on system call data since it represents a decent level of granularity. However, it must be noted that the more processes that are monitored, the larger the amount of collected data becomes. Regardless, it is still the most popular source of host-based IDS data.

OS Kernel

The OS kernel handles process and memory management, file systems and I/O communication. Depending on the exact location of the log triggering, higher or lower degree of coverage is possible. Some subsystems perform specific tasks such as file system management, while others perform very general tasks such as process scheduling. Regardless of the subsystem, all requests for service from any caller are captured by the inserted instrumentation. Inserting a data collection mechanism in the core subsystems provides access to process management, main and secondary memory management, file and I/O management as well as network management.

Discussion: OS kernel monitoring allows for monitoring privileged execution and provides system-wide information. By targeting the most general parts of the system, e.g., the process_task structure (Linux Audit Subsystem, 2004), all processes can be uniformly monitored. It is recommended that monitoring of the OS kernel is carefully conducted both with respect to the amount of data produced and the fact that the entire system may crash if monitoring is erroneously performed. Access to hardware constructs such as performance counters is useful program counter sampling for determining where programs spend their time, which, can be used to detect *rootkits*. Correlation between events is also easier since a uniform representation and a common clock can be used. In an architecture that permits inserting kernel modules, data collection can easily be performed dynamically. Most network monitoring tools operate in the OS kernel since this provides access to all data packets. The OS kernel is also the place where general purpose audit trail mechanisms, such as the (Linux Audit Subsystem, 2004; Sun Microsystems, 1995) are located. These mechanisms support a wide variety of events and are thus the opposite of application specific mechanisms. This data must be rich enough to promote several types of detection, therefore it is highly necessary that configuration of general purpose mechanisms is carefully performed to prevent being drowned in data.

Network-Based

Network locations include network interface cards on hosts, firewalls and routers, or other network equipment. The main sources of network data are TCP/IP packets and data link layer frames.

Location Relative Monitored Asset

The data collection mechanism can be *internal* or *external* to the monitored component.

Internal

An internal data collection mechanism is inserted directly into the code of the monitored component. The data collection is performed directly from inside the component.

Discussion: Internal data collection requires changes to the monitored component. This may or may not be feasible from an availability perspective, and it is advised that the collection mechanism is inserted before the component is deployed. However, mistakes in design or implementation of the mechanism may break the component or require run-time changes, which may lead to downtime. This is dependent on how the mechanism is realized. Internal collection mechanisms minimize the risk that data has been altered before delivery to the IDS and they cannot easily be modified.

External

An external mechanism is implemented in the code that is separate from the monitored component.

Discussion: External data collection mechanisms are less intrusive to the monitored component and do not require any changes. As such, they affect the operation of the asset and the host system less. For example, the UNIX *ps* utility program is an external data collection mechanism since disabling it does not imply that the kernel is correspondingly disabled. However, it is more prone to modification, e.g., by a *rootkit*, and can be instrumented to hide certain results.

Log Data

The following three categories of log data are covered: *application data, system data*, and *network data*.

Application Data

Application data is produced by an application during its execution. Application data includes contents of used data structures and function call traces.

Discussion: Application data can be collected from both within the application itself and from any other location that is invoked during execution. If data from only a specific application is desired it is more efficient to use a log trigger which triggers on actions performed by that application only. This promotes a low degree of pre-processing and a more accurate and efficient data delivery. If data for a larger set of applications is required, the trigger can be inserted in any other location, i.e., a helper library, the OS interface, or the OS kernel. This may be useful if a uniform representation of several different applications is desired, e.g., for correlation. A frequently used approach to analyze the behavior of applications is inserting a data collection mechanism at the OS interface, i.e., collecting system calls. This provides a uniform representation of all applications, and each application that requires higher privileges during execution must use system calls. Therefore, security relevant behavior can be collected.

System Data

System data is produced by the OS kernel. This data includes resource usage statistics such as CPU activity, number of software and hardware interrupts, and various times. It also includes system events and system structure contents, such as the current system configuration. Finally, it includes data generated by interrupts from software and hardware.

Discussion: Mechanisms that collect system data must be inserted in the OS interface or OS kernel. The kernel operation is normally only invoked by applications through the OS interface. It is therefore not possible to put a log trigger in an application to monitor events occurring in the kernel.

Network Data

Network data is data contained in network protocol stacks, network services, network device drivers or firmware in network interface cards. The data itself is either data packets or data related to handling of data packets such as interface characteristics and counts of sent and received packets. Furthermore, network enabled applications can also be a source of network data.

Discussion: Network data can be collected in both applications and the OS kernel, and all applications that want to use the network resources must use system calls, e.g., send() and receive() to access the network. Most detection systems rely on network data collected by the *libpcap* packet capturing library which provides access to raw network data from the network interface card. The OS kernel contains a network subsystem which parses and distributes packets to listening applications.

OPERATIONAL CONSIDERATIONS

This section discusses a few operational considerations that may arise when deploying a data collection infrastructure. In particular, it is discussed how data collection mechanisms affect the monitored resource and host system. Additionally, a listing of common pitfalls and recommendations to how to avoid the issues is provided.

Impact on Resources

A host-based collection mechanism consumes resources from the host system. In particular, it uses disk space to store collected data and CPU cycles to operate. Furthermore, depending on its realization, it may affect the availability of the monitored components or the host system.

Storage and Performance

When data collection mechanisms are deployed, they will inevitably consume resources of the host system. First, a collection mechanism consumes CPU cycles. Thus, the amount of CPU cycles available for production purposes decreases. Each deployed mechanism imposes a basic performance penalty. Furthermore, an additional penalty is imposed when the mechanism is triggered to collect data. Second, the collected data will occupy disk space. Data that is not directly analyzed must be stored on disk until it can be processed.

Recommendation: Consider the complete data requirement and remember that all mechanisms occupy resources. Try to minimize the number of active mechanisms. Primarily use mechanisms that have low performance penalty when inactive. Make sure that the selected mechanism is tailored to the requirements of the IDS. If the target is a single process, do not use a mechanism which monitors this process only.

Availability

The availability of the monitored component may be affected by the data collection mechanism. For example, a data collection mechanism may need to be taken offline to be reconfigured. Reconfiguration includes patching the mechanism software, changing the output format, or writing more informative log messages. For an internal data collection mechanism, reconfiguration means that the monitored component must be stopped and then restarted. The reconfiguration introduces a collection downtime, which is dependent on how long time the resource is interrupted from its normal operation. A mechanism with a large reconfiguration time may have a small impact on availability if the time between reconfigurations is short.

Recommendation: To avoid availability penalties and downtime, use a mechanism that is introduced during runtime, e.g., *strace* or *Dtrace*. Another option is to use an existing audit subsystem. Most audit subsystems are installed with the OS. These systems support a transparent reconfiguration which does not affect the availability of the monitored components.

Common Pitfalls

In this section we focus on reducing the amount of excess data, i.e., data that is collected but that is not subsequently analyzed by the IDS. This section describes three situations where excess data is produced. For each situation, it also provides a recommendation for how to reduce the amount of excess data.

Example 1: Mechanisms are not Tailored to the IDSs

The *mod_log_config* module provides logging facilities for the Apache web server. An IDS uses the access logs created by *mod_log_config* to scan for the "GET /cgi-bin/test-cgi? *" string. In this case, the access log does not have to contain more information than the request string. If the access log contains more information, this information must be filtered by a pre-processor before the IDS can use the data.

Recommendation: Investigate the input data requirement for each IDS and make sure that no more information than what is required by the IDS is collected.

Example 2: Mechanisms cannot be Tailored to the IDSs

Consider that an IDS operates on sequences of system call names, as described in, e.g., Forrest et al. (Forrest et al., 1996). A mechanism such as the Linux audit subsystem readily provides the system call name, but also 15 other attributes, e.g., UID and EUID. These attributes are not used by the IDS and are therefore excess data.

Recommendation: Always consider different mechanisms when collecting data for intrusion detection. There are several mechanisms available and if one mechanism cannot be properly configured, there may be several alternatives. A classification of 50 data collection mechanisms is available in Appendix. These mechanisms have roughly the same characteristics and can thus be used interchangeably.

Example 3: Mechanisms are Active when they are not Needed

Assume that a host connected to the Internet runs a web server that listens to ports 80 and 443. An IDS monitor's ports 80 and 443 in order to detect intrusion attempts against the web server. If the web server is taken offline for maintenance, the IDS is temporarily no longer required and the data collection can be temporarily disabled. However, if packets would still be collected, we have excess data production.

Recommendation: Make sure that data collection mechanisms and IDSs are only active when they are needed. If there is no need for data collection, the collection mechanism should be disabled. A suggestion for how to create an architecture which supports enabling and disabling of data collection mechanisms is presented in Larson et al. (Larson et al., 2008b).

DEPLOYMENT STRATEGY

This section provides a four step strategy for achieving efficient data collection inspired by Wetmore (Wetmore, 1993). For each item in the list, a reference to a section in this document is provided. The referenced section contains additional information which is useful when making the decisions.

1. Determine which types of data that should be collected (sections *determining what data to collect* and *a taxonomy of deployment considerations*).
2. Determine an appropriate set of IDSs.
    This item is outside the scope of this chapter, but relevant information can be found in, e.g., (Axelsson, 2000; Debar et al., 1999). Furthermore, an indication of what intrusion detection models are appropriate for specific audit data is discussed by Lee and Xiang (Lee & Xiang, 2001).
3. Determine which characteristics are required from the mechanism, taking the desired data and applicable resource restrictions in consideration (sections *a taxonomy of mechanisms characteristics*, *a taxonomy of deployment considerations*, and *operational considerations*).
4. Determine how the data collection framework should be established and deployed (section *a taxonomy of deployment considerations*).

FUTURE CHALLENGES

Future challenges for data collection with respect to intrusion detection include (1) reconfigurable internal collection mechanisms and (2) new data collection mechanisms for security in embedded systems. These two topics are discussed below.

Internal collection mechanisms (Zamboni, 2001) have several useful characteristics for intrusion detection. For example, they produce little excess data and they are not easily subverted. However, on the downside, the monitored component must be taken offline when the collection mechanism is reconfigured. To mitigate this availability reduction, the mechanisms should be transparent to the monitored component. This strategy is similar to the transparent data collection strategies proposed in Cantrill et al. (Cantrill et al., 2004). These mechanisms only impose a small performance penalty for the monitored component when they are disabled and they do not affect availability. A combination of internal and transparent collection mechanisms would eliminate some of the issues with internal mechanisms. They would then be more useful for detection. Thus, the applicability should therefore be further investigated.

Security in embedded systems is a novel field with respect to security. However, it is highly important since previously and isolated embedded systems and networks are opened up for external communication. Two examples are process control systems and automobile in-vehicle networks. Recent security analyses of a generic in-vehicle network (Nilsson and Larson, 2008a; Nilsson and Larson, 2008b) have shown that the communication protocols and node computers deployed in the network have no protection against most security threats. Furthermore, methods for data collection and intrusion detection are missing. Therefore, research of new methods for data collection and intrusion detection that fits the embedded environment is needed.

CONCLUDING REMARKS

This chapter has provided a structured overview of how to select data collection mechanisms for intrusion detection. A theoretical part discusses the basics of data collection and is thus useful for newcomers to the field. Furthermore, a practical part discusses some operational considerations and common pitfalls. It also provides a collection mechanism deployment strategy and a classification of 50 data collection mechanisms and techniques. The practical part is useful for designers and operators who must select, configure, and deploy suitable collection mechanisms for their IDSs.

ACKNOWLEDGMENT

The work at Chalmers University of Technology is financially supported by the Swedish Emergency Management Agency. The work at the Norwegian University of Science and Technology is financially supported by the research council of Norway.

REFERENCES

Albari, M. Z. (2005). *A taxonomy of runtime software monitoring systems*. Retrieved August 9, 2008, from http://www.informatik.uni-kiel.de/~wg/Lehre/Seminar-SS05/ Mohamed_Ziad_Abari/vortrag-handout4.pdf.

Almgren, M., Jonsson, E., & Lindqvist, U. (2007). A comparison of alternative audit sources for Web server attack detection. In *Proceedings of the 12ᵗʰ Nordic Workshop on Secure IT Systems (NordSec 2007)* (pp. 101–112), Reykjavik, Iceland.

Anderson, J. M., Berc, L. M., Dean, J., Ghemawat, S., Henzinger, M. R., Leung, S. A., & Weihl, W. E. (1997). Continuous profiling: Where have all the cycles gone? *ACM SIGOPS Operating Systems Review, 31*(5), 1–14. doi:10.1145/269005.266637

Anderson, J. P. (1980). *Computer security threat monitoring and surveillance (Tech. Rep.)*. Fort Washington, PA: James P. Anderson Company.

Apache mod_log_config. (2010). *Apache mod_log_config module*. Retrieved November 25, 2010, from http://httpd.apache.org/docs/2.2/mod/mod_log_config.html.

Aranya, A., Wright, C. P., & Zadok, E. (2004). Tracefs: A file system to trace them all. In *Proceedings of the 3ʳᵈ USENIX Conference on File and Storage Technoligies (FAST 2004)* (pp. 129–145). San Francisco, CA: USENIX Association.

Ariel, T., & Miller, B. P. (1999). Fine-grained dynamic instrumentation of commodity operating system kernels. In *Proceedings of the 3ʳᵈ Symposium on Operating Systems Design and Implementation (OSDI'99)* (pp. 117–130), New Orleans, LA.

Axelsson, S. (2000). *Instrusion detection systems: A survey and taxonomy* (Tech. Rep. 99-15). Göteborg, Sweden: Chalmers University of Technology.

Axelsson, S., Lindqvist, U., Gustafson, U., & Jonsson, E. (1998). An approach to UNIX security logging. In *Proceedings of the 21ˢᵗ National Information Systems Security Conference* (pp. 62–75), Arlington, VA.

Baker, M. G., Hartman, J. H., Kupfer, M. D., Shirriff, K. W., & Ousterhout, J. K. (1991). Measurements of a distributed file system. *ACM SIGOPS Operating Systems Review, 25*(5), 198–212. doi:10.1145/121133.121164

Baxter, I. D. (2002). *Branch coverage for arbitrary languages made easy* (Tech. Rep.). Austin, TX: Semantic Designs. Retrieved November, 2010, from http://www.semdesigns.com/Company/Publications/TestCoverage.pdf

Bishop, M. (1987). Profiling under UNIX by patching. *Software, Practice & Experience, 17*(10), 729–739. doi:10.1002/spe.4380171006

Bishop, M. (1989). A model of security monitoring. In *Proceedings of the 5th Annual Computer Security Applications Conference* (pp. 46–52), Tucson, AZ, USA.

Bishop, M., Wee, C., & Frank, J. (1996). *Goal-oriented auditing and logging.* Retrieved November, 2010, from http://seclab.cs.ucdavis.edu/papers/tocs-96.pdf.

Borg, A., Kessler, R. E., & Wall, D. W. (1990). Generation and analysis of very long address traces. In *Proceedings of the 17th Annual Symposium on Computer Architecture (ISCA-17)* (pp. 270–279), Seattle, WA, USA.

Braden, R. T. (1988). A pseudo-machine for packet monitoring and statistics. *ACM SIGCOMM Computer Communication Review, 18*(4), 200–209. doi:10.1145/52325.52345

Buck, B., & Hollingsworth, J. K. (2000). An API for runtime code patching. *Journal of High Performance Computing Applications, 14*(4), 317–329. doi:10.1177/109434200001400404

Cantrill, B. M., Shapiro, M. W., & Leventhal, A. H. (2004). Dynamic instrumentation of production systems. In *Proceedings of the annual conference on USENIX Annual Technical Conference (ATEC'04)* (pp. 15–28). Boston, MA: USENIX Association.

Chuvakin, A., & Peterson, G. (2010). *How to do application logging right.* Retrieved November 24, 2010, from http://www.computer.org/cms/Computer.org/Computing-Now/homepage/2010/1010/W_SP_ApplicationLogging.pdf.

Common Criteria. (2005). *Common criteria for Information Technology security evaluation: Part 2: Security functional requirements, Version 2.3.* Retrieved November 25, 2010, from http://www.commoncriteriaportal.org/files/ccfiles/ccpart2v2.3.pdf.

Crosbie, M., & Spafford, E. (1995). Defending a computer system using autonomous agents. In *Proceedings of the 18th National Information Systems Security Conference.*

Curry, T. W. (1994). Profiling and tracing dynamic library usage via interposition. In *Proceedings of the USENIX Summer 1994 Technical Conference (USTC '94)* (pp. 267–2780). Boston, MA, USA: USENIX Association.

Debar, H., Dacier, M., & Wespi, A. (1999). *A revised taxonomy for intrusion-detection systems (Tech. Rep.)*. Rüschlikon, Switzerland: IBM Zürich Research Laboratory.

Delgado, N., Gates, A. Q., & Roach, S. (2004). A taxonomy and catalog of runtime software-fault monitoring tools. *IEEE Transactions on Software Engineering, 30*(12), 859–872. doi:10.1109/TSE.2004.91

Denning, D. E. (1986). An intrusion-detection model. In *Proceedings of the 1986 IEEE Symposium on Security and Privacy* (pp. 118–131). Oakland, CA, USA: IEEE.

Dongarra, J., London, K., Moore, S., Mucci, P., & Terpstra, D. (2001). *Using PAPI for hardware performance monitoring on Linux system*s. In Conference on Linux Clusters: The HPC Revolution, Urbana, IL.

Etsion, Y., Tsafrir, D., Kirkpatrick, S., & Feitelson, D. (2007). Fine grained kernel logging with Klogger: Experience and insights. In *Proceedings of the 2nd ACM SIGOPS/EuroSys European Conference on Computer Systems 2007* (pp. 259–272). Lisbon, Portugal: ACM.

Eustace, A., & Srivastava, A. (1994). *ATOM: A flexible interface for building high performace program analysis tools (Tech. Rep.)*. Palo Alto, CA: DEC Western Research Laboratory.

Fessi, B. A., BenAbdallah, S., Hamdi, M., Rekhis, S., & Boudriga, N. (2010). Data collection for Information Security System. In *Proceedings of the 2nd International Conference on Engineering Systems Management and Applications (ICESMA 2010)*, Sharjah, United Arab Emirates.

Forrest, S., Hofmeyr, S. A., Somayaji, A., & Longstaff, T. A. (1996). A sense of self for Unix processes. In *Proceedings of the 1996 IEEE Symposium on Research in Security and Privacy* (pp. 120–128). Oakland, CA, USA: IEEE.

Garfinkel, S., & Spafford, G. (1996). *Practical UNIX and Internet security* (2nd ed.). Sebastopol, CA, USA: O'Reilly.

GDB. (2010). *GDB: The GNU project debugger*. Retrieved November 25, 2010, from http://www.gnu.org/software/gdb/gdb.html.

Graham, S. L., Kessler, P. B., & McKusick, M. K. (1984). GPROF: A call graph execution profiler. *ACM SIGPLAN Notices, 39*(4), 49–57. doi:10.1145/989393.989401

Harrington, D., Presuhn, R., & Wijnen, B. (2002). *RFC 3411: An architecture for describing simple network management protocol (SNMP) management frameworks* (STD 62).

Hedbom, H., Kvarnström, H., & Jonsson, E. (1999). Security implications of distributed intrusion detection architectures. In *Proceedings of the 4th Nordic Workshop on Secure IT Systems* (pp. 225–243), Kista, Sweden.

Intersect Alliance. (2003). *Guide to snare for Linux*. Retrieved November 25, 2010, from http://www.intersectalliance.com/resources/Documentation/Guide_to_Snare_for_Linux-3.2.pdf.

Itzkowitz, M., Wylie, B. J. N., Aoki, C., & Kosche, N. (2003). Memory profiling using hardware counters. In *Proceedings of the 2003 ACM/IEEE Conference on Supercomputing (SC'03)* (pp. 17–29). Phoenix, AZ, USA: IEEE.

Jin, X., & Osborn, S. L. (2007). Architecture for data collection in database intrusion detection systems. In *Proceedings of the 4th VLDB Workshop on Secure Data Management (SDM 2007)*, Vienna, Austria.

Kad (2010). *Handling interrupt descriptor table for fun and profit*. Retrieved November 25, 2010, from http://www.phrack.org/issues.html?issue=59&id=4#article.

Kent, K., & Souppaya, M. (2006). *Guide to computer security log management: Recommendations of the National Institute of Standards and Technology* (NIST) (special publication 800-92). Retrieved November 24, 2010, from http://csrc.nist.gov/publications/nistpubs/800-92/SP800-92.pdf.

Killourhy, K. S., Maxion, R. A., & Tan, K. M. C. (2004). A defense-centric taxonomy based on attack manifestations. In *Proceedings of the International Conference on Dependable Systems and Networks (DSN 2004)* (pp. 102–111). Florence, Italy: IEEE.

Kuperman, B. A. (2004). *A categorization of computer security monitoring systems and the impact on the design of audit sources*. PhD thesis, Purdue University, West Lafayette, IN.

Kuperman, B. A., & Spafford, E. (1999). *Generation of application level audit data via library interposition (Tech. Rep. CERIAS TR 99-11)*. West Lafayette, IN: COAST Laboratory, Purdue University.

Larson, U. E., Jonsson, E., & Lindskog, S. (2008a). A revised taxonomy of data collection mechanisms with a focus on intrusion detection. In *Proceedings of the 3rd IEEE International Conference on Availability, Security, and Reliability (ARES 2008)* (pp. 624–629). Barcelona, Spain: IEEE.

Larson, U. E., Lindskog, S., Nilsson, D. K., & Jonsson, E. (2008b). Operator-centric and adaptive intrusion detection. In *Proceedings of the 4th International Conference on Information Assurance and Security (IAS'08)* (pp. 161–166). Naples, Italy: IEEE.

Larus, J. R. (1993). Efficient program tracing. *Computer, 26*(5), 52–61. doi:10.1109/2.211900

Larus, J. R., & Ball, T. (1994). Rewriting executable files to measure program behavior. *Software, Practice & Experience, 24*(2), 197–218. doi:10.1002/spe.4380240204

Lee, W., Stolfo, S., & Chan, P. (1997). Learning patterns from Unix process execution traces for intrusion detection. In *AI approaches to fraud detection and risk management* (pp. 50–60). Providence, RI: AAAI Press.

Lee, W., & Xiang, D. (2001). Information-theoretic measures for anomaly detection. In *Proceedings of the 2001 Symposium on Research in Security and Privacy* (pp. 130–143), Oakland, CA.

Levon, J., & Elie, P. (2009). *Oprofile: A system-wide profiler for Linux systems.* Retrieved November 25, 2010, from http://oprofile.sourceforge.net/news/.

Linux Audit Subsystem. (2004). *Linux audit subsystem design documentation for Kernel 2.6.* Retrieved November 25, 2010, from http://www.uniforum.chi.il.us/slides/HardeningLinux/LAuS-Design.pdf.

Love, R. (2005). *Linux kernel development* (2nd ed.). Utah, USA: Novell Press.

Ltrace. (2002). *ltrace – Default branch.* Retrieved November 25, 2010, from http://freshmeat.net/projects/ltrace/.

Luk, C.-K., Cohn, R., Muth, R., Patil, H., Klauser, A., & Lowney, G. …Hazelwood, K. (2005). Pin: Building customized program analysis tools with dynamic instrumentation. In *Proceedings of the 2005 ACM SIGPLAN Conference on Programming Language Design and Implementation (PLDI'05)* (pp. 190–200). Chicago, IL, USA: ACM.

Lundin Barse, E. (2004). *Logging for intrusion and fraud detection.* PhD thesis, Chalmers University of Technology, Göteborg, Sweden.

Lundin Barse, E., & Jonsson, E. (2004). Extracting attack manifestations to determine log data requirements for intrusion detection. In *Proceedings of the 20th Annual Computer Security Applications Conference (ACSAC 2004)* (pp. 158–167). Tucson, AZ, USA: IEEE.

Maggi, F., Robertson, W., Kruegel, C., & Vigna, G. (2009). Protecting a moving target: Addressing Web application concept drift. In *Proceedings of the 12th International Symposium on Recent Advances in Intrusion Detection (RAID 2009)*, Saint-Malo, Brittany, France.

Mathew, S., Petropoulos, M., Ngo, H. Q., & Upadhyaya, S. (2010). A data-centric approach to insider attack detection in database systems. In *Proceedings of the 13th International Symposium on Recent Advances in Intrusion Detection (RAID 2010)*, Ottawa, Ontario, Canada.

McCanne, S., & Jacobson, V. (1993). The BSD packet filter: A new architecture for user-level packet capture. In *Proceedings of the USENIX Winter 1993 Conference (USENIX'93)* (pp. 259–270). San Diego, CA, USA: USENIX Association.

McKusick, M. K., Bostic, K., Karels, M. J., & Quarterman, J. S. (1996). *The design and implementation of the 4.4BSD operating system*. Boston, MA: Addison-Wesley.

Mogul, J. C., Rashid, R. F., & Acetta, M. J. (1987). The packet filter: An efficient mechanism for user-level network code. *ACM SIGOPS Operating Systems Review*, *21*(5), 39–51. doi:10.1145/37499.37505

Moore, R. J. (2001). A universal dynamic trace for Linux and other operating systems. In *Proceedings of the FREENIX Track: 2001 USENIX Annual Technical Conference* (pp. 297–308). Boston, MA: USENIX Association.

National Computer Security Center. (1988). *A guide to understanding audit in trusted systems* (Tech. Rep. NCSC-TG-001). National Computer Security Center (NCSC).

Nilsson, D. K., & Larson, U. E. (2008a). Conducting forensic investigations of cyber attacks on automobile in-vehicle networks. In *Proceedings of the 1st ACM International Conference on Forensic Applications and Techniques in Telecommunications, Information and Multimedia (e-Forensics 2008)* (pp. 1–6). Adelaide, Australia: ACM.

Nilsson, D. K., & Larson, U. E. (2008b). Simulated attacks on CAN-buses: Vehicle virus. In *Proceedings of the 5th IASTED Asian Conference on Communication Systems and Networks (AsiaCSN 2008)* (pp.66–72). Langkawi, Malaysia: IASTED.

Ousterhout, J. K., Costa, H. D., Harrison, D., Kunze, J. A., Kupfer, M., & Thompson, J. G. (1985). A trace-driven analysis of the UNIX 4.2 BSD file system. *ACM SIGOPS Operating Systems Review*, *19*(5), 15–24. doi:10.1145/323627.323631

Panchamukhi, P. S. (2004). *Kernel debugging with Kprobes*. Retrieved November 25, 2010, from http://www.ibm.com/developerworks/linux/library/l-kprobes.html.

Peisert, S. P. (2007). *A model of forensic analysis using goal-oriented logging.* PhD thesis, University of California, San Diego, CA.

Price, K. E. (1997). *Host-based misuse detection and conventional operating systems' audit data collection.* Master's thesis, Purdue University, West Lafayette, IN.

Punti, G., Gil, M., Martorell, X., & Navarro, N. (2002). *Gtrace: Function call and memory access traces of dynamically linked programs in ia-32 and ia-64 Linux* (Tech. Rep. UPC-DAC-2002-51). Barcelona, Spain: Polytechnic University of Catalonia.

Risso, F., & Degioanni, L. (2001). An architecture for high performance network analysis. In *Proceedings of the 6ᵗʰ IEEE Symposium on Computers and Communications (ISCC'01)*. Hammamet, Tunisia: IEEE.

Rubini, A., & Corbet, J. (2001). *Linux device drivers* (2nd ed.). Sebastopol, CA, USA: O'Reilly.

Russinovich, M., & Cogswell, B. (2010). *Process monitor.* Retrieved November 25, 2010, from http://technet.micrsoft.com/en-us/sysinternals/bb896645.aspx.

Russinovich, M. E., & Solomon, D. A. (2005). *Microsoft Windows internals* (4th ed.). USA: Microsoft Press.

SANS. 2006). *SANS consensus project Information System audit logging requirements.* Retrieved November 24, 2010, from http://www.sans.org/resources/policies/info_sys_audit.pdf.

Schroeder, B. A. (1995). On-line monitoring: A tutorial. *Computer, 28*(6), 72–78. doi:10.1109/2.386988

Smith, M. D. (1991). *Tracing with pixie* (Tech. Rep. CSL-TR-91-497). Palo Alto, CA: Stanford University.

Strace. (2010). *Strace – Default branch.* Retrieved November 25, 2010, from http://sourceforge.net/projects/strace.

Sun Microsystems. (1988). SunOS Reference Manual: *The Network interface tap.*

Sun Microsystems. (1995). *SunSHIELD basic security module guide.* CA: Mountain View.

Syscalltrack. (2010). *Syscalltrack.* Retrieved November 25, 2010, from http://syscalltrack.sourceforge.net.

Tan, K. M. C., Killourhy, K. S., & Maxion, R. A. (2002). Undermining an anomaly-based intrusion detection system using common exploits. In *Proceedings of the 5th International Symposium on Recent Advances in Intrusion Detection* (pp. 54–73). Zurich, Switzerland: Springer-Verlag.

Tcpdump. (2010). *Tcpdump/libpcap*. Retrieved November 25, 2010, from http://www.tcpdump.org.

Vogels, W. (2000). File system usage in Windows NT 4.0. *ACM SIGOPS Operating Systems Review, 34*(2), 17–18. doi:10.1145/346152.346177

Wagner, D., & Soto, P. (2002). Mimicry attacks on host-based intrusion detection systems. In *9th ACM Conference on Computer and Communications Security* (pp. 255–264). Washington, DC: ACM.

Wall, D. W. (1989). *Link-time code modification (Tech. Rep.-Res. Rep. 89/17)*. Palo Alto, CA: DEC Western Research Laboratory.

Wetmore, B. R. (1993). *Paradigms for the reduction of audit trails*. Master's thesis, University of California Davis, Davis, CA.

Yaghmour, K., & Dagenais, M. R. (2000). Measuring and characterizing system behavior using kernel-level event logging. In *Proceedings of the USENIX Annual Technical Conference (ATEC'00)*. San Diego, CA, USA: USENIX Association.

Zamboni, D. (2001). *Using internal sensors for computer intrusion detection*. PhD thesis, Purdue University, West Lafayette, IN.

Zhang, X., Wang, Z., Gloy, N., Chen, J. B., & Smith, M. D. (1997). System support for automatic profiling and optimization. In *Proceedings of the 16th ACM Symposium on Operating Systems Principles (SOSP'97)* (pp. 15–26). New York, NY, USA: ACM.

Zhou, S., Costa, H. D., & Smith, A. J. (1985). *A file system tracing package for Berkeley UNIX (Tech. Rep.)*. Berkeley, CA: University of California at Berkeley.

ADDITIONAL READING

Amoroso, E. (1999). *Intrusion Detection: An Introduction to Internet Surveillance, Correlation, Trace Back, Traps, and Response*. Sparta, NJ, USA: Intrusion.Net Books.

Anderson, R. J. (2008). *Security Engineering: A Guide to Building Dependable Distributed Systems* (2nd ed.). New York, NY: John Wiley & Sons.

Axelsson, S. (2000). The base-rate fallacy and the difficulty of intrusion detection. [TISSEC]. *ACM Transactions on Information and System Security, 3*(3), 186–205. doi:10.1145/357830.357849

Axelsson, S. (2004). Visualising intrusions: Watching the Webserver. In *Proceedings of the 19th IFIP International Information Security Conference (SEC2004)* (pp. 259–274). Tolouse, France: Springer.

Cheswick, W. R., Bellovin, S. M., & Rubin, A. D. (2003). *Firewalls and Internet Security: Repelling the Wily Hacker* (2nd ed.). Upper Saddle River, NJ: Addison Wesley.

Cheung, S., Dutertre, B., Fong, M., Lindqvist, U., Skinner, K., & Valdes, A. (2007). Using model-based intrusion detection for SCADA networks. In *Proceedings of the SCADA Security Scientific Symposium*, Miami, FL, USA.

CIDF. (2010). *Common intrusion detection framework.* Retrieved November 25, 2010, from http://gost.isi.edu/cidf/.

Durst, R., Champion, T., Witten, B., Miller, E., & Spagnuolo, L. (1999). Testing and Evaluating Computer Intrusion Detection Systems. *Communications of the ACM, 42*(7), 53–61. doi:10.1145/306549.306571

Erbacher, R. F. (2004). Analysis and management of intrusion data collection. In *Proceedings of the 2004 International Conference on Security and Management (SAM'04)* (pp. 179–185). Las Vegas, NV, USA.

Erbacher, R. F., & Augustine, B. (2002). Intrusion detection data: Collection and analysis. In

Fisch, E. A., White, G. B., & Pooch, U. W. (1994). The design of an audit trail analysis tool.

Gollmann, D. (2006). *Computer Security* (2nd ed.). West Sussex, England: John Wiley & Sons.

In *Proceedings of the 10th Annual Computer Security Applications Conference (ACSAC 1994)* (pp.126–132), Orlando, FL, USA.

Jaquith, A. (2007). *Security metrics: Replacing fear, uncertainty, and doubt.* Upper Saddle River, NJ: Addison Wesley.

Kemmerer, R. A., & Vigna, G. (2002). Intrusion detection: A brief history and overview. *Computer, 35*(4), 27–30. doi:10.1109/MC.2002.1012428

Kurose, J. F., & Ross, K. W. (200x). *Computer networking: A top-down approach featuring the Internet, 5th edition.* Upper Saddle River, NJ: Addison-Wesley.

Larson, U. E. (2009). *On adapting data collection to intrusion detection.* PhD thesis, Chalmers University of Technology, Göteborg, Sweden.

Larson, U. E., Lundin Barse, E., & Jonsson, E. (2005). METAL: A tool for extracting attack manifestations. In *Proceedings of the 2nd Conference on Detection of Intrusions and Malware, and Vulnerability Assessment (DIMVA 2005) (LNCS 3548)* (pp. 85–102). Vienna, Austria: Springer-Verlag.

Lindqvist, U. (1999). *On the fundamentals of analysis and detection of computer misuse.* PhD thesis, Chalmers University of Technology, Göteborg, Sweden.

McHugh, J. (2000). Testing intrusion detection systems: A critique of the 1998 and 1999 DARPA intrusion detection system evaluations as performed by Lincoln Laboratory. [TISSEC]. *ACM Transactions on Information and System Security, 3*(4), 262–294. doi:10.1145/382912.382923

Pfleeger, C. P., & Pfleeger, S. L. (2006). *Security in Computing* (4th ed.). Upper Saddle River, NJ: Prentice Hall.

Proceedingsof the2002International Conference on Security and Management (SAM'02) (pp. 3–9), Las Vegas, NV, USA.

Ragsdale, D., Carver, C., Humphries, J., & Pooch, U. (2000). Adaptation techniques for intrusion detection and intrusion response systems. In *Proceedings of the 2000 IEEE International Conference on Systems, Man, and Cybernetics* (vol. 4, pp. 2344–2349). Nashville, TN: IEEE.

Sebring, M. M., Shellhouse, E., Hanna, M., & Whitehurst, R. (1988). Expert systems in intrusion detection: A case study. In *Proceedings of the 11th National Information Systems Security Conference* (pp.74–81), Arlington, VA, USA.

Silberschatz, A., Galvin, P., & Gagne, G. (2009). *Operating system concepts* (8th ed.). Hoboken, NY: John Wiley & sons.

Stallings, W., & Brown, L. (2007). *Computer security: Principles and practice.* Upper Saddle River, NJ: Prentice Hall.

Vigna, G., Robertson, W., & Balzarotti, D. (2004). Testing network based intrusion detection signatures using mutant exploits. In *Proceedings of the 11th ACM Conference on Computer and Communications Security (CCS 2004)* (pp 21–30). Washington D.C.: ACM.

KEY TERMS AND DEFINITIONS

Audit Data: A chronological record of system activities.

Data Collection: The process of capturing events in a computer system. The result of a data collection operation is a log record. The term logging is often used as a synonym for data collection.

Intrusion: The term intrusion is in this context simply defined as an attack on a computer system, resulting in a breach.

Intrusion Detection: Intrusion detection is the process of identifying attacks or attack attempts. This process could be performed either manually or automatically.

Intrusion Detection System (IDS): An automated system used to warn operators of intrusions or intrusion attempts. An IDS is implemented in software and/ or hardware.

Security Log: A security log stores log record in chronological order. The terms security log and audit trail are often used interchangeably within the security community.

Taxonomy: Taxonomy is the science and practice of classification. Taxonomies are used when categorizing real-life as well as artificial phenomenon and the aim is to make systematic studies easier.

APPENDIX: CLASSIFICATION OF MECHANISMS AND TECHNIQUES FOR DATA COLLECTION

Table 1 provides an overview of 50 classified mechanisms and techniques for data collection. Each *row* in Table 1 represents the classification of one mechanism. The table contains dimensions from the taxonomies, i.e., *log data, location with respect to environment (Location), time of introduction (ToI), granularity of log trigger (Gr), trigger (Tr)*, and *action (Ac)*. The final column provides a reference to Table 2 which contains additional information.

Table 1. Mechanisms classified according to selected dimensions of the two taxonomies

Log data	Location	Realization		Behavior		Reference
		ToI	Gr	Tr	Ac	(see Table 2)
Network	OS Kernel	Pre-runtime	Program	Event	Retrieve attributes	1
Network	OS Kernel	Pre-runtime	Program	Event	Occurrence	2
System	OS Kernel	Pre-runtime	Program	Time	Occurrence	3
System	OS Kernel	Runtime	Program	Time	Occurrence	4
System	OS Kernel	Pre-runtime	Instruction	Event	Retrieve attributes	5
System	OS Kernel	Pre-runtime	Instruction	Event	Retrieve attributes/ Occurrence	6
System	OS Interface	Pre-runtime	Instruction	Event	Retrieve attributes/ Occurrence	7
System	OS Interface	Pre-runtime	Program	Event	Retrieve attributes	8
System	OS Kernel	Pre-runtime	Program	Event	Retrieve attributes	9
System	OS Kernel	Runtime	Program	Event	Retrieve attributes	10
System	OS Kernel	Pre-runtime	Program	Event/ Time	Retrieve attributes/ Occurrence	11
Application	Application	Pre-runtime	Instruction	Event	Retrieve attributes/ Occurrence	12
Application	Application	Pre-runtime	Program	Event	Occurrence	13
Application	Application	Runtime	Instruction	Event	Retrieve attributes/ Occurrence	14

continued on next page

Table 1. Continued

Log data	Location	Realization		Behavior		Reference
		ToI	Gr	Tr	Ac	(see Table 2)
Application	Application	Runtime	Instruction	Event	Occurrence	15
Application	Helper library	Runtime	Program	Event	Retrieve attributes/ Occurrence	16
Application	Application	Pre-runtime	Instruction	Event/ Time	Retrieve attributes/ Occurrence	17
Application	OS Kernel	Pre-runtime	Program	Time	Occurrence	18
Application	Application	Pre-runtime	Program	Event	Retrieve attributes	19
Application	OS Kernel	Runtime	Program	Time	Occurrence	20
System/ Application	OS Kernel	Runtime	Instruction	Event	Retrieve attributes/ Occurrence	21
System/ Application	OS Kernel	Pre-runtime	Program	Time	Occurrence	22
System/ Application	OS Kernel	Pre-runtime	Program	Event/ Time	Retrieve attributes/ Occurrence	23
System/ Application	OS Kernel	Runtime	Instruction	Event/ Time	Retrieve attributes/ Occurrence	24
System/ Application	OS Kernel	Pre-runtime	Program	Event	Retrieve attributes	25
System/ Application	OS Interface	Pre-runtime	Program	Event	Retrieve attributes	26
System/ Application	OS Kernel	Pre-runtime	Program	Event	Retrieve attributes/ Occurrence	27
System/ Application	OS Kernel	Pre-runtime	Program	Event	Retrieve attributes	28

Table 2. Translation for the references in Table 1

Reference	Source of information
1	(McCanne & Jacobson, 1993; Mogul et al., 1987; Risso & Degioanni, 2001; Sun Microsystems, 1988; tcpdump, 2010)
2	(Braden, 1988; Harrington et al., 2002; Rubini & Corbet, 2001)
3	(McKusick et al., 1996)
4	(Itzkowitz et al., 2003)
5	(Panchamukhi, 2010)
6	(Etsion et al., 2007; Moore, 2001)
7	Ousterhout et al. (1985), Zhou et al. (1985)
8	(kad, 2010)
9	(Love, 2005)
10	(Aranya et al., 2004; Russinovich & Cogswell, 2010)
11	(Baker et al., 1991; Vogels, 2000)
12	(Borg et al., 1990; Eustace & Srivastava, 1994; Larus & Ball, 1994; Smith, 1991; Wall, 1989)
13	(Baxter,2001)
14	(Buck & Hollingsworth, 2000; gdb, 2010; ltrace, 2010; Luk et al., 2005; Punti et al., 2002; strace, 2010)
15	(Bishop, 1987)
16	(Curry, 1994; Kuperman & Spafford, 1999)
17	(Graham et al., 1984)
18	(Zhang et al., 1997)
19	(Apache mod_log_config, 2010; Garfinkel & Spafford, 1996)
20	(Anderson et al., 1997)
21	(Ariel & Miller, 1999)
22	(Levon & Elie, 2010)
23	(Dongarra et al., 2001)
24	(Cantrill et al., 2004)
25	(Russinovich & Solomon, 2005)
26	(syscalltrack, 2010)
27	(Yaghmour & Dagenais, 2000)
28	(Linux Audit Subsystem, 2010; Sun Microsystems,1995)

Chapter 2
Protecting Enterprise Networks:
An Intrusion Detection Technique Based on Auto-Reclosing

Nana K. Ampah
Jacobs Engineering Group, USA

Cajetan M. Akujuobi
Alabama State University, USA

ABSTRACT

Designing, planning and managing telecommunication, industrial control and enterprise networks with special emphasis on effectiveness, efficiency and reliability without considering security planning, management and constraints have made them vulnerable. They have become more vulnerable due to their recent connectivity to open networks with the intention of establishing decentralized management and remote control (Chunmei, Mingchu, Jianbo, & Jizhou, 2004; Chi-Ho Tsang & Kwong, 2005; Amanullah, Kalam, & Zayegh, 2005; Motta Pires & Oliveira, 2006; Haji, Lindsay, & Song, 2005; Car & Jakupovic, 2005; Pollet, 2002; Farris & Nicol, 2004; Dagle, Windergren, & Johnson, 2002). They are now real targets for terrorists and therefore need urgent attention (Bridis & Sullivan, 2007; McMillan, 2008). Existing Intrusion Prevention and Detection Systems (IPS and IDS) do not guarantee absolute security.

Our new IDS, which employs both signature-based and anomaly detection as its analysis strategies, will be able to detect both known and unknown attacks and further isolate them. An auto-reclosing technique used on long rural power lines and multi-resolution techniques were used in developing these IDS, which will help

DOI: 10.4018/978-1-60960-836-1.ch002

Copyright ©2012, IGI Global. Copying or distributing in print or electronic forms without written permission of IGI Global is prohibited.

update existing IPSs. It should effectively block SYN-flood attacks; distributed denial of service attacks (DDoS) based on SYN-flood attacks, and helps eliminate four out of the five major limitations of existing IDSs and IPSs.

INTRODUCTION

Enterprise networks are the main targets for hackers or intruders due to the fact that most financial transactions take place online and the networks also handle vast amounts of data and other resources (Satti & Garner, 2001). Handling transactions online is on the increase everyday because it makes life easier for both the customers as well as the enterprises offering services (Jou et al., 2000; Yau & Xinyu Zhang, 1999; Ko, 2003; Tront & Marchany, 2004). Enterprise networks also have lots of bandwidth, which is very attractive to hackers because they take advantage of that by using those networks as launching pads to attack others (Tront & Marchany, 2004; Janakiraman, Waldvogel, & Qi Zhang, 2003). It therefore becomes very difficult for the IDSs and IPSs at the receiving end to detect and prevent the attacks or hackers, since the packet header information will indicate legitimate senders. This is the main reason why most IPSs are easily bypassed by hackers (Tront & Marchany, 2004; Paulson, 2002; Weber, 1999). Intrusion prevention, which is a proactive technique, prevents the attacks from entering the network. Unfortunately, some of the attacks still bypass the intrusion prevention systems. Intrusion detection on the other hand, detects attacks only after they have entered the network.

Although attacks are generally assumed to emanate from outside a given network, the most dangerous attacks actually emanate from the network itself. Those are really difficult to detect since most users of the network are assumed to be trusted people. The situation has necessitated drastic research work in the area of network security, especially in the development of intrusion detection and prevention systems intended to detect and prevent all possible attacks on a given network (Akujuobi & Ampah, 2007; Akujuobi, Ampah, & Sadiku, 2007). These IDSs use either anomaly or signature-based detection techniques. Anomaly detection techniques detect both known and unknown attacks, but signature-based detection techniques detect only known attacks. The main approaches of anomaly detection techniques are statistical, predictive pattern generation, neural networks, and sequence matching and learning. The main approaches of signature-based detection techniques are expert systems, keystroke monitoring, model-based, state transition analysis, and pattern matching (Biermann, Cloete, & Venter, 2001). There is no existing IDS or IPS that can detect or prevent all intrusions. For example, configuring a firewall to be 100% foolproof compromises the very service provided by the network. The use of conventional encryption algorithms and system level security techniques have helped to some extent, but not to the levels expected (Fadia, 2006; Leinwand &

Conroy, 1996; Stallings, 2003). The following are the five limitations associated with existing IDSs (Satti & Garner, 2001):

1. **Use of central analyzer:** Whenever the central analyzer is attacked by an intruder the whole system will be without protection, so it becomes a single point of failure (Janakiraman, Waldvogel, & Qi Zhang, 2003);
2. **Limited scalability:** Processing all data at a central point limits the size of the entire network that can be monitored and controlled at a time. Data collection in a distributed fashion also causes excessive traffic in the network (Kayacik, Zincir-Heywood, & Heywood, 2004);
3. **Effectiveness:** The ability of existing IDSs/IPSs to detect and prevent intrusion is still not clearly established because of high false positive and false negative rates (Chunmei, Mingchu, Jianbo, & Jizhou, 2004);
4. **Efficiency:** Quantifying resources like time, power, bandwidth, and storage used by existing IDSs will be a critical success factor (Khoshgoftaar & Abushadi, 2004); and
5. **Security:** Securing the security data itself from intruders is also a very important limitation to existing IDSs.

It is still an open problem to develop IDSs and IPSs to detect and prevent SYN-flood attacks, Distributed Denial of Service (DDoS) attacks based on SYN-flood attacks, and also eliminate some or all of the limitations of existing IDSs. Although many IDS and IPS techniques have been proposed for securing networks from attacks, problems with SYN-flood attacks and DDoS attacks based on SYN-flood attacks have not been resolved. Also, there is no research work that has attempted to solve the above problems nor have there been attempts to eliminate the majority or all of the five major problems of existing IDSs. Most research works solved only one or two of the major problems. Our approach will resolve the above problems through the following steps:

1. Design an IDS technique based on a well established model (i.e., auto-reclosing), which specifically targets SYN-flood attacks and DDoS attacks based on SYN-flood attacks; and
2. Transmit all security data from the network directly to the central detection point for analysis instead of transmitting them through the network itself.

Step one aims at solving the problems with effectiveness of existing IDSs. Step two aims at solving the problems with efficiency (i.e., saving bandwidth), security (i.e., securing security data from intruders), and limited scalability (i.e., reducing traffic in the network). These are the objectives of our approach.

BACKGROUND

The following major approaches are used to manage network security problems:

1. Intrusion Detection (traditional); and
2. Intrusion Prevention (proactive).

The basic techniques used by the two approaches are as follows:

1. Signature based detection system (Attack patterns are considered as signatures);
2. Anomaly detection system (Anything unusual is considered as suspect);
3. Distributed intrusion detection system (Data is collected and analyzed in a distributed fashion); and
4. Centralized intrusion detection system (Data is collected in a distributed fashion but analyzed centrally).

The use of intrusion detection and prevention techniques in addition to other authentication techniques has become very necessary in managing enterprise network security. A layer approach is often used since there is no single technique that guarantees absolute security against all attacks on a given network. Very strong authentication techniques will also help prevent attacks from within the network. Depending on where the IDS software is installed, it can be referred to as network based intrusion detection system (NIDS) or host based intrusion detection system (HIDS). NIDS ensures preventive control of a given system, whiles HIDS ensures detective control. The following are some existing NIDS: Internet Security Systems Real Secure, Network Security Wizard Dragon IDS, Symantec Net Prowler, Cisco Systems Net Ranger, Network Flight Recorder Intrusion, Detection Appliance, Network Ice Black Ice Defender, CyberSafe Centrax, and Snort. The following are some existing HIDS: Internet Security Systems Real Secure, Symantec Intruder Alert, CyberSafe Centrax, and Tripwire.

Securing information on data networks and the networks themselves have become very difficult tasks considering the diverse types and number of intrusions being recorded daily. There is a lot of ongoing research work in the area of data network security management to develop techniques to combat intruders because of the financial losses incurred by enterprises due to activities of intruders (Paez & Torres, 2009; Jing-Wen, Mei-Juan, Ling-Fang, & Shi-Ru, 2009; Kui, 2009; Lixia, Dan, & Hongyu, 2009; Momenzadeh, Javadi, & Dezfouli, 2009; Jing, HouKuan, ShengFeng, & Xiang, 2009; Ihn-Han & Olariu, 2009; Cannady, 2009; Changxin & Ke, 2009; Wei, Xiangliang, Gombault, & Knapskog, 2009). This effort should seriously include securing networks also, and that is exactly what this IDS proves to do. Research work in network security can be categorized into three major areas: intrusion detection systems only; intrusion prevention systems only; and combined intrusion detection and intrusion prevention systems.

INTRUSION DETECTION SYSTEMS

Intrusion detection, which is a traditional technique, detects attacks only after they have entered the network. The analysis of IDSs in terms of advantages and disadvantages was done in (Vokorokos, Kleinova, & Latka, 2006). This study was purely theoretical and it was proposed to consider different types of IDSs based on attack types, and whether attacks are directed towards a whole network, a sub network or a host. It will finally consider at the implementation stage, the important criterion for determining which layers of the ISO/OSI model will be covered by the IDSs including their ranges of operation. The importance of an automated intrusion response and further proposal on a dynamic intrusion response known as Gnipper vaccine was highlighted in (Zhaoyu & Uppala, 2006). This is a countermeasure, which uses dynamic agents to mitigate denial of service attacks. Although the approach provided an efficient and effective response to an intrusion with very little overhead, future work in this effort will focus on developing an efficient "trust model." A pattern matching NIDS, which consists of four modules: collection module, analysis module, response module and attack rule library was developed in (Zhou, Liu, & Zhang, 2006).

The system is based on Common Intrusion Detection Framework (CIDF) architecture and mature intrusion detection technology. Although efficient and effective, the system has to include anomaly detection in the future. An intrusion detection engine based on neural networks combined with a protection method, also based on watermarking techniques, was presented in (Mitrokotsa, Komninos, & Douligeris, 2007). This engine exploits two research areas, that is, visual representation and watermarking, which have not been used in mobile ad hoc network (MANET) in the past. The advantages of eSOM and visual representation in achieving intrusion detection were demonstrated. The use of the proposed engine with various routing protocols, for detecting various types of attacks and testing real MANET in the future was emphasized. An approach to combat threats from worms, insiders, and attackers with a toehold was discussed in (Weaver, Paxson, & Sommer, 2007). This was done by exploiting the VLAN capabilities of modern switches to enforce that all LAN communications must traverse and meet the approval of an intrusion detection monitor that operates separately from the switch. Two benefits were realized here: deployment and operation in today's enterprise networks without requiring replacement of existing infrastructure, and the use of highly flexible, commodity PCs for

LAN monitoring, rather than algorithms embedded in difficult-to-reprogram custom hardware. Further work is required in the development of a mechanism capable of processing WAN traffic and not only LAN traffic as described here.

A novel feature classification scheme for features that can be extracted by sniffing the network was introduced in (Onut & Ghorbani, 2006). It further gives a better understanding for real-time features that can be extracted from packets in order to detect intrusions. Preliminary results are promising for mapping the network features into the network attack domain. Future work will introduce statistical analysis of subsets of features versus specific attacks and attack categories in order to determine the necessary set of features to be analyzed by an IDS/IPS. Research into the question as to whether one can detect attacks without keeping per-flow state was initiated in (Ramana, Singh, & Varghese, 2007). It suggests that a tradeoff between performance and completeness may not be as Draconian as is commonly thought. Some progress has been made for bandwidth-based and partial completion DoS attacks, and scan-based attacks including worms, but the general problem still remains very difficult. Further work is needed concerning issues of "behavioral aliasing" and "spoofing" in such scalable solutions. An introduction to new evasion methods, presentation of test results for confirming attack outcomes based on server responses, and proposal of a methodology for confirming response validity were discussed in (Chaboya, Raines, Baldwin, & Mullins, 2006). These methods must be implemented as either analyst guidance or preferably in a NIDS plug-in or similar software solution. Also, these methods lead to the development of payload-size and shell-code-matching filters for Snort. Future work looks promising in reducing both the analyst workload and the risk from evasion attacks.

A framework for internet banking security using multi-layered, feed-forward artificial neural networks was outlined in (Bignell, 2006). Anomaly detection techniques applied for transaction authentication and intrusion detection within internet banking security architectures were utilized. This comprehensive fraud detection model via networks technology has the potential to significantly limit present level of financial fraud experienced with existing fraud prevention techniques. A prototype for this neural network will be developed to quantitatively validate the effectiveness of this machine learning technique. An innovative approach to the design and implementation of a VoIP specific honeypot was presented in (Nassar, State, & Festor, 2007). Simulation results from using this Session Initiation Protocol (SIP) specific honeypot look promising in relation to the effectiveness of the information gathering tools and the correctness of the inference engine deductions. Attempts to reduce false positive rates generated by cooperative Intrusion Detection Systems (IDSs) in MANETs were discussed in (Otrok, Debbabi, Assi, & Bhattacharya, 2007). This was done by analyzing the intrusion detected by mobile nodes within a cooperative game theoretic framework. Simulation results provided better results compared to existing methods.

An Incident Response Support System (IRSS) that correlates past and present events in order to classify attacks was introduced in (Capuzzi, Spalazzi, & Pagliarecci, 2006). This also serves as a preliminary report on a system to support the incident response activities of a security administrator. So far, a prototype has been implemented, but a massive set of experiments in order to evaluate the effectiveness of this system is underway. Plans to investigate new similarity metrics (for response retrieval) and more sophisticated adaptation algorithm will be dealt with in the future. A suit of detection techniques to identify fraudulent usage of mobile telecommunications services by exploiting regularities demonstrated in users' behaviors was presented in (Sun, Xiao, & Wang). This leads to the creation of an end user's profile for anomaly detection in wireless networks.

The intrusion detection problem is formulated as a multi-feature two-class pattern classification problem, which applies Bayes Decision Rule to the collected data. Both algorithms can achieve good performance depending on the input parameters as indicated by results from simulation studies. More features need to be considered in the future so as to make the system more general and robust. A fully automated technique for detecting, preventing and reporting SQL Injection Attacks (SQLIAs) incidents was discussed in (Muthuprasanna, Ke, & Kothari, 2006). Preliminary evaluation results of a prototype developed against various performance metrics affecting web server performance was also provided. Solutions for these critical security issues in web applications ensure easy transition towards next generation web services.

INTRUSION PREVENTION SYSTEMS

Intrusion prevention, which is a proactive technique, prevents the attacks from entering the network. Unfortunately, some of the attacks still bypass the intrusion prevention systems. A simple methodology for testing dynamic intrusion-prevention systems for McAfee Entercept version 5.0 and the Cisco Security Agent version 4.5 was developed in (Labbe, Rowe, & Fulp, 2006). Although test results showed that neither of the products stood up to their required effectiveness, the Cisco product did better. This test even supports the fact that effectiveness is one of the major problems of existing IDSs and IPSs. A multiple joint prevention technique of information security in Storage Area Networks (SAN) environment was presented in (Zheng-De, Zhi-Guo, Dong, & Fei-Teng, 2006). Although this technique can greatly improve the ability of preventing intrusion, issues with misreporting of intrusion prevention in IDS and filch of information in SAN need to be considered in future. A novel pattern-matching algorithm, which uses ternary content addressable memory (TCAM) and capable of matching multiple patterns in a single operation was considered in (Weinberg, Tzur-David, Dolev, & Anker, 2006). This system is compatible with Snort's rules syntax, which is the de facto standard for intrusion prevention systems. This Network Intrusion Prevention System (NIPS) presents several advantages over existing NIPS devices.

The necessary and sufficient conditions for the application of Byzantine agreement protocol to the intrusion detection problem were investigated in (Colon Osorio, 2007). This was done by developing a secure architecture and fault-resilient engine (SAFE), which is capable of tolerating such problems. This IPS eliminates some of the common shortcomings of existing IPSs. Both the implementation and evaluation stages are complete and require extra research work in relation to masquerading, distribution and protection of sensitive data, scalability and implementation issues. The link between concepts of the immune system in relation to the Danger Theory and components of operating system (such as application processes and sockets) was investigated in (Krizhanovsky & Marasanov, 2007). Although it is expected to develop intrusion prevention systems out of this link, more work needs to be done for this to be achieved. A framework for protecting against buffer overflow attacks, the oldest and most pervasive attack technique was introduced and discussed in (Piromsopa & Enbody, 2006a). It was used to create an effective, hardware, buffer overflow prevention tool. A formal argument made here was that "a necessary condition for preventing buffer-overflow attacks is the prevention of the integrity of addresses across domains." A further description of how the above statement supports a variety of successful hardware-based methods to prevent buffer overflow attacks was given.

Arbitrary copy, a type of buffer-overflow attack that is capable of bypassing most buffer-overflow solutions was introduced in (Piromsopa & Enbody, 2006b)]. Work is still ongoing to extend Secure Bit, which is one of the most promising buffer-overflow protection techniques, to protect against buffer-overflow of non-control data. A better solution for Information Security management by designing Preventive Information Security Management (PrISM) aimed at developing and deploying an indigenous Information Security Management System (ISMS) with intrusion prevention capabilities was proposed in (Anwar, Zafar, & Ahmed, 2007). This solution is based on reverse engineering of Open Source Security Information Management (OSSIM) system. A new strategy for dealing with the impossible path execution (IPE) and mimicry attack in the N-gram base Host Intrusion Detection System (HIDS) model was introduced in (Bruschi, Cavallaro, & Lanzi, 2007). This is also a novel defensive technique, represented by the obfuscator module, which works in a transparent way and low overhead of 5.9% with the higher accuracy than the state of the art HIDS. Future work will consider using the obfuscator module in order to reduce the false rate and to detect other kinds of IPE attacks.

COMBINED INTRUSION DETECTION AND PREVENTION SYSEMS

Combined intrusion detection and prevention systems take advantage of both the traditional and proactive approaches with the aim of eliminating some of the limitations of both systems. The use of active traffic splitters on the traffic with the goal of reducing the load on sensors, thereby improving performance in the detection and prevention of intrusion was presented in (Xinidis, Charitakis, Antonatos, Anagnostakis, & Markatos, 2006). Some improvements were made in terms of sensor performance for each of the methods used. The overall cost of the approach was also reasonable. An intelligent agent based intrusion detection and prevention system for mobile ad hoc networks was studied in (Sampathkumar, Bose, Anand, & Kannan, 2007). Although the developed system worked efficiently and detected intrusion at multiple levels, namely, user and packet levels, there is the chance of improving the efficiency in terms of time reduction and effectiveness in terms of increased prediction rate of the system by using training with more instances. A Session Initiation Protocol (SIP) intrusion detection and prevention architecture was implemented as an extension of the very popular open-source software Snort in (Niccolini, Garroppo, Giordano, Risi, & Ventura, 2006). The results indicated that the quality of service experienced by clients did not decrease, hence signaling a good basis for further development of more advanced VoIP IDS/IPS solutions. The effective detection of both known and unknown attacks by means of unified real-time analysis of network traffic introduced by ESIDE-DEPIAN based on Bayesian Belief Networks concepts was established in (Bringas, 2007). This is referred to as a unified Intrusion Detection paradigm.

An application-based intrusion detection and intrusion prevention (ID/IP) system coupled with data mining and mobile agent technologies was introduced in (Yee, Rao, & Radha, 2006). This hybrid system, consisting of a core engine with data sensor, detector, configuration device and alert and response device as its main components, uses both signature-based and anomaly based mechanisms in detecting and preventing intrusions. It further uses data mining and mobile agent technologies in providing a real-time adaptive and responsive ID and IP systems. An examination of integrated multiple intrusion detection sensors, which seek to minimize the number of incorrect-alarms was designed and implemented in (Beheshti & Wasniowski, 2007). The system was implemented using Open Software whenever possible such as Snort, Honeypot, MySQL, etc. This information fusion based intrusion detection and prevention model, which is a prototype, needs to include database design allowing for more efficient data fusion from multiple sensors.

Proactive screening of the health of a corporate network and performing first aid by systematically monitoring vital signs of mobile devices within the network was outlined in (Ransbottom & Jacoby, 2006). Some of the vital signs to be used to detect and prevent system intrusion were registry content changes, active processes, open ports, power usage thresholds, and power signatures. This system provides a comprehensive overall assessment of a network, which leads to building broader immunities to help maintain the health of any enterprise network. A security model to protect IP Multimedia Subsystem (IMS) Service Delivery Platform (SDP) from different time independent attacks, e.g., SQL injection and media flow attacks was developed in (Sher & Magedanz, 2007). This is an Intrusion Detection and Prevention (IDP) system for detecting and preventing message tempering and media flow attacks for IMS Service Delivery. The performance results at Open IMS Tested Fraunhofer show the processing delay of the IDP as very small. In the next section, we discuss a unified approach to network information security which is the main focus of this chapter.

THE INTRUSION DETECTION SYSTEM TECHNIQUE

The intrusion detection system (IDS) technique is an approach that is based on auto-reclosing technique employed on long rural electrical lines and generally targets SYN-flood attacks and distributed denial of service attacks based on SYN-Flood attacks. It makes use of parameters like packet interarrival time and packet arrival rate to block suspicious attacks on data networks. This IDS will identify new attacks and further help update existing IPSs. It will also eliminate most of the five major shortcomings of existing IDSs and IPSs. Traditionally, most IPSs and IDSs depend on packet header information for prevention and detection respectively, but this approach additionally considers using quantitative parameters such as packet arrival rate and time interval between packets.

Monitoring such parameters can lead to signature-based detection or/and anomaly detection. Monitoring port probes or packets that look at specific virtual ports that all computers have when connected to the internet, will help detect hackers trying to link up with Back Orifice software running on computers they want to take control of. If the parameters captured match values of known attacks, then, signature-based detection should be flagged (Anjum, Subhadrabandhu, Sarkar, & Shetty, 2004; Guan, Liu Da-Xin, & Cui Bin-Ge, 2004). On the other hand, a sudden surge in traffic on a certain port for no apparent reason indicates a network anomaly, therefore anomaly detection should be flagged (Guan, Liu Da-Xin, & Cui Bin-Ge, 2004).

In addition to logging information about attacks and issuing alerts that an attack has occurred, this technique will further block or log off all sources of attack. Information about new or unknown attacks gathered by this IDS will be used to reprogram firewalls or generally used to update the list of known attacks already existing in the IPSs (Nadkarni & Mishra, 2004; Schmoyer, Yu Xi Lim, & Owen, 2004).

DENIAL OF SERVICE ATTACKS

There are so many dangerous types of attacks commonly used by attackers of data networks. It has been established, that, the most dangerous and commonly used attacks are denial of service (DoS) attacks. A denial of service attack is an attack that blocks large parts of the memory of the target system, such that it can no longer serve its users. This situation leads to crashing, rebooting or denial of services to legitimate users. Almost every server experiences DoS attacks at a given time during its operations. Some of the popular DoS attacks are Ping of death, Teardrop, SYN-flood, Land, Smurf, UDP-flood, Distributed DoS, and Modem-disconnect attacks. Although a well-configured firewall is an effective countermeasure against nearly all DoS attacks, it also affects normal network traffic. There are existing countermeasures to protect data networks and systems from all the DoS attacks with the exception of SYN-flood attacks and Distributed DoS attacks based on SYN-flood attacks. SYN-flood attacks basically flood the target system with connection requests from spoofed source addresses making it very difficult or impossible to trace the origin of the attacks.

In an attempt to establish full connections with all the requests, the memory of the target gets used up and prevented from serving legitimate users. It exploits the three-way handshake process that takes place any time two systems across the network initiate a TCP/IP connection. The client should send a SYN packet to the host, then, the host should reply with a SYN packet and acknowledge the client's packet by sending an ACK packet (i.e., SYN/ACK packet), and finally the client should send an ACK packet to acknowledge the SYN/ACK packet sent by the host (i.e.,, ACK/SYN/ACK packet). A TCP/IP connection is established only after the above three steps are completed.

Under SYN-flood attacks, all SYN/ACK packets from the targeted host are sent into the void, since all the SYN packets are sent from invalid source IP addresses. While the targeted host waits in vain for the ACK/SYN/ACK packets from the client (i.e., attacker in this case), additional SYN packets or connection requests queue up behind the first set of requests. These repeated cycles of requests use up all the memory of the targeted host, preventing it from answering requests from legitimate clients. TCP/IP protocol enables the targeted host to free part of its used up memory by discarding queued up connection requests after a time out period. But the attacker sends the connection requests from the spoofed addresses faster than the earlier connection requests can be timed out, thereby continuously using up the target host's memory. This means, the packet arrival rate will rapidly increase or the packet interarrival time will rapidly decrease for subsequent connection requests. These were the two parameters used as threshold values for detection in the automated IDS technique discussed in this chapter.

Although there is no single reliable countermeasure to protect a host from SYN-flood attacks, the following steps can be taken to minimize the risk of damage caused by them: reducing the "timed out" period (this can lead to disconnecting legitimate clients); increasing acceptable number of connection requests by the host (this leads to additional memory and system resources consumption); installing vendor-specific updates and patches (this can be time consuming and not always guaranteed); using firewall (this can lead to blocking legitimate clients).

Distributed DoS (DDoS) attacks have proved to be the most dangerous DoS attack because unlike SYN-flood attacks, they leave no trails behind after disabling large networks, thereby making it impossible to trace the attackers. They are even more dangerous than viruses and worms. A DDoS attack is basically the execution of any other DoS attack in a distributed fashion. The attacker takes full control of a less secured network of about 50 computers and installs DDoS attack tools on each of them. The attacker will then launch the DDoS attack from the 50 computers on the real target system with a single command line instruction. This raises the ratio of number of attackers to number of targets from 1:1 to 50:1, thereby making it more effective than all other DoS attacks. A combination of countermeasures is used to counter DDoS attacks, since there is no single existing reliable countermeasure. This was the main reason why the IDS technique discussed in this chapter was developed based on automated detection (Fadia, 2006).

METHOD OF APPROACH

As described above, additional SYN packets or connection requests are sent faster than the earlier connection requests can be timed out during SYN-flood attacks. This situation leads to an increase in packet arrival rate at the targeted host or node. Our method of approach is to detect these changes in packet arrival rate, classify them as anomalies and further block their sources. Detection and blocking of the additional SYN packets will be based on auto-reclosing technique.

MODELING TECHNIQUE

This is an automated IDS technique based on the mechanisms of auto-switches or auto-reclosers used extensively on long rural power lines. An auto-recloser prevents unnecessary disconnection of a long rural power line from the entire grid due to an over-current caused by a fault (e.g., short circuit) anywhere along that particular line. It differentiates between transient (temporal) and permanent faults, thereby managing outage time efficiently (Gans, 1996; Shepherd, Lane, & Steward, 1990). This technique reduces outage time thereby reducing revenue losses. The operations of a typical auto-recloser can be described as follows:

1. A short circuit occurs on any portion of the power line being protected;
2. Auto-recloser signals circuit breaker to open in order to block fault current from flowing through the power line;
3. Auto-recloser again signals circuit breaker to close after a set time (i.e., dead time);
4. If short circuit is cleared (i.e., transient fault), then, circuit breaker remains closed. This is referred to as successful reclosure; and
5. If short circuit persists (i.e., permanent fault), then, auto-recloser again signals circuit breaker to open, but lock out permanently until fault is cleared. This is referred to as unsuccessful reclosure (Luxenburger & Schegner, 2004).

The application of such mechanisms in data networks will not only reduce outage time and revenue losses, but also help reduce high false positive and false negative rates in existing IDSs/IPSs. The main task here was to look for a parameter, which could help achieve the above stated goals. The auto-recloser uses current levels as threshold values for detecting a fault, but this new approach used packet arrival rate and/or packet interarrival time to detect an intrusion. (Please refer to the previous section for further details).

All models for the simulation studies based on our algorithm were developed with the help of Optimized Network Engineering Tools (OPNET) 14.0. OPNET is the most widely used platform by the communications industry for network packet analysis. This software is based on Proto C (i.e., a special version of C language for OPNET), C, and C++ languages (Dale, Weems, & Headington, 2002).The simulation studies involved two stages: blocking analysis and sensitivity analysis. Blocking analysis investigated the possibility of blocking packet streams temporarily or permanently and further determined the effectiveness of its implementation. Sensitivity analysis investigated the sensitivity of the developed IDS technique. The following were the assumptions made for this model during the blocking analysis:

1.   The packet interarrival time for normal packets was assumed to be 40 seconds (i.e., the packet arrival rate was assumed to be 0.025 packet per second); and
2.   The packet interarrival time for attack packets was assumed to be 1 second (i.e., the packet arrival rate was assumed to be 1 packet per second).

Please note that the interarrival time, which is simulation time and not real time, was chosen based on the total simulation time of 1,000s just for the sake of clarity. In reality, it was in the order of a few microseconds (i.e., around 40 μs for normal packets and 1 μs for attack packets). This means that the packet arrival rates were also very high (i.e., around 25,000 packets per second for normal packets and 1,000,000 packets per second for attack packets or 50kbps and 2Mbps respectively, since each packet consists of 2 bits). Figure 1 describes the algorithm for the automated IDS technique. The IDS temporarily blocked the packet stream (i.e., the packet stream with an increased packet arrival rate or decreased interarrival time) such that, in-

Figure 1. Algorithm for the developed automated IDS technique

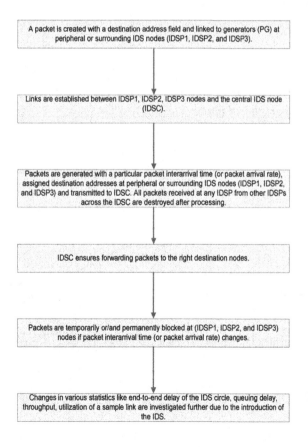

formation about the attack packet could be analyzed and decisions made quickly. The automated IDS technique was modeled around a major node, where the node itself was classified as the central IDS node (i.e., IDSC) and each of the connecting or surrounding nodes was referred to as the peripheral IDS node (i.e., IDSP). Figure 2 shows the network model of the automated IDS technique and details of a typical connection between two IDSPs (i.e., IDSP1 and IDSP3) across the IDSC.

The algorithm in Figure 1 can be described further with the help of Figure 2. For example, a stream of packets is created or generated with a particular packet arrival rate at IDSP1 and assigned a destination address such that it is forwarded by IDSC to IDSP3 in Figure 2. Figure 2 also shows details of the links between IDSP1, IDSC, IDSP3 and their respective packet generators (PG), receivers (RP, R1 and R3), and transmitters (TP, T1 and T3). The role of the IDSC is to ensure packets are sent to the right destination. Various statistics like end-to-end delay, throughput, utilization and queuing delay are captured from the packets at IDSP3 before they are destroyed. When the packet arrival rate is increased, partial blocking or/and full blocking are effected at IDSP1 and the above statistics are recaptured and compared to the previous ones for further analysis. The auto-reclosing set in during and also after the analysis.

Figure 2. Network model of the automated IDS technique and a typical connection between two IDS peripheral nodes

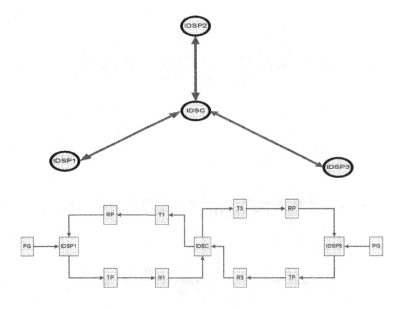

1.   The packet interarrival time for attack packets was assumed to be 1, 10, 20, 30, 40, 50, and 100 seconds (i.e., the packet arrival rate was assumed to be 1, 0.1, 0.05, 0.033, 0.025, 0,02, 0.01 packet per second). Please note also that these are all simulation times and not real times.

Figure 3 shows an overview of the implementation scheme for the automated IDS technique. The implementation steps will be presented at the end of this chapter.

Only two IDSC nodes can be efficiently implemented for this sample network. Each IDSC node is linked to four IDSP nodes for detection. Please note that LAN 1 does not form part of the IDS nodes because it is not linked directly to any of the chosen central IDS nodes. All security data from the IDSC and IDSP nodes will be directly transmitted to the central detection point for analysis. This is done using multiresolution techniques.

RESULTS FROM THE SIMULATION STUDIES

Three scenarios were considered during the initial part of the first stage of the simulation studies. Scenario 1 did not implement the automated IDS technique, that is, packet arrival rate or packet interarrival time remained the same throughout the simulation. Scenario 2 implemented the automated IDS technique partially, that is, packet arrival rate or packet interarrival time changed, but the automated IDS technique only blocked the next interrupt of the packet stream (i.e., only one interrupt

Figure 3. Overview of implementation scheme for the automated IDS

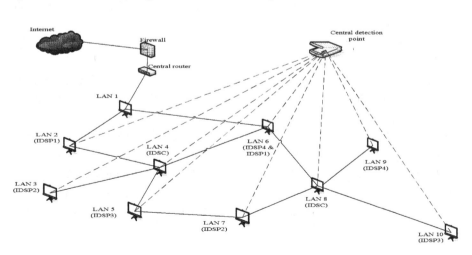

was blocked). Blocking the packet stream temporarily will give the central detection point time to analyze information about the attack or intrusion and subsequently take decisions. Scenario 3 implemented the automated IDS technique permanently, that is, packet arrival rate or packet interarrival time changed, but the automated IDS technique blocked the packet stream indefinitely.

INITIAL RESULTS

This subsection presents the initial results obtained from the first stage of the simulation studies. Please note that the same models were used for all the three scenarios and all times were simulation times and not real times. All the network performance statistics obtained from the simulation studies were averages. The packet interarrival time and packet arrival rate for normal packets used in all the three scenarios were assumed to be 10 seconds and 0.1 packet per second, respectively. The packet arrival rate for attack packets used for blocking in scenarios 2 and 3 was 0.025 packets per second. Please note also that although the packet arrival rate of the attack packets was far less than that for the normal packets, the main test at this stage was to verify whether blocking could be effected whenever the packet arrival rate was changed. The simulation speed and duration were set at 21 events per second and 1000 seconds respectively for both stages of the simulation studies.

A comparison of network performance statistics (in averages) like end-to-end delay from one IDSP to the other IDSP across the IDSC, queuing delay, throughput, and utilization of one of the links (in the IDS circle) obtained from all three scenarios is presented here. Please note that the end-to-end and queuing delays relate to only the IDSC and its surrounding IDSPs (i.e., in the IDS circle). Those delays will form part of the global ETE Delay of the entire system or network to be determined at the central detection point. Table 1 summarizes all the obtained performance statistics (averages) from the three scenarios.

ETE delay increased from 0.279s to 40.4s after the automated IDS was used temporarily, but it didn't exist when used permanently. Queuing delay (from IDSP to IDSC) did not change after the automated IDS was used temporarily, and it didn't exist when used permanently.

Queuing delay (from IDSC to IDSP) changed slightly after the automated IDS was used temporarily, but it didn't exist when used permanently. Throughput (from IDSP to IDSC) dropped from 101bps to 93bps after the automated IDS was used temporarily, but fell to zero when used permanently. Throughput (from IDSC to IDSP) rose from 80bps to 85bps after the automated IDS was used temporarily,

Table 1. Comparison of scenarios

	Scenario 1: No blocking	Scenario 2: Temporal blocking	Scenario 3: Permanent blocking
ETE Delay in seconds	0.279	40.4	Did not exist
Queuing delay in seconds (From IDSP to IDSC)	0.119	0.119	Did not exist
Queuing delay in seconds (From IDSC to IDSP)	0.129	0.13	Did not exist
Throughput in bits/second (From IDSP to IDSC)	101	93	0
Throughput in bits/second (From IDSC to IDSP)	80	85	0
Utilization in percent (From IDSP to IDSC)	113	104	0
Utilization in percent (From IDSC to IDSP)	90	94	0

but fell to zero when used permanently. Utilization (from IDSP to IDSC) dropped from 113% to 104% after the automated IDS was used temporarily, but fell to zero when used permanently.

Please note that utilization values greater or equal to 100% imply growth in the queue size at the node as time increases. Utilization (from IDSC to IDSP) rose from 90% to 94% after the automated IDS was used temporarily, but fell to zero when used permanently. Throughput and utilization generally dropped in the direction of IDSP towards IDSC and increased in the direction of IDSC towards IDSP because packets were only blocked at the IDSP nodes but not at the IDSC nodes, in favor of traffic flow in the direction of IDSC towards IDSP after removing the temporal block. The packet stream was blocked for about 80 simulation seconds (i.e., far less than 1 second in real time) in scenario 2.

FURTHER RESULTS

This subsection presents results obtained from the rest of the first stage and the second stage of the simulation studies. Only the possibility of blocking packet streams temporarily or permanently due to changes in the packet inter-arrival time or packet arrival rate has been investigated so far. That proved to be possible from the initial results obtained. The following were investigated here:

Blocking analysis

1. To determine the required type(s) and sequence of blocking;
2. To determine the required number of blockings; and
3. To determine the duration of each blocking.

Sensitivity analysis

1. To determine how the performance of this IDS relates to packet arrival rate or packet interarrival time; and
2. To discuss how the performance of this IDS technique will be linked to the following metrics:
    a. False positive rate (FPR);
    b. False negative rate (FNR); and
    c. Crossover error rate (CER).

BLOCKING ANALYSIS

Six scenarios were considered under this analysis as follows:

1. No blocking;
2. One partial blocking;
3. Two or more successive partial blockings;
4. One full blocking;
5. Two or more successive full blockings; and
6. One successive partial and full blocking.

Please note that the packet interarrival time used for normal packets was 40 seconds (i.e., the packet arrival rate was 0.025 packets per second). Also, the packet interarrival time used for attack packets was 1 second (i.e., the packet arrival rate was 1 packet per second). Both average and instantaneous statistics were considered for better clarification at this stage. Only throughput and end-to-end delay statistics were used for the rest of this analysis due to space. Table 2 summarizes results from all the 6 scenarios followed by brief discussions.

Table 2. Blocking Analysis - All scenarios

No Blocking						
Packet Inter-arrival Time (seconds)	Packet Arrival Rate (packets/second)	Packet Arrival Rate (bits/second)	Throughput (Average) (bits/second)	Throughput (Instantaneous) (bits/second)	Time Interval Between Successive Packets (seconds)	End-To-End Delay (seconds)
1	1	2	1010	1040	0	0.265
40	0.025	0.05	26	104/0	20	0.25
One Partial Blocking						
1	1	2	510	515	0	0 - 0.248
40	0.025	0.05	13	104/0	65	0 - 0.24
Two or More Successive Partial Blockings						
1	1	2	510	515	0	0 - 0.248
40	0.025	0.05	13	104/0	65	0 - 0.24
One Full Blocking						
1	1	2	2	104/0	0	0
40	0.025	0.05	2	104/0	0	0
Two or More Successive Full Blockings						
1	1	2	2	104/0	0	0
40	0.025	0.05	2	104/0	0	0
One Successive Partial and Full Blocking						
1	1	2	2	104/0	0	0
40	0.025	0.05	2	104/0	0	0

Scenario 1 (Without Blocking)

Attack packet: The average throughput was almost the same as the instantaneous throughput because there were no time intervals between successive packets. The end-to-end delay was virtually constant.

Normal packet: The average throughput was far less than the instantaneous throughput because of the presence of time intervals (or dips to zero) between successive packets. The end-to-end delay was virtually constant.

Scenario 2 (With One Partial Blocking)

Attack packet: The average throughput was almost the same as the instantaneous throughput because there were no time intervals between successive packets. The end-to-end delay increased steadily from 0s to 0.248s.

Normal packets: The average throughput was far less than the instantaneous throughput because of the presence of larger time intervals (or dips to zero) between successive packets. The end-to-end delay increased steadily from 0 s to 0.24s. Please note that the time intervals between successive packets increased from 20s (i.e., in scenario 1) to 65s because an interrupt or a packet stream was blocked partially. This difference of 40s equals to the duration of one spike cycle (i.e., when there was no blocking: scenario 1) and depicts that a packet stream or an interrupt was blocked within that period. The number of spikes decreased by about half from 25 (i.e., in scenario 1) to 13 due to the blocking. The average throughput also dropped from 26 (1010) bps to 13 (510) bps as a result of the partial blocking. Please note that the numbers in parenthesis relate to normal packets.

Comparison: The average throughput values in this scenario decreased by about half compared to those of scenario 1. Only the instantaneous throughput of the attack packets was reduced by about half. The instantaneous throughput for the normal packets remained the same.

Scenario 3 (With Two or More Successive Partial Blockings)

All results were the same as obtained in scenario 2.

Scenario 4 (With One Full Blocking)

Attack packet: Instantaneous throughput spiked once initially to 104bps and dropped sharply to 0bps throughout. This was why the average throughput remained at 2bps and not 0 bps. The packet stream was blocked permanently, so time interval between successive packets and end-to-end delay did not exist.

Normal packets: The situation was the same as in the case of attack packets. Comparison: Please note that the average throughput values in this scenario dropped from 1010bps in scenario 1 to virtually 0bps because the packet stream was blocked fully. The instantaneous throughput of the attack packets dropped to the level for the normal packet in scenario 1. The instantaneous throughput for the normal packets remained the same.

Scenario 5 (With Two or More Successive Full Blockings)

All results were the same as obtained in scenario 4.

Scenario 6 (With One Successive Partial and Full Blocking)

All results were the same as obtained in scenario 4.

RECOMMENDATIONS

Two partial blockings and one full blocking are recommended based on the above study. This is how the new IDS will make use of the auto-reclosing technique. Auto-reclosers installed on power lines temporarily isolate the power lines twice and move into a state of lockout permanently until the fault on the line is cleared by a fault team. The outage time between the two isolations is roughly 0.3333s. Considering the high packet rate in communications networks (i.e., 100Mbps) compared to the frequency of power systems (i.e., 60 Hz), the recommended blocking time should be in microseconds and must also be less than the lower end-to-end delay in scenario 1 (i.e., without blocking). Please note that the values of end-to-end delay for the entire simulation studies need to be divided by thousand in order to get closer to the real delays. The recommended time between blockings was therefore 250 µs. Please note that end-to-end delay at any stage of the entire simulation studies referred to the time for a packet to travel from one IDSP to the other and not the global end-to-end delay of the entire network. This outage time value should be less than the time out period of the three-way handshake process required for establishing a TCP/IP connection between two nodes within a particular network.

SENSITIVITY ANALYSIS

This subsection investigated and discussed how the performance of this IDS technique is linked to false positive rate (FPR), false negative rate (FNR), and crossover error rate (CER). Any or a combination of the above metrics can be used to determine the performances of IDSs. The same setup was used at this stage as before but this time, the packet interarrival time for attack packets was varied from 1s up to 100s in order to establish the sensitivity of the IDS technique in relation to packet arrival rate or packet interarrival time. The statistics collected were end-to-end delay, time interval between successive packets, average throughput, and instantaneous throughput. Three scenarios were considered at this stage: no blocking, one partial

Table 3. Sensitivity analysis – All scenarios

No Blocking						
Packet Inter-arrival Time (seconds)	Packet Arrival Rate (packets/second)	Packet Arrival Rate (bits/second)	Throughput (Average) (bits/second)	Throughput (Instantaneous) (bits/second)	Time Interval Between Successive Packets (seconds)	End-To-End Delay (seconds)
1	1	2	1040	1040	0	0.265
10	0.1	0.2	104	104	0	0.26
20	0.05	0.1	52	104	2	0.255
30	0.033	0.67	34	104	10	0.25
40	0.025	0.05	26	104	20	0.25
50	0.02	0.04	21	104	35	0.25
100	0.01	0.02	11	104	80	0.249
One Partial Blocking						
1	1	2	510	515	0	0 - 0.248
10	0.1	0.2	51	0	0	0 - 0.245
20	0.05	0.1	26	0	20	0 - 0.24
30	0.033	0.67	17	0	40	0 - 0.24
40	0.025	0.05	13	0	65	0 - 0.24
50	0.02	0.04	11	0	80	0 - 0.225
100	0.01	0.02	5	0	180	0 - 0.2
One Full Blocking						
1	1	2	2	0	0	0
10	0.1	0.2	2	0	0	0
20	0.05	0.1	2	0	0	0
30	0.033	0.67	2	0	0	0
40	0.025	0.05	2	0	0	0
50	0.02	0.04	2	0	0	0
100	0.01	0.02	2	0	0	0

blocking, and one full blocking. Table 3 summarizes the results from all 3 scenarios followed by brief discussions.

Scenario 1 (Without Blocking)

Discussion: There was a general increase in time interval between successive packets as packet arrival rate decreased. Average throughput also decreased as the packet arrival rate decreased. The instantaneous throughput generally remained constant at 104bps apart from the high initial value of 1040bps when packet interarrival time was 1s. The end-to-end delay virtually remained constant throughout.

Scenario 2 (With One Partial Blocking)

Discussion: The effect of partial blocking reduced with increasing packet arrival rate as indicated by the time interval between successive packets (i.e., increasing from 0s to 180s). Instantaneous throughput followed the same trend as in scenario 1 (i.e., drastic decrease from 515bps to 0bps).

Scenario 3 (With One Full Blocking)

Discussion: All the above four statistics did not exist. The average throughput will be 0bps in reality as described in scenario 4 under blocking analysis. It was around 2bps just because of the initial spike. Figures 4, 5, 6, and 7 depict the graphs of the four chosen statistics against packet interarrival time/packet arrival rate for all the three scenarios. Figures 4 to 6 supported the fact that this IDS technique was very sensitive when the packet arrival rate was 0.2bps and lower (i.e., because both the instantaneous and average throughput values dropped quickly to 0bps in this case and at the same time, the time interval between successive packets increased drastically) as compared to when the packet arrival rate was above 0.2bps (i.e., because both the instantaneous and average throughput values dropped steadily and not quickly to 0bps in this case and at the same time, the time interval between

Figure 4. Instantaneous throughput for all 3 scenarios

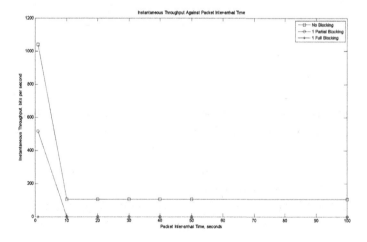

Figure 5. Average throughput for all 3 scenarios

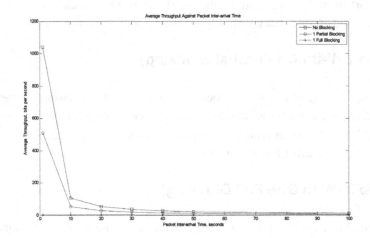

Figure 6. Time interval between successive packets for all 3 scenarios

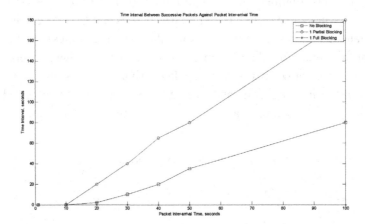

successive packets remained constant at around 0s). It is clear from Figure 7 that the end-to-end delay was virtually constant for scenarios 1 and 2, but didn't exist for scenario 3. This outcome will also help determine the range of packet arrival rate within which this IDS can be implemented.

A detailed sensitivity analysis requires testing this IDS technique by introducing attacks to a particular node in a real network (i.e., during the implementation stage). Some of the metrics that can be used to assess the performance of an IDS technique due to changes in sensitivity are false positive rate (FPR), false negative rate (FNR),

Figure 7. End-to-end delay for all 3 scenarios

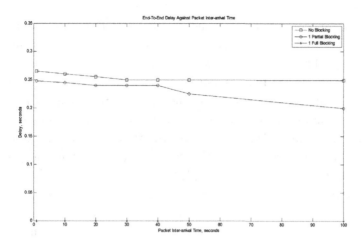

and crossover error rate (CER). The sensitivity of the IDS will be varied by varying the range of the threshold values of the IDS. FPR is the frequency with which the IDS reports malicious activity in error. It generally increases as the sensitivity increases. FNR is the frequency with which the IDS fails to raise an alarm when a malicious activity actually occurs. It generally decreases as the sensitivity increases. CER is the frequency value at which FPR is equal to FNR. If it is required to achieve a balance between FPR and FNR, then the best choice must be the IDS with the lowest CER. If it is required to detect every single attack, then the best choice will be the IDS with the lowest FNR or highest FPR. Please note that this choice may lead to an increase in administrative overhead associated with the FPR.

MULTIRESOLUTION TECHNIQUES

A multiresolution technique is an application of wavelet transform, which decomposes an image and reconstructs it after transmission, with the aim of reproducing the exact image. The decomposition (or decimation) process involves convolving data samples from the image with low pass and high pass wavelet coefficients (i.e., h0 and h1, respectively). This process is also known as sampling. The reconstruction (or interpolation) process involves convolving the received data after decomposition and transmission with the transformed (i.e., reflection in the line y = x or 180° rotation about the origin) low pass and high pass wavelet coefficients. This process is also known as upper-sampling. The high pass portion of the multiresolution technique eliminates any noise associated with the two major processes. The low pass portion of the technique, which contains no noise, is therefore projected further. It contains much of the energy content of the original data samples. Data received from the two portions of the technique are finally summed up to reproduce the original image.

Only the signal processing applications of wavelets was taken advantage of in this research work. In the field of signal analysis, the methods of wavelet transform have wide applications because of their unique merit. One of the important applications is multiresolution technique, which was used to decompose, transmit and reconstruct signals or data from the enterprise network to a Central Detection Point for further analysis. Multiresolution technique simultaneously represents segments of an image or data by multiple scales and further consists of two very important concepts, that is, dilation and translation.

Multiresolution Haar transform, which is a multiresolution technique using Haar wavelets coefficients, produces detail information of segments from an image or data as described in (Yung-Da & Paulik, 1996). Transmission of traffic from the network nodes to the central detection point for the technique developed in this research work was done using a one-dimensional, two-stage multiresolution technique. Haar Wavelets was applied here. The effectiveness of multiresolution Haar transform was also taken advantage of in (Piscaglia & Maccq, 1996).

FUTURE RESEARCH DIRECTIONS

Further investigation should be done in the following areas to enhance this automated IDS technique: modeling the automated IDS such that a generator can generate a packet stream with variable interarrival times; and repeating the simulation for increasing simulation run times and analyzing the outcome.

IMPLEMENTATION OF IDS TECHNIQUE

Implementation of this IDS technique involves two major parts: "set-up inside the network" and "set-up at the central detection point." The following should be the steps under the "set-up inside the network" part:

1. Group all the nodes in the network into various IDS circles (i.e.,, each IDS circle consists of one central IDS or IDSC and all the peripheral IDSs or IDSPs linked to it);
2. Install a detector (i.e., software on a computer) at each IDSP for determining the packet arrival rate etc. at that node; and

3. Install a transmitter at each IDSP for sending the packet arrival rate data etc. to the central detection point by multiresolution techniques.

The following should be the steps under the "set-up at the central detection point" part:

1. Install OPNET 14.0 at the central detection point (i.e., software on a computer);
2. Replicate the actual network in OPNET 14.0 at the central detection point with reference to Figure 3 or the actual implementation scheme for the IDS;
3. Install a receiver at the central detection point to receive the packet arrival rate data etc. from the network (i.e., at the end of the multiresolution techniques);
4. Furnish the replica of the actual network developed in OPNET with the packet arrival rate data etc. of all the IDSP nodes; and
5. Carry out all the steps discussed under the simulation studies above.

CONCLUSION

It was clear from the discussions under this IDS technique that although the packet stream was blocked temporarily, the average performance statistics did not change that much from the scenario without the automated IDS. Zero values obtained for all statistics from scenario 3 of the first stage of the simulation studies explained the fact that the packet stream was really blocked, thereby preventing the attack packets (i.e., packets with arrival rate of 1 packet per second) from getting to their target destinations. This automated IDS was very effective because it instantly prevented the attack packets from leaving the IDSP node as shown in the results obtained from scenario 2 (i.e., All performance statistics before time t = 80 seconds were zero). The implementation scheme makes the automated IDS technique efficient because bandwidth will be saved for normal network activities by transmitting security data separately. This indicates that this IDS technique also guaranteed security for the security data itself. This implies that four out of the five limitations of existing IDSs/IPSs have so far been eliminated by this technique.

CONTRIBUTION

Results obtained so far from this IDS technique look promising. They seek to eliminate the following limitations: limited scalability (i.e., partly by reducing traffic in the network); efficiency (i.e., saving bandwidth for network operation); and security (i.e., securing security data) because security data was sent directly to the central detection point using multiresolution techniques; effectiveness (i.e., reducing false positive and false negative rates) because of the use of auto-reclosing technique. They also seek to show how the IDS counters DDoS attacks based on SYN-flood attacks or distributed attacks in general and also SYN-flood attacks in particular.

REFERENCES

Akujuobi, C. M., & Ampah, N. K. (2007). Enterprise network intrusion detection and prevention system. *Society of photographic instrumentation engineers defense and security symposium* (vol. 6538, pp. 1-12).

Akujuobi, C. M., Ampah, N. K., & Sadiku, M. N. O. (2007). An intrusion detection technique based on change in hurst parameter with application to network security. *International Journal of Computer Science and Network Security, 5*(7), 55–64.

Amanullah, M. T. O., Kalam, A., & Zayegh, H. (2005). Network security vulnerabilities in SCADA and EMS. *Transmission and Distribution Conference and Exhibition: Asia and Pacific* (pp. 1-6).

Anjum, F., Subhadrabandhu, D., Sarkar, S., & Shetty, R. (2004). *On optimal placement of intrusion detection modules in sensor networks* (pp. 690–699). BroadNets.

Anwar, M. M., Zafar, M. F., & Ahmed, Z. (2007). A proposed preventive Information Security System. *International Conference on Electrical Engineering* (pp. 1-6).

Beheshti, M., & Wasniowski, R. A. (2007). Data fusion support for intrusion detection and prevention. *International Conference on Information Technology* (p. 966).

Biermann, E., Cloete, E., & Venter, L. M. (2001). A comparison of intrusion detection systems. *Computers & Security, 8*(20), 676–683. doi:10.1016/S0167-4048(01)00806-9

Bignell, K. B. (2006). Authentication in the Internet banking environment; Towards developing a strategy for fraud detection. *International Conference on Internet Surveillance and Protection* (p. 23).

Bridis, T., & Sullivan, E. (2007). US video shows hacker hit on power grid. *Associated Press Writers* Retrieved September, 27, 2007, from http://www.physorg.com/news110104929.html

Bringas, P. G. (2007). Intensive use of Bayesian Belief Network for the unified, flexible and adaptable analysis of misuses and anomalies in network intrusion detection and prevention systems. *International Conference on Database and Expert Systems Applications* (pp. 365-371).

Bruschi, D., Cavallaro, L., & Lanzi, A. (2007). An effective technique for preventing mimicry and impossible paths execution attacks. *International Conference on Performance, Computing, and Communications* (pp. 418-425).

Cannady, J. (2009). Distributed detection of attacks in mobile ad hoc networks using learning vector quantization. *3rd International Conference on Network and System Security* (pp. 571–574).

Capuzzi, G., Spalazzi, L., & Pagliarecci, F. (2006). IRSS: Incident response support system. *International Symposium on Collaborative Technologies and Systems* (pp. 81-88).

Car, J., & Jakupovic, G. (2005). SCADA system security as a part of overall security of deregulated energy management system. *International Conference on Computer as a Tool* (pp. 338-341).

Chaboya, D. J., Raines, R. A., Baldwin, R. O., & Mullins, B. E. (2006). Network intrusion detection: Automated and manual methods prone to attacks and evasion. *Security and Privacy Magazine, 6*(4), 36–43. doi:10.1109/MSP.2006.159

Changxin, S., & Ke, M. (2009). Design of intrusion detection system based on data mining algorithm. *International Conference on Signal Processing Systems* (pp. 370–373).

Chunmei, Y., Mingchu, L., Jianbo, M., & Jizhou, S. (2004). Honeypot and scan detection in intrusion detection system. *Canadian Conference on Electrical and Computer Engineering* (pp. 1107–1110).

Colon Osorio, F. C. (2007). Using Byzantine agreement in the design of IPS systems. *International Conference on Performance, Computing, and Communications* (pp. 528-537).

Dagle, J. E., Windergren, S. E., & Johnson, J. M. (2002, January). *Enhancing the security of supervisory control and data acquisition (SCADA) systems: The lifeblood of modern energy infrastructure.* Paper presented at the Power Engineering Society Winter Meeting, New York, NY.

Dale, N., Weems, C., & Headington, M. (2002). *Programming and problem solving with C.* Sudbury, MA: Jones and Bartlett.

Fadia, A. (2006). *Network security: A hacker's perspective*. Boston, MA: Thomson Course Technology.

Farris, J. J., & Nicol, D. M. (2004). *Evaluation of secure peer-to-peer overlay routing for survivable SCADA systems*. 2004 Winter Simulation Conference (pp. 308-317).

Gans, M. (1996). *Development of a pole-mounted RTU for use on rural power lines*. Power System Control and Management Conference (pp. 103–107).

Guan, J., Liu, D.-X., & Cui, B. G. (2004). *An intrusion learning approach for building intrusion detection models using genetic algorithms*. World Congress on Intelligent Control and Automation (pp. 4339–4342).

Haji, F., Lindsay, L., & Song, S. (2005). *Practical security strategy for SCADA automation systems and networks*. Canadian Conference on Electrical and Computer Engineering (pp. 172-178).

Ihn-Han, B., & Olariu, S. (2009). *A weighted-dissimilarity-based anomaly detection method for mobile wireless networks*. International Conference on Computational Science and Engineering (pp. 29–34).

Janakiraman, R., Waldvogel, M., & Zhang, Q. (2003). *Indra: A peer-to-peer approach to network intrusion detection and prevention*. International Workshops on Enabling Technologies: Infrastructures for Collaborative Enterprises (pp. 226-231).

Jing, Z. HouKuan, H., ShengFeng, T., & Xiang, Z. (2009). *Applications of HMM in protocol anomaly detection*. International Joint Conference on Computational Sciences and Optimization (pp. 347–349).

Jing-Wen, T., Mei-Juan, G., Ling-Fang, H., & Shi-Ru, Z. (2009). Community intrusion detection system based on wavelet neural network. *International Conference on Machine Learning and Cybernetics* (vol. 2, pp. 1026 – 1030).

Jou, Y. F., Gong, F., Sargor, C., Wu, S., Wu, S. F., Chang, H. C., & Wang, F. (2000). Design and implementation of a scalable intrusion detection system for the protection of network infrastructure. *Defense Advanced Research Projects Agency Information Survivability Conference and Exposition* (vol. 2, pp. 69–83).

Kayacik, H. G., Zincir-Heywood, A. N., & Heywood, M. I. (2004*). On dataset biases in a learning system with minimum A Priori information for intrusion detection*. Communication Networks and Services Research Conference (pp. 181–189).

Khoshgoftaar, T. M., & Abushadi, M. E. (2004). *Resource-sensitive intrusion detection models for network traffic*. High Assurance Systems Engineering Symposium (pp. 249–258).

Ko, C. (2003). System health and intrusion monitoring (SHIM): Project summary. *Defense Advanced Research Projects Agency Information Survivability Conference and Exposition* (vol. 2, pp. 202–207).

Krizhanovsky, A., & Marasanov, A. (2007). *An approach for adaptive intrusion prevention based on the danger.* 2nd International Conference on Availability, Reliability and Security (pp. 1135-1142).

Kui, Z. (2009). *A danger model based anomaly detection method for wireless sensor networks.* 2nd International Symposium on Knowledge Acquisition and Modeling (pp. 11–14).

Labbe, K. G., Rowe, N. G., & Fulp, J. D. (2006). *A methodology for evaluation of Host-Based intrusion prevention systems and its application.* Information Assurance Workshop (pp. 378-379).

Leinwand, A., & Conroy, K. F. (1996). *Network management: A practical perspective.* New York, NY: Addison-Wesley.

Lixia, X., Dan, Z., & Hongyu, Y. (2009). *Research on SVM based network intrusion detection classification.* 6th International Conference on Fuzzy Systems and Knowledge Discovery (pp. 362–366).

Luxenburger, R., & Schegner, P. (2004). A new intelligent auto-reclosing method considering the current transformer saturation. *8th International Conference on Developments in Power Systems Protection* (vol. 2, pp. 583-586).

McMillan, R. (2008). *CIA says hackers pulled plug on power grid. IDG News Service*, Retrieved January 19, 2008, from http://www.networkworld.com.

Mitrokotsa, A., Komninos, N., & Douligeris, C. (2007). *Intrusion detection with neural networks and watermarking techniques for MANET.* International Conference on Pervasive Services (p. 966).

Momenzadeh, A., Javadi, H. H. S., & Dezfouli, M. A. (2009). *Design an efficient system for intrusion detection via evolutionary fuzzy system.* 11th International Conference on Computer Modeling and Simulation (pp. 89–94).

Motta Pires, P. S., & Oliveira, L. A. H. G. (2006). *Security aspect of SCADA and corporate network interconnection: An overview.* International Conference on Dependability of Computer Systems (pp. 127-134).

Muthuprasanna, M., Ke, W., & Kothari, S. (2006). *Eliminating SQL injection attacks – A transport defense mechanism.* 8th International Symposium on Web Site Evolution (pp. 22-23).

Nadkarni, K., & Mishra, A. (2004). *A novel intrusion detection approach for wireless ad hoc networks*. Wireless Communications and Networking Conference (pp. 831–836).

Nassar, M., State, R., & Festor, O. (2007). *VoIP honeypot architecture*. International Symposium on Integrated Network Management (pp. 109-118).

Niccolini, S., Garroppo, R. G., Giordano, S., Risi, G., & Ventura, S. (2006). *SIP intrusion detection and prevention: Recommendation and prototype recommendation*. 1st Workshop on VoIP Management and Security (pp. 47-52).

Onut, I. V., & Ghorbani, A. A. (2006). *Toward a feature classification scheme for network intrusion detection*. 4th Annual Communication and Networks and Service Research Conference (p. 8).

Otrok, H., Debbabi, M., Assi, C., & Bhattacharya, P. (2007). *A cooperative approach for analyzing intrusion in mobile ad hoc networks*. 27th International Conference on Distributing Computing Systems Workshops (p. 86).

Paez, R., & Torres, M. (2009). *Laocoonte: An agent based intrusion detection system*. International Symposium on Collaborative Technologies and System (pp. 217–224).

Paulson, L. D. (2002). Stopping intruders outside the gates. *Computer, 11*(35), 20–22. doi:10.1109/MC.2002.1046967

Piromsopa, K., & Enbody, R. J. (2006). *Arbitrary copy: Buffer-overflow protections*. International Conference on Electro/Information Technology (pp. 580-584).

Piromsopa, K., & Enbody, R. J. (2006). *Buffer-overflow protection: The theory*. International Conference on Electro/Information Technology (pp. 454-458).

Piscaglia, P., & Maccq, B. (1996). Multiresolution lossless compression scheme. *International Conference on Image Processing* (vol. 1, pp. 69-72).

Pollet, J. (2002). *Developing a solid SCADA security strategy*. 2nd International Society of Automation Sensors for Industry Conference (pp. 148-156).

Ramana, R. K., Singh, S., & Varghese, G. (2007). On scalable attack detection in the network. *Association for Computing Machinery Transactions on Networking, 1*(15), 31–44.

Ransbottom, J. S., & Jacoby, G. A. (2006). *Monitoring mobile device vitals for effective reporting*. Military Communication Conference (pp. 1-7).

Sampathkumar, V., Bose, S., Anand, K., & Kannan, A. (2007). *An intelligent agent based approach for intrusion detection and prevention in ad hoc networks*. International Conference on Signal Processing Communications and Networking (pp. 534-536).

Satti, M. M., & Garner, B. J. (2001). *Information security on Internet enterprise managed intrusion detection system (EMIDS)*. International Multi-topic Conference (pp. 234-238).

Schmoyer, T. R., Lim, Y.-X., & Owen, H. L. (2004). *Wireless intrusion detection and response: A classic study using main-in-the-middle attack.* Wireless Communications and Networking Conference (pp. 883 – 888).

Shepherd, A. D., Lane, S. E., & Steward, J. S. (1990). *A new microprocessor relay for overhead line SCADA application.* Distribution Switchgear Conference (pp. 100–103).

Sher, M., & Magedanz, T. (2007). *Protecting IP Multimedia Subsystem (IMS) server delivery platform from time independent attacks.* 3rd International Symposium on Information Assurance and Security (pp. 171-176).

Stallings, W. (2003). *Cryptography and network security: Principles and practices.* India: Pearson Education, Inc.

Sun, B., Xiao, Y., & Wang, R. (2007). Detection of fraudulent usage in wireless networks. *Transactions on Vehicular Technology, 6*(56), 3912–3923. doi:10.1109/TVT.2007.901875

Tront, J. G., & Marchany, R. C. (2004). *Internet security: Intrusion detection and prevention.* 37th Annual Hawaii International Conference on System Sciences (p. 188).

Tsang, C.-H., & Kwong, S. (2005). *Multi-agent detection system in industrial network using ant colony clustering approach and unsupervised feature extraction.* International Conference on Industrial Technology (ICIT '05) (pp. 51–56).

Vokorokos, L., Kleinova, A., & Latka, O. (2006). *Network security on the intrusion detection system level.* International Conference on Intelligent Engineering Systems (pp. 534-536).

Weaver, N., Paxson, V., & Sommer, R. (2007). *Work in progress: Bro-LAN Pervasive network inspection and control for LAN traffic* (pp. 1–2). Securecomm and Workshops.

Weber, W. (1999). *Firewall basics.* 4th International Conference on Telecommunications in Modern Satellite, Cable and Broadcasting Services (vol. 1, pp. 300-305).

Wei, W., Xiangliang, Z., Gombault, S., & Knapskog, S. J. (2009). *Attribute normalization in network intrusion detection.* 10th International Symposium on Pervasive Systems, Algorithms, and Networks (pp. 448–453).

Weinberg, Y., Tzur-David, S., Dolev, D., & Anker, T. (2006). *High performance string matching algorithm for a network intrusion prevention system.* Workshop on High Performance Switching and Routing (p. 7).

Xinidis, K., Charitakis, I., Antonatos, S., Anagnostakis, K. G., & Markatos, E. P. (2006). An active splitter architecture for intrusion detection and prevention. *Transactions on Dependable and Secure Computing, 1*(3), 31–44. doi:10.1109/TDSC.2006.6

Yau, S. S., & Zhang, X. (1999). *Computer networks intrusion detection, assessment and prevention based on security dependency relation.* Computer Software and Applications Conference (pp. 86–91).

Yee, C. G., Rao, G. V. S., & Radha, K. (2006). *A hybrid approach to intrusion detection and prevention business intelligent applications.* International Symposium on Communications and Information Technologies (pp. 847-850).

Yung-Da, W., & Paulik, M. J. (1996). A discrete wavelet model for target recognition. *39th Midwest Symposium on Circuit and Systems* (vol. 2, pp. 835-838).

Zhaoyu, L., & Uppala, R. (2006). *A dynamic countermeasure method for large-scale network attacks.* International Symposium on Dependable, Autonomic and Secure Computing (pp. 163-170).

Zheng-De, Z., Zhi-Guo, L., Dong, Z., & Fei-Teng, J. (2006). *Study on joint prevention technique of information security in SUN.* International Conference on Machine Learning and Cybernetics (pp. 2823-2827).

Zhou, C., Liu, Y., & Zhang, H. (2006). *A pattern matching based Network Intrusion Detection System.* 9th International Conference on Control, Automation, Robotics and Vision (pp. 1-4).

ADDITIONAL READING

Erramilli, A., Roughan, M., Veitch, D., & Willinger, W. (2002). Self-similar traffic and network dynamics. *Proceedings of the Institute of Electronics and Electrical Engineers, 5*(90), 800–819.

Garcia, R. C., Sadiku, M. N. O., & Cannady, J. D. (2002). WAID: wavelet analysis intrusion detection. *Midwest Symposium on Circuits and Systems* (vol. 3, pp. 688–691).

Graps, A. (1995). An introduction to wavelets. *Computing in Science & Engineering*, *2*(2), 50–61. doi:10.1109/99.388960

Kay, S. M. (1993). *Fundamentals of statistical signal processing - Estimation theory*. Upper River Saddle, New Jersey: Prentice Hall.

Nash, D. A., & Ragsdale, D. J. (2001). Simulation of self-similarity in network utilization patterns as a precursor to automated testing of intrusion detection systems. *Transactions on Systems, Man and Cybernetics. Part A: Systems and Humans*, *4*(31), 327–331. doi:10.1109/3468.935051

Qinghua, S., & Xiongjian, L. (2003). The fractal feature of telecommunication network. *International Conference on Communication Technology* (vol. 1, pp. 77–80).

Shibin, S., Nh, J. K.-Y., & Bihai, T. (2004). Some results on the self-similarity property in communication networks. *Transactions on Communications*, *10*(52), 1636–1642.

Ziemer, R. E., & Tranter, W. H. (5). (2002). *Principles of communications: Systems, modulation and noise*. Wiley.

KEY TERMS AND DEFINITIONS

Anomaly Detection: An approach which considers any unusual pattern as an anomaly and therefore an attack. It helps in detecting both known and unknown attacks.

Auto-Reclosing: A technique which protects sections of electrical power systems from transient and permanent faults through the isolation of faulted parts from the rest of the electrical network. It prevents unnecessary disconnection of a long rural power line from the entire grid due to an over-current caused by a fault anywhere along that particular line.

Centralized Intrusion Detection: An intrusion detection technique, whereby data is collected in a distributed fashion, but analyzed centrally.

Denial of Service Attack: An attempt to block large parts of the memory of a target system, such that it can no longer serve its users. This situation leads to crashing, rebooting or denial of services to legitimate users.

Distributed Intrusion Detection: An intrusion detection technique, whereby data is collected and analyzed in a distributed fashion.

Distributed SYN-Flood Attack: A SYN-flood attack implemented in a distributed fashion. This is one of the most dangerous distributed denial of service attacks known.

Intrusion Detection: A traditional technique which detects actions that attempt to compromise the confidentiality and integrity of a resource in information security. It is used only after an attack has already entered a given system.

Intrusion Prevention: A proactive technique which detects actions that attempt to compromise the confidentiality and integrity of a resource in information security. This is used to prevent an attack from entering a given system.

Signature Based Detection: An approach which considers attack patterns as signatures and further compares signatures of known attacks to incoming attacks for detection. It helps in detecting only known attacks.

SYN-Flood Attack: An attempt to flood a target system with connection requests from spoofed source addresses making it very difficult or impossible to trace the origin of the attacks. This is one of the most dangerous denial of service attacks known.

Chapter 3

Usage of Broadcast Messaging in a Distributed Hash Table for Intrusion Detection

Zoltán Czirkos
Budapest University of Technology and Economics, Hungary

Gábor Hosszú
Budapest University of Technology and Economics, Hungary

ABSTRACT

In this chapter, the authors present a novel peer-to-peer based intrusion detection system called Komondor, more specifically, its internals regarding the utilized peer-to-peer transport layer. The novelty of our intrusion detection system is that it is composed of independent software instances running on different hosts and is organized into a peer-to-peer network. The maintenance of this overlay network does not require any user interaction. The applied P2P overlay network model enables the nodes to communicate evenly over an unstable network. The base of our Komondor NIDS is a P2P network similar to Kademlia. To achieve high reliability and availability, we had to modify the Kademlia overlay network in such a way so that it would be resistent to network failures and support broadcast messages. The main purpose of this chapter is to present our modifications and enhancements on Kademlia.

DOI: 10.4018/978-1-60960-836-1.ch003

Copyright ©2012, IGI Global. Copying or distributing in print or electronic forms without written permission of IGI Global is prohibited.

INTRODUCTION

Network security is one of the most important problems of today's Internet. This article presents a novel application, which uses the network itself to enhance security of the hosts it protects. The hosts create a specially featured Application Level Network (ALN). Nodes connected to this ALN send reports to each other about suspicious events they detect using their system logs and other means of intrusion detection. By combining and analyzing these reports, they are capable of detecting network-level intrusion attempts, and notifying each other to enhance their security.

In this article we present a *novel peer-to-peer based intrusion detection and prevention system* called Komondor, and specifically its internals regarding the P2P transport layer utilized. Many different security systems, for example Snort (Snort, 2002), use the network for communication. The novelty of our intrusion detection system is that it is composed of independent software instances running on different hosts and they are organized into a Peer-to-Peer (P2P) network (Hosszú & Czirkos, 2007), in such a way that they create a virtual overlay network on application level. The maintenance of this overlay network does not require any user interaction.

The applied P2P overlay network model enables the nodes to communicate even over an unstable network. The base of our Komondor NIDS is a P2P network similar to Kademlia. To achieve high reliability and availability, we had to modify the Kademlia overlay network in such a way that it is more resilient to network failures and supports broadcast messages. The main purpose of this article is to present the modifications and enhancements.

BACKGROUND

Intrusion Detection Systems

Network Intrusion Detection Systems (NIDS) are capable of supervision and protection of company-scale networks. One commercially available product is RealSecure (RealSecure, 2006), while Snort is an open source solution (Snort, 2002). Snort is based on a description language, which supports investigation of signatures, network application level protocols, anomalies, and even the combination of these. It realizes a probe which is able to check network traffic. It is a well configurable system, automatically refreshing its rule set regularly through the Internet. In this way, new signatures and rules added by developers and users can be immediately added to the database of the software.

Information collected by probes installed at different points of the network is particularly important for protection against network scale attacks. Data collected by one probe alone may not be enough to consider an attack manifested, but an extensive analysis of all sensors' information can reveal the fact that the system is under attack. By the aid of sensors communicating in the network, the Intrusion Detection Working Group (IDWG) of the Internet Engineering Task Force (IETF) has developed the Intrusion Detection Message Exchange Format (IDMEF) (IETF, 2006).

Data Collected in Distributed Intrusion Detection

Intrusion detection has tradeoffs even on standalone hosts, especially for the quantity of data to be processed. Larger quantity of data needs more computational power. On the other hand, too little data means that some intrusions will not be detected. This also applies to distributed systems – useless data does not only slow down processing, but it will load the network as well. Types of data to be collected can therefore be categorized in the following three groups:

1. Data which is useless for intrusion detection.
2. Data which can be used for intrusion detection also on standalone hosts. To process this group, a distributed system is not needed; however, the network can be used to alert other participants of the possible danger.
3. Data of events which do not imply an intrusion by themselves, but collected and processed in a distributed manner, small pieces of information together can indicate an intrusion.

Distributed intrusion detection can increase efficiency for the second and third type. The third type of events can only be handled and interpreted by a distributed system.

Detectable events which imply an intrusion are called manifestations of an ongoing attack (Mutz, Vigna & Kemmerer, 2003). These usually can only be detected at the host that is actually under attack – for example, usually the host itself can only tell whether a particular user name and password pair is correct. Detecting events is therefore most efficient at the endpoints. These events must be, however, at least partially processed at the endpoints. An event log cannot state something like 'missing file'. With different systems, different applications, services, this error message can be of different importance. In case of a web server, this might mean an incorrectly typed filename – however, the configuration file of a firewall missing is a serious problem.

A possible attack scenario is when an attacker is some kind of worm software, which tries to guess passwords of users. In this case, only the end hosts directly attacked can know if the name and password are correct. For this reason, the intrusion attempt data is generated at different hosts under attack. This data, when collected, can be used to indicate the network-scale attack. The correlation is usually done in a centralized manner.

Data Processed in Distributed Intrusion Detection

Processing data collected by the sensors has other problems, too (Peng, Cui & Reeves, 2002). In the case of a centralized server, all data connected to intrusion attempts is stored in a single database. When using distributed processing, pieces of data related to a single intrusion can be stored at various places in the network, making global processing and interpreting more complicated.

According to our research, three properties of events detected can be used to correlate pieces of data:

1. The source of the event, e.g. the attacker itself.
2. The method of attack.
3. The destination of the attack.

Unfortunately, a complex attack is probably started from various sources; this information might not be enough to correlate attacks (Mutz, Vigna & Kemmerer, 2003).

Peer-to-Peer Networks

Participants of the P2P network are either called peers or nodes. The two main types of P2P overlay networks are structured and unstructured networks. In unstructured types, one node can be easily dispensed; the overlay handles quitting and failing nodes flexibly. Queries for data items can be handled by any node in these networks, by means of mechanisms built into the application. Gnutella (Gnutella, 2003), Freenet (Freenet, 2004) and FastTrack are typical examples for unstructured overlays.

Structured P2P networks use DHTs (distributed hash tables); these overlays store key–value pairs, and allow quick retention of any value associated with a precisely given key. Connections between nodes, the topology of the network are accurately defined. Every key–value pair is stored by a node selected by a given algorithm. Each node is assigned a Node IDentifier (NodeID) from a large range of integer numbers, for example, 160-bit long binary numbers. Similarly, pieces of information are also assigned a key, which can be, for example, a hashed value of that file name, which contains the information in question. This is a File IDentifier (FileID), which has the same number of bits as the NodeID. Every node stores those key–value pairs, which have their hashed keys closest to its own NodeID. This way, given a precise key, the exact location of a file can be determined by all participants.

Peer-to-Peer Based Intrusion Detection Systems

The intrusion protection system named PROMIS (and its previous version, Netbiotic) builds a partly decentralized network using the JXTA framework for its nodes to be able to share data of intrusion attempts (Vlachos & Spinellis, 2007). The nodes of the PROMIS system receive information from other nodes about the number of suspected intrusion attempts detected, and they automatically fine-tune the security level of the Web browser integrated into the operating system. This method provides some general protection about malicious software, but also decreases usability. This approach is similar to the prevention of epidemics in daily life.

The spam filter system named Spamwatch is built on a Tapestry peer-to-peer network (Zhou, Zhuang, Zhao, Huang, Joseph & Kubiatowicz, 2003). The program is a plugin of the e-mail client. Information about e-mails marked by the users as spam is collected in a DHT; the same spam message can be automatically deleted on other users' computers. By using the DHT, this lookup is fast, and only generates a small amount of network traffic.

Komondor: Our Distributed Intrusion Detection System

In the Komondor system, detection of intrusion attempts is distributed, by means of a DHT's based on the Kademlia network (Maymounkov & Mazieres, 2002). The following goals were important during the development of the system:

1. Building a stable overlay network to exchange information.
2. The data should be exchanged as quickly as possible.
3. Decentralization of the system, enabling nodes to be missing.
4. Masking the security holes of nodes based on intrusion attempts detected.

The several hosts running the Komondor software create an application level network. The speed of exchanging data about intrusion attempts largely depends on the network model employed. The system is built on a peer-to-peer (P2P) based overlay to ensure decentralization and stability, in contrast to the client-server model with a much higher risk of failure.

In the Komondor system, a DHT is employed to store data of intrusion attempts. Keys are IP addresses of attackers, values are the information of intrusion attempts. Report of intrusion attempts from a specific attacker will be sent to a single node, as all nodes use the same hash functions. If that node analyzes the reports and sees that the IP address in question belongs to an attacker, it initiates a broadcast message, to alert other Komondor nodes of the possible danger. Every node is interested in receiving information which enables it to strengthen its protection. Compared to PROMIS, the protection built up by Komondor is not general; rather it is against the recognized attackers only.

Detection at multiple points and collection of data can be very efficient. Consider the following example. There is an attacker who is trying to find an open, badly configured SMTP server to send junk e-mail. It tries to connect to many nodes protected by the Komondor system to find out which nodes have an SMTP service at all. One node sees an incoming connection which is immediately lost. From the viewpoint of a single host, a sole event like this does not necessarily indicate an attacker. It could possibly be a lost connection caused by some link failure. But if this event is detected on many of the nodes, then it immediately becomes suspicious. In the Komondor system, the IP address of the attacker determines which node will be the collector of information. That node will be responsible for processing data about a specific attacker; so sharing information about every suspicious event is necessary.

The Kademlia Overlay: Implementation Details

Routing in the Kademlia overlay is based on prefix-matching. Consider two nodes, e.g. A and B. If node A forwards a query, destined to node B, to the node in the routing table of node A that has the smallest XOR-distance (Maymounkov & Mazieres, 2002). This "smallest distance" is the basis of the "closeness" in this XOR metric. The symmetry of the XOR metric is an advantage compared to other systems, e.g. Chord (Stoica, Morris, Karger, Maashoek & Balakrishnan, 2001), since in Kademlia, if node A is close to node B, then node B is also close to node A. In this way, incoming messages also help keeping the routing table of a node fresh, as outgoing messages have the same distribution as incoming ones.

The entries in the routing tables are called contacts and are kept in an unbalanced, binary routing tree. This makes the overlay scalable, as any node P stores only a few contacts to nodes that are far away in the overlay but increasingly more contacts to nodes as the query gets closer P (Figure 1). For a given prefix distance, node P knows not only a single node but a list of contacts, called k-buckets. Each k-bucket can contain up to k contacts, in order to deal with node churn in a more efficient and reliable way without the need to periodically check if the contacts are still online. This list of contacts also enables nodes to send queries to more nodes

Figure 1. Routing table of a small Kademlia overlay

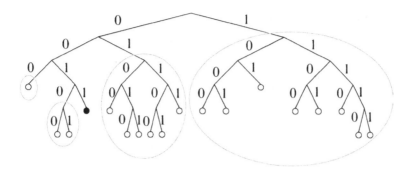

at once, and to choose nodes to which they have a fast network connection, based on (round trip time selection).

Routing to a specific NodeID is done in an iterative way, which means that each node on the way to the destination returns the coordinate of the next hop to the sending node. While iterative routing experiences a slightly higher delay than recursive routing, it offers increased robustness against message loss.

RELIABILITY OF KADEMLIA

Our test of the DHT-based Komondor software revealed that replication in Kademlia is more important than in other overlay networks. Some nodes might be unable to connect each other because of packet losses, packet filtering or network address translation (Bhagwan, Savage & Voleker, 2003; Chu, Labonte & Levine, 2002). As not all nodes are able to connect to the one that is closest to the key in identifier address space, it is possible for reports about a specific attacker to end up at different locations.

For the Komondor system we had to enhance the Kademlia network to make sure it meets the reliability standards which are demanded by an intrusion detection application. Replication can solve the problem of reliability mentioned above. If data is not only stored at one node, but at k nodes, the probability for the node sets to have a common node in their intersection is much higher. Replication also helps if the routing tables are partially incorrect. This might be the case in high churn networks, where nodes join and quit the network frequently (Rhea, Geels, Roscoe & Kubiatowicz, 2004).

To verify this statement we developed an application specific simulator, Kadsim. The program simulates the reports sent in a Komondor overlay, but the results are applicable for any Kademlia-based network. The most important requirement of

Figure 2. Storing keys in Kademlia, replication k=16, failing links: 20%

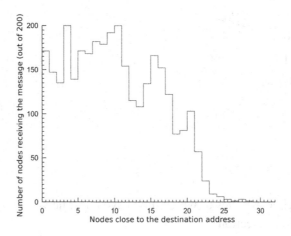

the Komondor system is for every report about a specific attacker to be collected by one node. Therefore Kadsim models the case, when all nodes in the overlay detect a suspicious event from the same IP address. The IP address is hashed using the SHA-1 function (FIPS 2008). In this aspect, the attacker is modeled by a randomly generated identifier. In the overlay simulated by Kadsim, every node looks up the node closest to this key, not counting nodes which are unreachable. Lookups in any Kademlia network are similar to this procedure; the task is to find nodes that are close to the key in identifier space.

At the end of the simulation, Kadsim sorts nodes by their distance to the hashed key, and plots the number of messages received by each. Ideally, if all network connections work, the function is a single step: the *k* closest nodes receive n messages, and others receive zero, where n is the number of all nodes in the overlay. Figure 2 shows the results for a simulation with 20% of the links failing, and replication *k=16*.

Simulation results show that relatively low, for example *k=8* replications already ensure that there is a node, which is able to collect all attack report. This might look too much for an overlay counting a hundred of participants. But increasing the number of nodes here is no need to increase the level of replication, the level required is only influenced by the ratio of failing links. With high probability, there will be a node, which is reachable by everybody (Figure 3).

Kademlia as the Substrate of Komondor

The choice of Kademlia being the substrate of our intrusion detection system Komondor greatly enhances the response time of intrusion detection and prevention.

Figure 3. Successful lookups in a Kademlia overlay

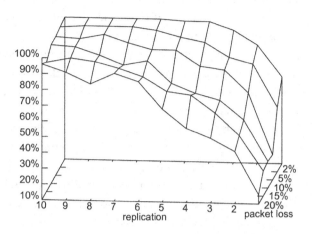

In the Kademlia network, there are no fixed, session based (TCP) connection between nodes, rather they use UDP packets. When a key–value pair is stored in the network, first the IP address of the node storing the pair has to be looked up. This can take tens of seconds, if the network and the nodes are loaded with traffic – but after that, the message which is sent as a store request will reach the destination node in less than a second. Due to the nature of network intrusions, we can expect that more than one report signaling a possible intrusion is generated within a short timeframe. If this is the case, the IP address of the node storing the reports does not have to be looked up again, as the node generating the report will still have the address in one of its *k*-buckets. This is the reason why Kademlia is the best choice for Komondor, and why it reduces the response time of intrusion detection to seconds.

Broadcast in P2P Overlays

Implementing broadcast (one to all) messages in P2P networks is rare, due to the large number of nodes. Still, there are applications, which require this type of communication (Chu, Ganjam, Ng, Rao, Sripanidkulchai, Zhan & Zhang, 2003); Komondor is also an example (Hosszú & Czirkos, 2007). When one of the nodes has collected enough information about an attacker, so that it can decide whether it imposes real danger or not, it initiates a broadcast message on the overlay. One-to-all messages are also used in DHT networks to implement partial keyword searches, for example, part of a filename.

The inherit topology of structured networks is a useful substrate to implement an efficient broadcast service. As messages can be duplicated at any node, the broadcast will take place in logarithmically many steps and logarithmic time. There is no need to initiate new connections during broadcast; the recently seen node lists can be used. That is also an advantage of the Kademlia overlay. The topology of the overlay is essentially an implicit multicast tree.

In the following section, three different algorithms for implementing broadcast service in Kademlia will be presented. In our tests, our packet losses are terminal, i.e. nodes do not try to detect and resend lost packets. This way, we can study how the algorithms perform in a short timeframe. Detecting a packet loss usually takes many seconds; that is enough for a complete broadcast sequence to take place, as the number of nodes receiving the message grows exponentially in time.

First algorithm: broadcast using flooding. Each node sends received messages to any other nodes it knows. As a specific message can be received in duplicates, every broadcast should be tagged with a unique identifier. Known messages (i.e. messages that were previously seen and processed) are dropped by nodes. This solution is simple, but it generates a lot of network traffic, especially when k-buckets are large. It has no practical use, but is rather a reference; by simulating this method on an overlay, one can see the time the broadcast requires.

Second algorithm: broadcast using the topology. Every subtree in the Kademlia overlay is assigned a node, which is responsible for broadcasting the message in its own tree. In Figure 4 the node *00110* (black dot) initiates the broadcast. It sends it to another freely chosen one from each of its k-buckets (normal arrows). These nodes are *11000*, *01010*, *00100* and *00000*. The nodes receiving the message are responsible for sending them on in their own subtrees that are *1*****, *01****, *000*** and *0010**. This is shown using dashed lines. Broadcast using this method will be finished in logarithmic time.

Nodes forwarding messages must know which subtree they are responsible for. Every message is tagged with a small integer, which denotes the height of the sub-

Figure 4. The proposed broadcast algorithm for Kademlia

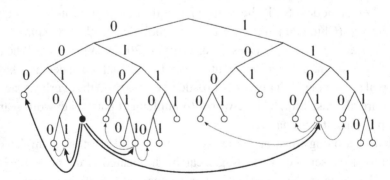

List 1. The proposed broadcast algorithm for Kademlia

```
broadcast(text, height)
     for i=height to number of bits
          if bucket i is not empty, then
               select a random node from bucket i
               send the message to the node: text, i+1
          endif
     endfor
```

tree; this shows how many bits the address of the subtree should share its prefix with the NodeID. The Kademlia protocol makes sure that at least one node is always known for every subtree; there is no need to maintain an auxiliary routing table for the broadcast. Messages are forwarded to the subtree and all smaller trees, as the List 1 presents.

This method is very cost-efficient since there are no duplicate messages. Problems can arise when there are packet losses on the network, as not only single nodes, but complete subtrees will miss the broadcast. Messages are actually directed to subtrees in this method: the original sender sends the message to the other half tree, and is itself responsible for his own half tree. Then it sends to the other quarter of the overlay, and is responsible for its own quarter and so on. Every subtree has a single responsible node.

Figure 5 shows a simulation of this method. Nodes shown as white dots received the message, while black ones did not. As one can see, there are complete subtrees drawn in black. It is possible for such a message to be lost, which was sent to a high subtree. In a worst case scenario, the number of nodes not getting the message can be more than 50%, independent from the packet loss ratio. Although the network is decentralized, this algorithm is not in its essence; as the importance of messages is vastly different, depending on which subtree they are addressed to.

Third algorithm: broadcast using the topology with replication. Addressing the problem mentioned above, the two algorithms can be combined. This algorithm is similar to the second one, but from every subtree, not a single, rather multiple nodes are selected to be responsible for forwarding the message. This way, the probability of skipping a subtree is falling rapidly. Duplicate messages are possible in this case, so a unique identifier is required for all broadcasts initiated. Replication level can vary from two to k, the size of k-buckets.

Figure 5. Errors of the implicit tree broadcast algorithm. As messages are directed to subtrees, losing one of them causes complete subtrees in the overlay to be missed.

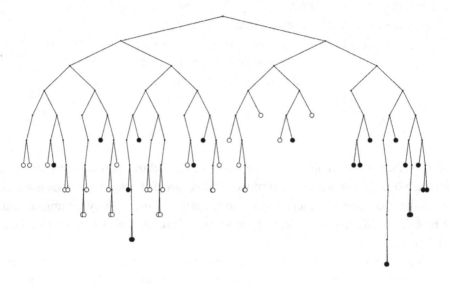

Comparison of Broadcast Algorithms

To evaluate the algorithms presented above, we developed a simple, application specific simulator (the internals of which are not discussed here). The application records the following data:

- The number of all messages sent,
- The number of messages per node,
- The number and ratio of nodes receiving the broadcast,
- The time required for sending the message to as many nodes as possible.

In terms of traffic costs, flooding gives the worst results. The number of messages grows rapidly with increasing the node count or sizes of k-buckets. The second algorithm using the implicit multicast tree evidently results one message for each node. For the third method, the number of messages grows rapidly for large k-buckets, but only slowly for increasing the number of nodes. For $k=5$, there were 7 messages/node for an overlay of 100 nodes, and only 9 for 1000 nodes.

To evaluate the reliability of the algorithms, we simulated an overlay of 200 nodes. Packet loss ratio varied from 0% to 20%, replication from one fold to fivefold. Flooding almost always yields perfect results; the error is smaller than line

Figure 6. Reliability of the broadcast algorithms

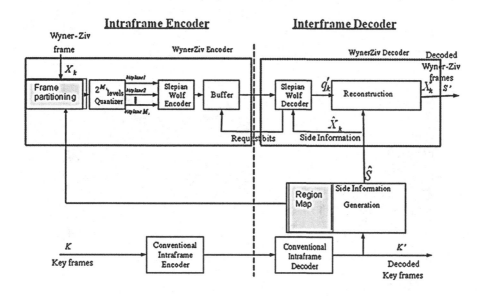

width on Figure 6. This is due to the enormous number of messages. The reliability of the enhanced algorithm is of course the same as the second for *k=1*, so it is not denoted individually. In turn, using *k=2*, this algorithm produces 90% reliability even for one fifth of the packets lost; *k=3* gives 97%.

RESULTS

Figure 7 shows attacks detected by our Komondor test network. Data shown was collected in three years. The numbers are the first eight bits (first octet) of the IP address. Dots show sources of different kind of attacks: SQL injections, virus activities, SSH worm propagation attempts. As Figure 7 shows, the distribution of sources of attacks is totally uneven over the Internet. By using hash functions on the whole IP addresses of attackers, we are able to evenly distribute intrusion data to be processed among Komondor nodes.

Our observation shows that the Komondor system is especially usable to create protection against systematic attacks against the every host of a certain IP-address range (for example, a corporate network), when it correlates attacks using the IP addresses of attackers. However, other correlation methods can also be applied.

Figure 7. Intrusion detections grouped by IP addresses

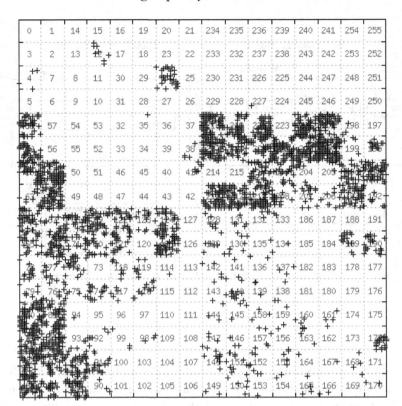

When correlating events by their attack types, the intensity of virus attacks can be determined by the collector nodes.

Protection is useful against attacks when multiple events can be detected. In our test network, which was composed of only five hosts, but collected data for two years, the following number of attacks was detected, as show on Table 1. The ratio is the number of network scale attacks divided by the number of all attacks. It estimates the ratio of cases when distributed intrusion detection can be superior to host-based detection, and may provide enhanced security to hosts.

Table 1. Attack types and network-scale attacks. The last row shows the ratio of cases, where distributed intrusion detection can provide enhanced security.

Type of attack	Number of events	Network scale	Ratio
SSH invalid password	3347	966	28%
CyberKit ICMP scan	1093	1032	94%
phpMyAdmin remote login attempt	215	152	70%

CONCLUSION

The DHT-based intrusion prevention system presented in our article is capable of creating a robust P2P application level overlay of the participant software entities. Using an appropriate structured overlay network, the intrusion detection is distributed among the peering software instances of the developed system called Komondor, but still it creates little processing and network traffic overhead. The reliability of the both of the two elementary services, namely sending attack reports and broadcasting alerts can be increased using replication. The substrate is affected only by one system-wide configuration parameter, namely the level of this replication. That can be determined in advance, with the methods presented in this article.

REFERENCES

Bhagwan, R., Savage, S., & Voelker, G. M. (2003). Understanding availability. *Peer-to-Peer Systems II* (LNCS 2735-2003).

Chu, J., Labonte, K., & Levine, B. N. (2002, July). Availability and locality measurements of peer-to-peer file systems. In *Proceedings of ITCom* (*Vol. 4868*). Scalability and Traffic Control in IP Networks II Conferences. Proceedings of SPIE.

Chu, Y. h., Ganjam, A., Ng, T. S. E., Rao, S. G., Sripanidkulchai, K., & Zhan, J. & Zhang, H. (2003, December). *Early experience with an Internet broadcast system based on overlay multicast* (Tech. Rep. CMUCS-03-214). Pittsburgh, PA: Carnegie Mellon University.

Federal Information Processing Standards Publication (FIPS PUB) 180-1. (1995, April). *Announcing the standard for secure hash standard.* Retrieved 2008 from http://www.itl.nist.gov/fipspubs/fip180-1.htm

Gnutella homepage. (2003). *Gnutella.* Retrieved August 16, 2010, from http://www.gnutella.org/

Hosszú, G., & Czirkos, Z. (2007). Network-based intrusion detection. In Freire, M., & Pereira, M. (Eds.), *Encyclopedia of Internet technologies and applications* (pp. 353–359). Hershey, PA: Information Science Reference. doi:10.4018/978-1-59140-993-9.ch050

IETF IDWG. (2006). *IETF Intrusion Detection Working Group* (IDWG). Retrieved January 4, 2006, from http://www.ietf.org/

Maymounkov, P., & Mazieres, D. (2002). A Peer-to-peer Information System based on the XOR Metric. In *Proceedings of IPTPS02*. Cambridge, USA: Kademlia.

Mutz, D., Vigna, G., & Kemmerer, R. (2003). An experience developing an IDS stimulator for the black-box testing of network intrusion detection systems. In *Annual Computer Security Applications Conference* (pp. 374-383), Las Vegas, NV.

Ning, P., Cui, Y., & Reeves, D. S. (2002, November). Constructing attack scenarios through correlation of intrusion alerts. In *CCS'02* (pp. 245-254), Washington, DC.

RealSecure. (2006). *IBM Internet security systems: Ahead of the threat*. Retrieved January 5, 2006, from http://www.iss.net/

Rhea, S., Geels, D., Roscoe, T., & Kubiatowicz, J. (2004, June). Handling churn in a DHT. In *Proceedings of USENIX Technical Conference*.

Snort. (2002). *Snort - The de facto standard for intrusion detection/prevention*. Retrieved August 16, 2010, from http://www.snort.org/

Stoica, I., Morris, R., Karger, D., Kaashoek, M. F., & Balakrishnan, H. (2001, March). *Chord: A scalable peer-to-peer lookup service for Internet applications* (Tech. Rep. TR-819). Cambridge, MA: MIT.

The Freenet Project. (2004). *Freenet: The free network*. Retrieved August 16, 2010, from http://freenetproject.org/

The giFT project. (2006). *Open-source implementation of the FastTrack protocol*. Retrieved August 16, 2010, from http://developer.berlios.de/projects/gift-fasttrack/

Vlachos, V., & Spinellis, D. (2007). A PROactive malware identification system based on the computer hygiene principles. *Information Management & Computer Security, 15*(4), 295–312. doi:10.1108/09685220710817815

Zhou, F., Zhuang, L., Zhao, B. Y., Huang, L., Joseph, A. D., & Kubiatowicz, J. (2003). Approximate object location and spam filtering on peer-to-peer systems. In *ACM Middleware*.

KEY TERMS AND DEFINITIONS

Ad-Hoc Network: This is a special type of the computer network, where the communication does not require any fixed computer network infrastructure, the nodes communicate directly with each other without access points. In the host-multicast the mobile peering hosts construct ad-hoc network.

Client-Server Model: A communicating way, where one host has more functionality than the other. It differs from the P2P network.

Hash Function: A mathematical formula, which is used to turn some data into a representing number, which can serve as a digital fingerprint. These formula can usually be applied to any data, and create a seemingly random, but reproducible identifier. Example algorithms for this are MD5 and SHA-1.

K-Bucket: A list of a node's neighbors in the Kademlia overlay.

Key-Value Pair: The fundamental unit of information stored in a hash table. Every piece of information content (value) is assigned an identifier (key), which is used for reference: values are mapped onto keys. An everyday example for this is a name of a file and its content.

Overlay Network: The applications, which create an ALN work together and usually follow the P2P model.

Peer-to-Peer (P2P) Network: A communication way where each node has the same authority and communication capability. They create a virtual network, overlaid on the Internet. Its members organize themselves into a topology for data transmission.

Replication: Storing a specific piece of information at many places, to increase availability and dependability.

Chapter 4
An Entropy–Based Architecture for Intrusion Detection in LAN Traffic

P. Velarde-Alvarado
Autonomous University of Nayarit, Mexico

A. Martinez-Herrera
ITESM-Campus Monterrey, Mexico

C. Vargas-Rosales
ITESM-Campus Monterrey, Mexico

D. Torres-Roman
Center for Investigation and Advanced Studies, Mexico

ABSTRACT

Information security has become a primary concern in enterprise and government networks. In this respect, Network-based Intrusion Detection System (NIDS) is a critical component of an organization's security strategy. This chapter is the result of the effort to design an Anomaly-based Network Intrusion Detection System (A-NIDS), which is capable of detecting network attacks using entropy-based behavioral traffic profiles. These profiles are used as a baseline to define the normal behavior of certain traffic features. The Method of Remaining Elements (MRE) is the core for the task of traffic profiling. In this method, a new measure of uncertainty called Proportional Uncertainty (PU) is proposed, which provides an important characteristic: the exposure of anomalies for those traffic slots related to anomalous

DOI: 10.4018/978-1-60960-836-1.ch004

Copyright ©2012, IGI Global. Copying or distributing in print or electronic forms without written permission of IGI Global is prohibited.

behavior. Moreover, PU increases the sensitivity for early detection, and allows detection of a wide range of attacks with respect to naïve entropy estimation. The performance evaluation of the proposed architecture was accomplished through MIT-DARPA dataset and also on an academic LAN by implementing real attacks. The results show that this architecture is effective in the early detection of intrusions, as well as some attacks designed to bypass detection measures.

INTRODUCTION

Nowadays, network infrastructures are crucial to the internal and external activities of an organization. It is vital that sensitive information and network assets that are handled through these networks should be protected from attacks by illegal users and malicious hackers. Examples of sensitive information include proprietary, privacy, financial, or classified government information. Therefore, it is important that an organization implements rigorous security strategies that meet the requirements of mission-critical applications. Mission-critical applications are those where failure of execution, or faulty execution, may have catastrophic results. In business environments, information systems managers would consider systems where failure could lead to loss of money (e.g. Banking & Telecom), serious inability to conduct business (e.g. online investment systems or accounting systems), or serious operational chaos (e.g. electronic trading systems or electronic data interchange systems), as being mission-critical.

According to the annual Computer Crime and Security Surveys, conducted by the Computer Security Institute (CSI, 2009), it has been observed a tendency that security threats have not only grown in volume, but also in sophistication and damage potential. In this context, conventional security measures have only been able to provide limited protection. Specifically, firewalls often cannot protect against an insider attack. They also cannot protect connections that do not go through the firewall, e.g. when someone connects to the Internet through a desktop modem and telephone. In essence, a firewall simply blocks traffic by enforcing access control policies. On the other hand, the rules used by Signature-based NIDS (S-NIDS) such as Snort (Roesch, 1999), can be created only if a new type of intrusion has been identified and analyzed. By the time this process has been completed, the attack could have time to disperse or be modified by its creators. Finally, in a traditional Anomaly-based NIDS (A-NIDS) a profile can be built around certain traffic features, for instance in terms of a threshold for the maximum volume of traffic. However, a clever attack may infiltrate if the volume of malign traffic remains within the threshold level. In such a case, the overall volume of traffic into the network looks normal. Respond by lowering the threshold for this type of attack can lead to a high false positives rate.

In order to resolve these shortcomings in traditional systems, a number of recent research studies have begun pointing the way toward new approaches to intrusion detection. These approaches used to address the anomaly detection, seek a better characterization of normal traffic behavior. The effectiveness of the detection scheme depends on the accuracy of the traffic model. The new trends are based on the use of statistical signal processing, artificial intelligence (AI) and entropy. Signal processing techniques have been successfully applied to analyze time series data obtained from network probes and filtering techniques. Thottan and Ji (Thottan & Ji, 2003) proposed a statistical signal processing technique based on abrupt change detection to solve the problem of anomaly detection. On the other hand, AI tools such as neural networks and fuzzy logic have been used to mine normal patterns from audit data. Pattern Recognition as a branch of AI has been proposed for detecting novel attacks using learning by example paradigms. Esposito et al. (Esposito, Mazzariello, Oliviero, Peluso, Romano, & Sansone 2008) presented a reference model for a real-time network Intrusion Detection System based on Pattern Recognition techniques with very low false alarm rate. Finally, entropy-based methods have been widely investigated and discussed in recent years. These methods have shown to be viable for the task of automatic intrusion detection because they offer more fine-grained insights of the structure and composition of network traffic (Nychis, Sekas, Andersen, & Zhang, 2008). Entropy-based characterizations are less affected by traffic sampling processes applied in high speed networks. Consequently, entropy methods become more robust for the task of intrusion detection in sampled environment, this is because entropy preserves the structure of an attack (Brauckhoff, Tellenbach, Wagner, & May, 2006). A variety of entropy-based network traffic profiling schemes for detecting security attacks have been proposed (Lee & Xiang, 2001; Nychis, Sekas, Andersen, & Zhhang, 2008; Velarde, Vargas, Torres, & Martinez, 2008; Xu, Zhang, & Bhattacharyya, 2008; Wagner & Plattner, 2005; Ziviani, Gomes, & Monsores, 2007). The argument is based on the fact that an attack changes the character of the network traffic in subtle but unavoidable ways. Such changes alter the entropy of the network in clearly measurable ways (Nucci & Bannerman, 2007). Velarde et al. (Velarde, Vargas, Torres, & Martinez, 2010) propose the Method of Remaining Elements (MRE), which is an entropy-based method that profiles the behavior of sequences of traffic features. MRE is applied to the early detection of probes, scans and floods. MRE highlights the traffic slots where attacks occur by means of a parameter called the exposure threshold. This method works at packet-level; hence is adequate to implement it to monitor LAN traffic.

In this chapter, architecture of an A-NIDS that uses entropy-based baseline models is proposed. These models describe the behavior of four intrinsic traffic features i.e. source IP address (*srcIP*), destination IP address (*dstIP*), source port (*srcPrt*) and destination port (*dstPrt*). The capabilities of this system will be discussed in the following sections. For instance, the simple entropy estimation for these features in traffic slots is not sufficient to detect certain anomalous conditions caused by an attack. Similarly, it is shown that some attacks attempt to evade detection by temporarily dispersing attack packets. The proposed solution includes the definition of two types of traffic slots. Furthermore, the incorporation of the balanced entropy estimator provides better results for attack detection and reduces the computational complexity as well. An important feature in this proposal is the exposure of anomalies, which highlights those traffic slots related to anomalous behavior by obtaining a visual element for the detection of attacks.

In summary, the proposal uses a methodology based on entropy for obtaining knowledge about the behavior of traffic features to perform anomaly detection tasks. This knowledge is obtained from training datasets for a subsequent comparison with the current traffic. To test the practical detection performance of this approach, three types of attacks and two scenarios were considered. The attacks were classified according to three types of activity performed on the victim: scan, probe, and flood. In the first scenario, true worm attacks were implemented within an academic LAN, which varied in their propagation rates as well as in their scanning techniques. The second scenario is defined by using the MIT-DARPA dataset. MIT-DARPA traffic traces allow setting up a performance study under extremely valuable intrusion detection public domain datasets, which provide a performance benchmark for detection and prevention systems (Wang, 2009).

BACKGROUND

There are two key concepts which are very important for the proposed architecture, entropy and Anomaly-based Intrusion Detection. Taken together, these two concepts support the integrated and comprehensive platform that addresses threat scenarios. These concepts are reviewed in this section.

Entropy

Entropy stems from the key idea that a probability distribution represents uncertainty, and that some distributions represent more uncertainty than others. A measure of this uncertainty was originally provided by (Shannon, 1948). For a discrete probability distribution, $p(x_k)$, Shannon's uncertainty measure H is given by Equation (1)

$$H(X) = -\sum_{k=1}^{M} p(x_k) \log p(x_k), \qquad (1)$$

where the discrete random variable X takes the value x_k, $1 \leq k \leq M$, and H is termed the entropy. Intuitively, the entropy is a measure of the diversity or randomness of the data coming over a stream. The entropy attains its minimum value of zero when all the items coming over the stream are the same, and attains its maximum value of $\log m$ when all the m items in the stream are distinct.

Entropy Estimation

In general, the probability distribution for a given stochastic problem is not known and only the datasets from which to estimate entropy are available. For example, consider the problem of estimating the entropy H in Equation (1) for a probability distribution $p(x_k)$, where the index k runs over M possibilities. In an experiment it is observed that in N samples each possibility k occurred n_k times. If $N >> M$, the probabilities by frequencies, $p(x_k) \approx \hat{p}(x_k) = n_k / N$ are approximated, and construct a naive estimate of the Shannon entropy,

$$H(X) \approx \hat{H}^{naive} = -\sum_{k=1}^{M} \hat{p}(x_k) \log \hat{p}(x_k) \qquad (2)$$

This is also a maximum likelihood estimator, since the maximum likelihood estimate of the probabilities is given by the frequencies.

It is well known that $\hat{H}^{naive}$ underestimates the entropy (Paninski, 2003). This is due to the nonlinear nature of the entropy. Specifically, the frequencies $\hat{p}(x_k)$ are unbiased estimators of the probabilities, i.e., their expectation value $\langle \hat{p}(x_k) \rangle$ (where $\langle . \rangle$ stands for ensemble average) coincides with the true value of the estimated quantity. In other words, the frequencies $\hat{p}(x_k)$ approximate the probabilities $p(x_k)$ with certain statistical error (variance), but without any systematic error (bias). In contrast, the naive entropy estimator, in which $p(x_k)$ are simply replaced by n_k / N, are always biased, i.e., it deviates from the true value of the entropy not only statistically but also systematically.

Recently, Bonachela et al. (Bonachela, Hinrichsen, & Muñoz, 2008) proposed an improved estimator which reduces either the bias or the variance of the estimate of the Shannon entropy. This estimator is called balanced estimator for the Shannon entropy which is shown in Equation (3).

$$\hat{H}^{bal}(X) = \frac{1}{N+2} \sum_{k=1}^{M} \left[(n_k + 1) \sum_{j=n_k+2}^{N+2} \frac{1}{j} \right] \qquad (3)$$

The second summation in Equation (3) can be represented as a partial harmonic series or equivalently, as a harmonic number. A harmonic number is a number of the form

$$H_n = \sum_{k=1}^{n} \frac{1}{k} \qquad (4)$$

Equivalently, a harmonic number can be expressed analytically as

$$H_n = \gamma + \Psi(n+1) \qquad (5)$$

where $\gamma = 0.5772156649$ is the Euler-Mascheroni constant, (Conway & Guy, 1996), and $\Psi(n+1)$ is the digamma function. The corresponding asymptotic expansion of H_n is

$$H_n \sim \log(n) + \gamma + (1/2)n^{-1}$$
$$-(1/12)\, n^{-2} + (1/120)\, n^{-4} - (1/250)\, n^{-6} + \cdots$$

$$H_n = \log(n) + \rho_n \qquad (6)$$

Using the definition of a harmonic number, the second summation in Equation (3) can be expressed in terms of two harmonic numbers as shown in Equation (7)

$$\sum_{j=n_k+2}^{N+2} \frac{1}{j} = \sum_{j=1}^{N+2} \frac{1}{j} - \sum_{j=1}^{n_k+1} \frac{1}{j} = H_{N+2} - H_{n_k+1}, \qquad (7)$$

using the compact form of the asymptotic expansion of H_n, this difference of harmonic numbers can be represented as shown in Equation (8)

$$H_{N+2} - H_{n_k+1} = \log\left(\frac{N+2}{n_k+1}\right) + \rho_{N+2} - \rho_{n_k+1}, \tag{8}$$

where ρ_{N+2} and ρ_{n_k+1} approach the same value C when N and n_k increase indefinitely, hence the difference $\rho_{N+2} - \rho_{n_k+1}$ approaches zero. A more computationally efficient expression for the balanced estimator can be obtained by replacing the second summation in Equation (3) by Equation (8) to get the Balanced Estimator-II,

$$\hat{H}^{bal-II}(X) = \frac{1}{N+2}\sum_{k=1}^{M}(n_k+1)\log\left(\frac{N+2}{n_k+1}\right) \tag{9}$$

The condition that maximizes the Balanced Estimator-II, occurs when x_k's frequencies are $n_k = 1$. Hence, the size of the alphabet is equal to the size of the dataset, i.e., $M = N$. Therefore, the maximum value of the Balanced Estimator-II is given by

$$\hat{H}_{MAX}^{bal-II}(X) = \frac{2M}{M+2}\log\left(\frac{M+2}{2}\right) \tag{10}$$

Proportional Uncertainty

The proportional uncertainty, PU, (Velarde, Vargas, Torres, & Martinez, 2009) is an index of uncertainty regarding the maximum value of Shannon's entropy in a dataset. For a discrete dataset X, PU is defined as,

$$PU(X) = \frac{\hat{H}^{bal-II}(X)}{\log(M)} \leq \lim_{M\to\infty}\frac{\frac{2M}{M+2}\log\left(\frac{M+2}{2}\right)}{\log(M)} = 2, for M > 1. \tag{11}$$

$PU_{\text{Max-rel}}$ is defined as the maximum PU for a given alphabet size M, its value is given by

$$1 \leq PU_{\text{Max-rel}}(X) = \hat{H}_{MAX}^{bal-II}(X)\big/\log(M) \leq 2 \tag{12}$$

Values of $PU_{\text{Max-rel}}$ for different alphabet sizes are shown in Figure 1.

Figure 1. PU maximum relative value for different size of alphabet

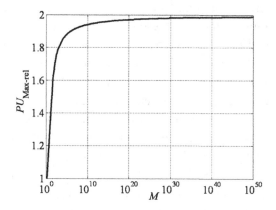

The proportional uncertainty is used to characterize the traffic-slot's normal behavior for a given traffic feature, which for simplicity, it is referred as r-feature, where $r = 1,2,3,4$ for *srcIP*, *dstIP*, *srcPrt*, and *dstPrt*, respectively. In summary, *PU* provides a measure of randomness in a dataset, the numeric quantification of randomness for an r-feature is within the interval [1, 2]. In reality, this range is narrower because it depends on the size of the alphabet. Consequently, the more random a dataset is, the more approaches to $PU_{Max-rel}$.

For an r-feature with an initial level of randomness *PU*, a maximum level of *PU* can be obtained by extracting its significant elements (i.e., those most frequently). In typical traffic conditions, r-features show an average maximum level of *PU*. It is called *exposure threshold,* which in the context of traffic analysis it is denoted as β_r. The exposure threshold is the parameter to characterize the behavior of the four traffic features in a given period of time.

Network Intrusion Detection Systems

An Intrusion Detection System (IDS) can be a combination of hardware/software that automates the process of monitoring the events occurring in a computer system or network. An IDS analyzes these events to find signs of intrusions or attempts to bypass the security mechanisms of a computer or network. IDS can be split into two categories – Host IDS (HIDS) and Network IDS (NIDS). HIDS protect an end system or network application, by auditing system and event logs. NIDS can be deployed on the network, monitoring network traffic for attacks. An NIDS can sit outside the firewall, on the demilitarized zone (DMZ), or anywhere inside the private network. Typically NIDS focus their efforts around one of two areas – Signature

Detection and Anomaly Detection. Signature-based (S-NIDS) e.g., Snort, (Roesch, 1999), employ pattern recognition techniques, i.e., they have a database with the known attack signatures and match these signatures with the analyzed data, when one similarity is found an alarm is activated. However, there are several drawbacks to be considered in the case of S-NIDS. The most important is related to detect new type of attacks. If a new type of attack appears, S-NIDS will not be able to detect such attack because it does not have reference in its database (Arvidson, Carlbark, 2003). It means that an S-NIDS needs sufficient time and resources to learn and store the main features of the new attack before detecting it. Nevertheless, it produces new administration drawbacks. Like antivirus software, it means to have a big database, download the updates and alerts to have the most recent references of new type of attacks, but such actions does not guarantee to be on-safe of new type of attacks because new variants of an attack or new attacks appear frequently. Such activities can lead to significantly affect the design requirements of a NIDS related to scalability (Besson, 2003). It implies to use sufficient and representative data to detect attacks without augment the complexity of the NIDS and this characteristic is desirable on constraint environments such as mobile devices. Zero day attacks are examples of attacks that S-NIDS is unable to detect.

Meanwhile, instead of having a database, A-NIDS first builds a statistic traffic profile which describes the typical behavior of the network. A-NIDS has some advantages. The first one is related to personalize the A-NIDS regards to the typical traffic profile of the network based on the main features. Building such traffic reference, an A-NIDS is capable to perform detection tasks only by making a comparison between the current traffic and the reference traffic. An alarm is enabled when the current traffic diverts from the reference. Instead of the time spent on reconfiguring an S-NIDS, It allows detecting zero-day attacks as soon as they appear. However, an A-NIDS needs to choose significant and relevant traffic features to perform its tasks. It allows reducing the rates of false positives and false negatives. Another disadvantage is to define which behavior is really "normal traffic behavior" (Arvidson, Carlbark, 2003). An additional issue is related to the unavailability of the features, e.g., encrypted traffic, which cannot be extracted from the current traffic. With respect to the generation of behavioral traffic profiles (IP source, packet size, type of protocol, payload, etc.), an entropy-based detection improves performance significantly over that of the traditional A-NIDS methods. In the following section, the focus is on the use and justification of an entropy-based anomaly detection method.

Entropy and Anomaly Detection

A number of recent empirical studies (Gu, McCallum, & Towsley, 2005; Nychis et al., 2008; Wagner et al., 2005; Xu et al., 2008) have suggested the use of entropy as a succinct means of summarizing traffic distributions for different applications, in particular, in anomaly detection and in fine-grained traffic analysis and classification. With respect to anomaly detection, the use of entropy for tracking changes in traffic distributions provides two significant benefits. First, the use of entropy can increase the sensitivity of detection to uncover anomalous incidents that may not manifest as volume anomalies. Second, using such traffic features provides additional diagnostic information into the nature of the anomalous incidents (e.g., making distinction among worms, DDoS attacks, and scans) that is not available from just volume-based anomaly detection (Lall, Sekar, Ogihara, Xu, & Zhangz, 2006).

Since entropy is a property of the probability distribution, if there is a change in the probability distribution there is also a change in its underlying entropy. Changes in the statistical behavior of the data could be caused by abnormal activities and represent an anomaly. In the particular case of traffic analysis, changes in the entropy of the traffic features were analyzed in a previous paper (Velarde, Vargas, Torres & Munoz, 2008), in that work, a LAN was subjected to real attacks of the worms W32.Blaster and W32.Sasser. A forensic analysis based on the estimation of the entropy for traffic traces indicated that the r-features showed anomalous behavior during the infection. The analysis suggested that the statistical tools, specifically, average value, Inter-Quartile Range (IQR), and the correlation coefficient applied to the entropy of the r-features captured the anomalies caused by the spread of worms. Moreover, the analysis introduced was robust to different maximum slot duration, t_d. As shown in the Figure 2, increment or decrement in the value of entropy, and changes in correlation of the entropy of srcIP vs. dstIP and srcPrt vs. dsrPrt, are the most evident characteristics during worm propagation. However, a subsequent observation of this work made evident that a change in the level of entropy is not

Figure 2. Behavior of the entropy of r-features during normal periods and worm attacks

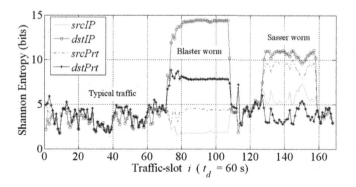

sufficient to detect an attack. This can be verified by observation of slots 2 - 4 in Figure 2, where a portscan attack occurred, but the entropy levels are maintained at normal levels, however, the anomalous behavior of the correlation captures the anomaly.

The empirical results show that the selection of features is important, but also an appropriate processing of them is required. The proposed methodology is based on learning the behavior of these r-features in order to recognize the subtle changes in traffic caused by different dynamics of attacks. The Method of Remaining Elements (Velarde et al., 2009; Velarde et al., 2010) is an effort aimed at providing traffic characterization in terms of entropy and a subsequent integration of the resulting model to an A-NIDS. The following section describes the details of this method.

Taxonomy for Computer Attacks

A Taxonomy of computer intrusions allows to classify attacks into groups that share common properties. Once these groups have been identified, the task of testing an IDS becomes more effective. Instead of developing a large number of attacks, it should be sufficient to pick a representative subset of each category of attacks. However, it is difficult to define an accurate taxonomy without knowing all possible types of attack and considering alternate approaches to grouping attacks. New attacks are constantly being discovered. There are numerous taxonomies that have been proposed. One of the best known taxonomies is the Defense Advanced Projects Agency (DARPA) attack taxonomy. This taxonomy was developed in 1998 for classifying attacks in order to simplify the process of evaluating an IDS.

Through this chapter, it is used the taxonomy proposed by Ye, Newman and Farley (2006) which extends and refines the taxonomy given by Howard and Longstaff (1998). Their classification framework simplifies the task of comparing and categorizing attacks, providing a useful tool for the design of an IDS. According to this taxonomy, network incidents can be ordered in terms of cause and effect. The overall incident begins with a threat, followed by an attack. A threat is composed of the three categories: objective, propagation and attack origin. On the other hand, the elements involved in the cause-effect chain of an attack are sorted in eight categories: objective, propagation, attack origin, action, vulnerability, asset, state effects and performance effects. The *action category* describes the specific activity the attack is performing on the victim: probe, scan, flood, authenticate, bypass, spoof, read, copy, termination, create processes, execute, steal, modify, delete, misdirect, and eavesdrop. Based on the type of activity carried out by an attack, the proposed architecture focuses on the timely detection of three *action subcategories*: *probes*, *scans* and *floods*, through statistical deviations with respect to a behavioral profile based on entropy for certain traffic features considering two time scales.

THE METHOD OF REMAINING ELEMENTS

MRE makes short-term observations in non-overlapping i-traffic slots. Traffic slot has a maximum duration of t_d seconds and is formed by a stream of W_i packets. On each slot a set of four sequences are generated, which are labeled as S_i^1, S_i^2, S_i^3, and S_i^4. In general, an S_i^r sequence represents a succession of IP source addresses (for $r = 1$), IP destiny addresses (for $r = 2$), source port numbers (for $r = 3$), and destiny port numbers (for $r = 4$). S_i^r sequence is identified as *input sequence* for the MRE algorithm (Algorithm 1). This algorithm performs an iterative process to remove the elements that contain highest frequencies in the underlying sequence. These removed elements are called *significant elements* and are grouped into another set. During the j-iterative process of removal of elements, the sequence is called *sequence in progress*. The notation used to label this sequence is $S_{i,j}^r$, where j is the iteration number. When MRE finishes, a *residual sequence* is obtained which is labeled as $\tilde{S}_i^r$. The cardinality of $\tilde{S}_i^r$ is denoted by R_i^r, where $R_i^r \geq 1$. Besides, the cardinality of the set of significant elements is denoted by I_i^r, where $I_i^r \geq 0$. An iterative process in MRE is performed while two conditions are fulfilled. 1) $PU(S_{i,j}^r) \leq \beta_r$, and 2) $|S_{i,j}^r| > 2$. Algorithm 1 describe the main steps to determine $\tilde{S}_i^r$, R_i^r, and I_i^r, for a given input sequence, S_i^r and an exposure threshold, β_r. The exposure threshold β_r is the maximum level of PU that should be reached by $S_{i,j}^r$ while MRE algorithm is performed.

However, it is not always possible that a sequence in progress reaches the exposure threshold when the MRE algorithm is applied. This occurs in two situations: (1) when S_i^r has low diversity, this implies that the entropy of the sequence in progress i.e., $\hat{H}^{bal-II}(S_{i,j}^r)$ is not increased as the significant elements are removed. In consequence, the condition $\hat{H}^{bal-II}(S_{i,j}^r)/\log(R_{i,j}^r) \geq \beta_r$ is not reached. In this situation, the iterative process will lead to $R_i^r = 2$. (2) When the cardinality of the input sequence is unitary, i.e., $|S_i^r| = 1$ then $R_i^r = 1$.

R_i^r and I_i^r values calculated by the MRE algorithm are determined by a exposure threshold, β_r which is specific for a maximum slot duration, t_d. This threshold is learned during the training phase using typical traffic traces. In short, the exposure threshold defines the condition of separation between significant and remaining elements for a given input sequence.

*Algorithm 1. Obtain $\tilde{S}_i^r$, R_i^r, and I_i^r given an input sequence S_i^r and β_r. Table **T**, consists of (a, b) value pairs, a means frequency and b is a particular r-instance (e.g., an IP address value).*

```
1:    Parameters: Sᵢʳ , βr
2:    define alphabet from Sᵢʳ, and Items = | Sᵢʳ |
3:    if Items == 1
4:        Iᵢʳ = 0
5:        Rᵢʳ = Items
6:    else
7:        compute PU( Sᵢʳ , βr)
8:        if PU >= βr
9:            Iᵢʳ = 0,  Rᵢʳ = Items
10:       else
11:           build table T
12:           sort T in decreasing order
13:           PU = 0,  j = 1,  Sᵢ,ⱼʳ = Sᵢʳ
14:           while PU <= βr && | Sᵢ,ⱼʳ | > 2 do
15:               Sᵢ,ⱼʳ = Sᵢ,ⱼʳ \ T(b (j))    %removing significant
elements
16:               compute PU ( Sᵢ,ⱼʳ , βr)
17:               j++
18:           end while
19:           Iᵢʳ = j -1
20:           Rᵢʳ = Items - Iᵢʳ ,
21:           S̃ᵢʳ = Sᵢ,ⱼʳ
22:       end if
23:   end if
```

Exposure of Anomalies

The exposure threshold, β_r determines the final characteristics of the residual sequences produced by the MRE algorithm. That residual sequence, $\tilde{S}_i^r$ whose proportional uncertainty is greater than the exposure threshold, exhibits a characteristic called *exposure of anomaly*. That is, sequences associated with anomalous behavior present residual cardinalities greater than two, i.e., $R_i^r > 2$. By means of the exposure of anomalies, the traffic slots whose residual sequences, $\tilde{S}_i^r$ exceed a certain level of entropy $H(\tilde{S}_i^r)$ for a given residual cardinality R_i^r are highlighted. The greater the residual cardinality, the greater is the anomaly in the input sequence. β_r is described by a two variable discrete function, where the proportion of entropy and cardinalities of the residual sequences satisfy Equation (13)

$$H(\tilde{S}_i^r)\big/\log(R_i^r) = \beta_r \tag{13}$$

For a given β_r there are pairs of values $H(\tilde{S}_i^r)$ and R_i^r associated with residual sequences that satisfy Equation (13), such values define a curve or function. In general, each function defines the conditions of both residual cardinality and entropy of residual sequences to determine the analyzed sequence's status (i.e., benign or anomalous).

The Anomaly Level Exposure (ALE) in a traffic slot i and for an r-feature is defined as Equation (14)

$$ALE_i^r = R_i^r - 2 \tag{14}$$

ALE offers a description of the behavior of a residual sequence, $\tilde{S}_i^r$ regards to a given exposure threshold, β_r. At normal conditions (i.e., without potential attacks), $\tilde{S}_i^r$ satisfies that $PU(\tilde{S}_i^r) \leq \beta_r$. According to MRE algorithm, it leads to a residual cardinality of $R_i^r = |\tilde{S}_i^r| = 2$. Therefore, in typical traffic conditions $ALE_i^r = 0$. Otherwise, a residual sequence with anomalous behavior shows $PU(\tilde{S}_i^r) > \beta_r$, and $R_i^r = |\tilde{S}_i^r| > 2$ and consequently, $ALE_i^r > 0$. ALE allows detecting anomalies on each $\tilde{S}_i^r$ if the conditions defined in the case of anomalous behavior are fulfilled.

MRE Support

It was found that there are attacks whose behaviors are not directly detectable by ALE. Concretely, two cases are considered. Case I occurs in those residual sequences that despite having $ALE_i^r = 0$, there is evidence of anomalous traffic in the sequence. This kind of anomalies or attacks are captured by the cardinality of the set of significant elements i.e., I_i^r. Thus, a new feature I_r is defined for profiling I_i^r, which consist to obtain the threshold of the maximum value of I_i^r. Case II occurs when there are attacks that lead to generate sequences of unitary cardinality with atypical lengths. Under these conditions, the traffic has unusual properties. It was observed in targeted attacks against a particular host and port. For this reason, a threshold for the lengths of sequences of unitary cardinality was defined. The threshold that defines the maximum length of sequences of unitary cardinality is denoted as U_r. In summary, both I_r and U_r define the support for MRE.

Exposure Threshold Algorithm

The obtaining of residual and significant cardinalities, i.e., R_i^r and I_i^r depend on the value of the exposure threshold that characterizes a given type of traffic slot. The type of traffic slot is determined by its maximum duration, denoted as t_d. In proposed architecture two types of traffic slot are used, $t_d = 0.5$ and $t_d = 60$ seconds, which will be explained later. MRE-based Intrusion Detection Architecture requires two phases of operation: training phase and detection phase. During the training phase, it is assumed that traffic is devoid of any attack and the characterization of traffic by β_r acts as a typical traffic profile. The behavior of R_i^r is defined implicitly by the exposure threshold. However, behavior of I_i^r must be profiling by *a posteriori* training.

Algorithm 2 describes the main steps to obtain the maximum proportional uncertainty reached by an input sequence. In each iteration, the algorithm tries to increase the proportional uncertainty of the sequence. The maximization of PU is an optimization problem: find the elements of the sequence that must be removed to reduce the cardinality and increase the entropy. Removed elements are related to higher frequencies (i.e. belong to significant elements set). *fnbeta* function receives two parameters: an input sequence, S_i^r and the value of proportional uncertainty PU_A that tries to achieve (target value). This function returns the maximum uncertainty as PU_B. The computation of the maximum proportional uncertainty begins with $PU_A = 1.0$. While the value delivered by the function is greater than the target value, i.e. $PU_B > PU_A$, the function calls will continue. Finally, the maximum proportional uncertainty for the sequence S_i^r is reported as β_i.

A training traffic processing generates a vector of β_i's denoted as $\beta_r^{trace} = [\beta_1 \ \beta_2 \ \cdots \ \beta_m]$, where m is the number of traffic slots that form the trace. Vector β_r^{trace} is statistically analyzed to determine the exposure threshold of the whole traffic trace. Basically, this analysis characterizes statistically the extreme values of β_r^{trace}. This process is summarized in Figure 3. The first stage decimates the input vector β_r^{trace} to remove the values that have a threshold $\beta_i = 1$, which is the minimum value of PU in the context of exposure of anomalies; the new vector is denoted as β_r^{D1}. Stage two explores the existence of outliers in β_r^{D1}; if there are no outliers, β_r^{D1} is transmitted to stage five, otherwise, an analysis of outliers (stage

Figure 3. Stages to obtain β_r^{trace}

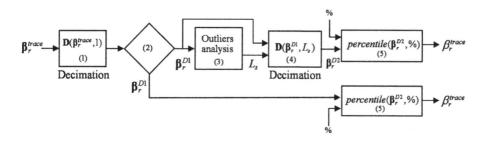

three and four) in β_r^{D1} is performed. Stage three sets the threshold for outliers, represented by the upper limit Ls. Thus, a $\beta_i \in \beta_r^{\text{trace}}$ such that $\beta_i > Ls$ is regarded an outlier. The upper limit is calculated as expressed in Equation (15)

$$Ls = Q_3 + w(Q_3 - Q_1), \tag{15}$$

here w is the maximum whisker length, and Q_k is the k-quartile. The default value for w is 1.5, which is equivalent to $\pm 2.7\sigma$, (Tukey, 1977), where σ is the standard deviation of β_r^{D1}. Stage four takes the vector β_r^{D1} as input and decimates it. After the decimation, all values below Ls are removed and a new vector is obtained as the output. Such vector is denoted as β_r^{D2} which contains the outliers of the input vector β_r^{D1}. Stage five takes the decimated vectors either β_r^{D1} or β_r^{D2} as input, to be characterized by a percentile. Each training trace produces an unique β_r^{trace} value, and the set of β_r^{trace} is averaged to obtain the exposure threshold for each r-feature, i.e.,

$$\beta_r = \overline{\beta}_r^{\text{trace}} \tag{16}$$

Architecture for Intrusion Detection Based on MRE

The architecture for an A-NIDS based on MRE is summarized in Figure 4. The training phase is responsible for building the behavioral profiles for two types of traffic slots: short-time traffic slot (STTS) and long-time traffic slot (LTTS). The profiles for an r-feature are represented by the following parameters: (1) the exposure threshold, β_r, (2) a threshold for the maximum value of I_i^r, denoted as I_r, and

Algorithm 2. Obtain maximum PU in an input sequence

```
1:    Input sequence: S_i^r for a given t_d
2:    PU_A = 1.0 // initial PU
3:    PU_B = fnbeta(S_i^r, PU_A)  // calling function
4:    while ( PU_B > PU_A ) do
5:        PU_A = PU_B
6:        PU_B = fnbeta(S_i^r, PU_B)
7:    end while
8:    β_i = max(PU_A, PU_B) // maximum PU
9:    // fnbeta function declaration
10:       function B = fnbeta(S_i^r, β)
11:       if    (| S_i^r | = = 1  ||  | S_i^r | = = 2)
12:           B = 0
13:       else
14:           PU = H( S_i^r ) / log (| S_i^r | )
15:           j = 0,   S_{i,j}^r = S_i^r
16:           while ( PU ≤ β && |S_{i,j}^r|>2 ) do
17:               j++
18:               S_{i,j}^r = S_{i,j-1}^r \ T(b(j))
19:               PU(S_{i,j}^r) = H(S_{i,j}^r) / log(| S_{i,j}^r |)
20:           end while
21:           B = PU
22:       end if
23:       end function fnbeta
```

(3) a threshold for the maximum value of U_i^r, denoted as U_r. Experimentally, it is shown that the fastest detection can be achieved with a t_d= 0.5 seconds; this type of slot is called STTS. Additionally, a longer traffic slot is required to detect attacks that attempt to evade detection by the temporary dispersion of malign traffic. The value of t_d = 60 seconds, which corresponds to the second type of traffic slot called LTTS. Having defined the profiles, the next step is obtaining the current traffic measurements, in order to determine the status of traffic slot i. The measurements are: (1) Cardinality of the set of the remaining elements, R_i^r. (2) Cardinality of the set of the significant elements, I_i^r. (3) Length of the unitary cardinality sequence, U_i^r. Diagnostic defines the status of a traffic slot based on any of the following

Figure 4. Architecture for an A-NIDS based on MRE

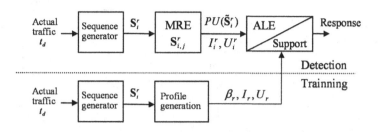

approaches for detection: (1) $PU(\tilde{\mathbf{S}}_i^r)$ versus β_r (ALE approach), (2) I_i^r versus I_r (significant elements approach), and (3) U_i^r versus U_r (unitary cardinality approach). The presented architecture does not need to compare chunks involving a fixed number of contiguous messages in order to detect anomalies. This feature is one of the most valuable elements of this architecture. It also does not need to analyze chunks with the same number of messages for the same purpose.

Experimental Platform, Dataset, and Tools

The evaluation of MRE was conducted in two different scenarios: scenario 1 (labeled as SC1) is an academic LAN which is subdivided into four subnets. There are 100 hosts running Windows XP SP2 mainly. One router connects the subnets with 10 Ethernet switches and 18 IEEE 802.11b/g wireless access points. The data rate of the core network is 100Mbps. A sector of the network is left vulnerable for worm propagation experiments with ten not patched Windows XP stations. In the experiments Blaster, Sasser, and Welchia worms were released in the vulnerable sector. Additionally, a port scanning attack was captured on the proxy server. The dataset was collected by a network sniffer tool based on libpcap library used by *tcpdump*, (Jacobson, Leres, & McCanne, 2001). The full dataset is comprised of 30 traces files corresponding to 30 days of standard traffic in user's typical working hours. These trace files were arranged into five datasets (SCx-D1 to SCx-D5) comprised of six trace files each (SCx-Dy-01 to SCx-Dy-06), to be used for training purposes. The trace files in this collection contain TCP traffic and a total of 32.6 million packets. In addition, the dataset SC1-D6 is comprised of four trace files; these traces correspond to a portscan attack and three types of worm attacks. All traces were cleaned to remove spurious data using *plab*, a platform for packet capture and analysis, (Peppo, 2006). Traces were split into segments using *tracesplit*, which is a tool that belongs to *Libtrace*, (Trac Project, 2003). The traffic files in ASCII format suitable

Table 1. Description of the attacks

Attack	Description	Action	Trace file
Portscan	Involves a remote host scanning TCP ports on victims machines running vulnerable services	scan	SC1-D6-01
Blaster	Network worm that propagates by exploiting the Microsoft Windows DCOM RPC Interface Buffer Overrun Vulnerability	probe	SC1-D6-02
Sasser	Network worm that attempts to exploit the vulnerability in LSASS. It spreads by IP random scanning	probe	SC1-D6-03
Welchia	Network worm that exploits multiple vulnerabilities, including: DCOM RPC and the WebDav vulnerabilities	probe	SC1-D6-04
Smurf	Smurf attack uses ICMP echo request packets to overload all hosts of a local network	flood	SC2-D1-01
Neptune	Also known as a SYN flood attack, this attack targets all TCP/IP implementations.	flood	SC2-D1-02
Portsweep	Surveillance sweep through many ports to determine which services are supported on a single host	scan	SC2-D1-03
Ipsweep	Surveillance sweep performing either a port sweep or ping on multiple host addresses	scan	SC2-D1-04
Satan	Network probing tool which looks for well-known weaknesses.	probe	SC2-D1-05
Nmap	Network mapping using the nmap tool. Mode of exploring network will vary—options include SYN	flood	SC2-D1-06
PoD	DoS attack which is created when an attacker sends IP packets larger than 65,536 bytes.	flood	SC2-D1-07
Back	Denial of service attack against apache webserver where a client requests a URL containing many backslashes	flood	SC2-D1-08

for perl and MATLAB® processing were created with *ipsumdump,* (Kohler, 2009). Scenario 2 (labeled as SC2), is based on a sub-set of the 1998 MIT-DARPA data, (Lincoln Laboratory, MIT, 1998), a public benchmark for testing NIDS. This data set adds eight more attacks to the experiments. Table 1 gives an overview of the attacks in their respective scenarios that were evaluated in this work.

PROFILING THE TRAFFIC

Table 2 presents an example of the results of processing the dataset SC1-D5 for a STTS. The exposure threshold β_r is obtained by means of the average β_r^{trace} in every r-feature. Table 3 summarize the evolution in five weeks of the exposure thresholds for the five training datasets that comprise the scenario one (SC1), obtained for STTS and LTTS.

Table 2. Traffic traces processed of dataset SC1-D5 to obtain β_r, for STTS

Trace file	β_r^{trace} (srcIP)	β_r^{trace} (dstIP)	β_r^{trace} (srcPrt)	β_r^{trace} (dstPrt)
SC1-D5-01	1.276	1.344	1.465	1.448
SC1-D5-02	1.379	1.409	1.497	1.482
SC1-D5-03	1.342	1.421	1.539	1.49
SC1-D5-04	1.354	1.379	1.517	1.577
SC1-D5-05	1.372	1.398	1.509	1.455
SC1-D5-06	1.349	1.379	1.530	1.490
$\beta_r = \overline{\beta_r}^{\text{trace}}$	**1.345**	**1.388**	**1.510**	**1.490**

Table 3. obtained from the training datasets in scenario 1 (SC1) for STTS and LTTS

Dataset	STTS				LTTS			
	$r=1$	$r=2$	$r=3$	$r=4$	$r=1$	$r=2$	$r=3$	$r=4$
SC1-D1	1.421	1.418	1.564	1.568	1.522	1.385	1.577	1.706
SC1-D2	1.415	1.392	1.526	1.555	1.519	1.359	1.573	1.702
SC1-D3	1.376	1.356	1.503	1.545	1.479	1.376	1.574	1.668
SC1-D4	1.366	1.354	1.493	1.513	1.421	1.387	1.602	1.616
SC1-D5	**1.345**	**1.388**	**1.510**	**1.490**	1.504	1.393	1.566	1.656

EXPERIMENTAL EVALUATION

For the evaluation of the proposed architecture two testing datasets were used: SC1-D6 and SC2-D1 which correspond to the scenarios 1 and 2, respectively. SC1-D6 dataset is comprised of four trace files of traffic going through the proxy server. Each of these trace files contain a combination of benign traffic and anomalous traffic caused by one of the following attacks: PortScan, Blaster.worm, Sasser worm, and Welchia.worm. Similarly, SC2-D1 dataset consists of eight trace files, each trace corresponds to a single attack attempt. The attacks included in this dataset are: Smurf, Neptune, Portsweep, Ipsweep, Satan, Nmap, Ping of Death, and, Back. The attacks in both scenarios fall into the following subcategories: probes, scans and floods. Table 4 summarizes the three types of anomalies caused by the activity of the attacks. The first two columns of the table correspond to the number of slot and r-feature compromised by the attack. The third column indicates the type of traffic slot in which the detection was achieved. The fourth column gives the value

Table 4. Summary of the analyzed attacks

| Compromised | | slot | ALE | I_i^r | U_i^r | Approach detection | Protocol | Scenario | Attack |
i	r								
95 to 162	1, 4	STTS	13 to 44	-	-	1	TCP	SC1	Portscan
195 to 4521	2, 4	STTS	22 to 336	-	-	1	TCP	SC1	Blaster
1 to 33	1, 2	LTTS	125 to 2334	-	-	1	TCP	SC1	Sasser
42 to 3875	2	STTS	49 to 452	-	-	1	ICMP	SC1	Welchia
2 to 71	1	STTS	326 to 503	-	-	1	ICMP	SC2	Smurf
5550	3	STTS	12	-	-	1	TCP	SC2	Neptune
7743	3, 4	STTS	65	-	-	1	TCP	SC2	Portsweep
607 to 698	3, 4	LTTS	18 to 27	-	-	1	TCP	SC2	Ipsweep
3997 to 4017	3, 4	STTS	34 to 1128	-	-	1	TCP	SC2	Satan
41 to 60	2	STTS	50 to 45	-	-	1	TCP	SC2	Nmap
10 and 11	1, 2	STTS	-1	-	406, 44	2	ICMP	SC2	PoD
328 to 338	3, 4	LTTS	NA	89 to 103	-	3	TCP	SC2	Back

or range of ALE corresponding to the compromised traffic slots. The fifth and sixth columns are support parameters. The seventh column indicates the detection approach used. The eighth column indicates type of traffic by protocol where the attack was present. The ninth column indicates the scenario where the attack took place. Finally, the tenth column shows the type of attack involved on each trace file. The architecture of detection was able to distinguish the anomalous traffic contained in the evaluation datasets. The anomalies were detected mainly by levels of $ALE > 2$, as shown in the first ten attacks in Table 4. The other two attacks were detected by MRE support, i.e. the cardinality of the set of significant elements and the length of sequences of unitary cardinality.

Left part of Figure 5 presents the variation of the remaining elements in sequences of source IP addresses for STTS. This testing trace shows levels of remaining greater than two in slots 95 to 162. In particular, 70 consecutive traffic slots have anomalous behavior with an $ALE_i^r > 0$. The anomaly was exposed during the compromised traffic slots and subsequently traffic returns to its normal behavior, because $ALE_i^r = 0$. According to the MIT-DARPA specifications, these traffic anomalies are caused by the Smurf attack. Right part of Figure 5 shows the behav-

Figure 5. Exposure of anomalies in two traces files. (left) Smurf attack detected in 70 consecutive traffic slots. (right) Satan attack detected in 20 traffic slots.

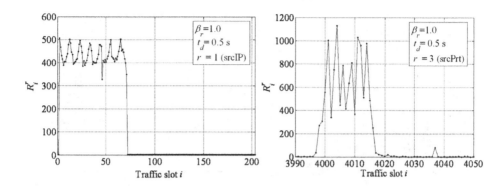

ior of the remaining elements in sequences of source ports during the propagation of Satan attack on scenario 2. This attack lasted 10 seconds and similarly its detection was handled with STTS. The following attacks: Portscan, Blaster, *Sasser*, *Welchia*, *Neptune*, *Portsweep*, *Ipsweep*, and *Nmap* were also timely detectable by the level of exposure as shown in Table 4.

The characterization of sequences S_i^r through a particular level of proportional uncertainty, i.e., β_r establishes levels of entropy for each alphabet size that these sequences must comply under typical traffic conditions. In this context, MRE performs a filtering process for those sequences whose levels of entropy for a given alphabet size are beyond the threshold set by the exposure threshold. An example of this entropy-based filtering can be seen in a trace file of scenario 2 which is related to the back attack. The left side of Figure 6 shows 800 traffic slots versus the value of remaining elements of the sequences S_i^r, where $r = 4$ (destination ports). The exposure threshold used is $\beta_r = 1$, with this exposure threshold is not possible to identify the anomalous behavior caused by the back attack. The right hand side of Figure 6 shows the same portion of traffic, but it is processed with a different value of the exposure threshold, i.e., $\beta_r = 1.22$. By applying this exposure threshold, the sequences formed in slots from 607 to 698 have a level of $ALE > 2$. Comparing both parts of Figure 6, it is possible to observe that the filtering process of the anomalous sequences does not depend on the value of remaining but the properties of entropy and alphabet size of such sequences.

In the experiments, other dynamics were found in the behavior of an attack that prevents the intrusion detection under the ALE approach. For these situations, a support for MRE through the approaches of unitary cardinality and significant elements was used. The approach of unitary cardinality defines a threshold for the

Figure 6. Entropy-based Filtering of anomalous sequences. (left) Inappropriate exposure threshold value becomes undetectable the attack. (right) The same portion of traffic using the appropriate threshold.

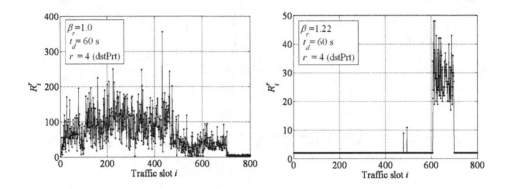

Figure 7. Detection through support of MRE. (left) Ping of death. (right) back attack.

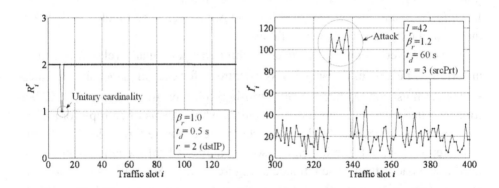

maximum length of a sequence with unitary cardinality, which is denoted by U_r. In addition, the approach of the significant elements defines a threshold for the typical level of significance, denoted by L_r. Our empirical observations on the training datasets allowed to determine the thresholds for the two above parameters as $U_r = 5$ and $I_r = 42$.

Scenario two allowed to evaluate the support for MRE, for example, the anomalies caused by Ping of death (*PoD*) attack generated two very long sequences of unitary cardinality in slots 10 and 11, and consequently an $ALE = -1$ as shows Figure 7(a). Concretely, input sequences in these slots have lengths of $U_{i=10}^{r=1} = 406$, and $U_{i=11}^{r=1} = 44$ for the feature of source IP address. Both traffic slots exceed the threshold $U_r = 5$, thus the attack was detected. Similarly, *Back* attack presents characteristics that also require the support of MRE. Back is a DoS attack; each attack session lasts 0.162 seconds that consists of 61 packets. The entire attack lasted about 11 minutes. However, this attack generates a large volume of packets that involve only two port values (80 and 28801). Consequently, the residual sequences for the features of source-destination port are not able to capture the anomaly. On the contrary, the component of significant elements (i.e. I_i^r) is able to capture the anomaly. The analysis of significant elements allowed to detect that the slots 328 to 338 for the features srcPrt and dstPrt deviates from the threshold $I_r = 42$, as shows Figure 7(b).

FUTURE RESEARCH DIRECTIONS

The algorithms described in this chapter could be improved regards to high volume of data processing. These improvements could be performed by applying complexity analysis. In some cases, the huge amount of traffic that is processed in a network could become the aforementioned algorithms in a complex process. Developing strategies to alleviate such tasks remain open in several scenarios, for instance, Ad-Hoc networks. Currently, new scenarios have emerged in this area. One of them is related to Ad-Hoc networks. Due to their special features, a NIDS should be a lightweight application to avoid waste of resources, treating to hold the same level of security.

One promising idea is to combine S-NIDS and A-NIDS. S-NIDS could be implemented as a preprocessing stage. S-NIDS could perform functions as a filter of known attacks. A-NIDS only could perform the tasks to detect new types of attacks. This improvement probably can reduce the amount of false positives.

CONCLUSION

An architecture developed to perform traffic profiling and intrusion detection based on the Method of Remaining Elements (MRE) was presented. The Anomaly-based NIDS proposed in this chapter uses training datasets to characterize the behavior for two types of traffic slots in terms of three thresholds: exposure threshold, cardinality of significant elements, and length of unitary cardinality sequences. Thus, changes in the properties of the sequences caused by activities of scanning, probing, and flooding can be detected. The experimental results carried out in two scenarios (an academic LAN and the MIT-DARPA dataset) showed that the traffic characterization by means of the exposure threshold (defined through an algorithm based on fixed-point iterations and a fixed point-like iterative process) provides a good sensitivity to detect intrusions. The taxonomy used shows that the number of selected features is sufficient to detect the three types of sub-categories listed in this work. An increase in the number of features increases the computational cost and response time of an IDS. Therefore, the proposal seeks to minimize the number of traffic features used. An improvement is with respect to the selection of additional traffic features, for instance header or content information. Thus, different types of attacks could be detected. In this context, it would be interesting to detect attacks related to other attacks subcategories of the taxonomy, that is, actions like authenticate, bypass, spoof, read, copy, termination, create processes, etc.

REFERENCES

Arvidson, M., & Carlbark, M. (2003). *Intrusion detection systems technologies, weaknesses and trends* (student thesis). Retrieved December 11, 2010, from http://liu.diva-portal.org/smash/record.jsf?pid=diva2:18938

Besson, J. L. (2003). *Next generation intrusion detection and prevention for complex environments* (Master Thesis in Computer Science). Retrieved December 11, 2010, from http://www.ifi.uzh.ch/archive/mastertheses/DA_Arbeiten_2003/Besson_Jean_Luc.pdf

Bonachela, J. A., Hinrichsen, H., & Muñoz, M. A. (2008). Entropy estimates of small data sets, *Journal of Physics A. Mathematical and Theoretical, 41*(20), 11.

Brauckhoff, D., Tellenbach, B., Wagner, A., & May, M. (2006, October). *Impact of packet sampling on anomaly detection metrics*. Paper presented at the Internet Measurement Conference 2006, Rio de Janeiro, Brazil.

Computer Security Institute. (2009). *2009 computer crime and security survey.* Retrieved from http://www.gocsi.com/

Conway, J. H., & Guy, R. K. (1996). *The book of numbers* (pp. 143 & 258-262). New York, NY: Springer-Verlag.

De Peppo, A. (2006). *Plab. Network tool for traffic traces.* Retrieved December 11, 2010, from http://www.grid.unina.it/software/Plab/

Esposito, M., Mazzariello, C., Oliviero, F., Peluso, L., Romano, S. P., & Sansone, C. (2008). Intrusion detection and reaction: An integrated approach to network security. *Intrusion Detection Systems* (pp. 171-210).Berlin, Germany: Springer Science+Business Media, LLC.

Gu, Y., McCallum, A., & Towsley, D. (2005). *Detecting anomalies in network traffic using maximum entropy estimation.* Paper presented at the 5th ACM SIGCOMM Conference on Internet Measurement, Berkeley, CA.

Howard, J. D., & Longstaff, T. A. (1998). *A common language for computer security incidents* (Tech. Rep. SAND98-8667). Albuquerque/Livermore, USA: Sandia National Laboratories.

Jacobson, V., Leres, C., & McCanne, S. (2001). *Tcpdump/libpcap.* Retrieved December 11, 2010, from http://www.tcpdump.org

Kohler, E. (2009). *IPsumdump: A traffic tool.* Retrieved December 11, 2010, from http://www.cs.ucla.edu/~kohler/ipsumdump

Lall, A., Sekar, V., Ogihara, M., Xu, J., & Zhangz, H. (2006). *Data streaming algorithms for estimating entropy of network traffic.* Paper presented in International Conference on Measurement and modeling of computer systems, Saint Malo, France.

Lee, W., & Xiang, D. (2001). Information-theoretic measures for anomaly detection. In *Proceedings of IEEE Symposium on Security and Privacy* (pp. 130-143).

Lincoln Laboratory. (1998-2000). *MIT. DARPA intrusion detection data.* Retrieved December 11, 2010, from http://www.ll.mit.edu/mission/communications/ist/corpora/ideval/data/index.html

Nucci, A., & Bannerman, S. (2007). Controlled chaos. *IEEE Spectrum, 44*(12), 42–48. doi:10.1109/MSPEC.2007.4390022

Nychis, G., Sekar, V., Andersen, D., Kim, H., & Zhang, H. (2008). *An empirical evaluation of entropy-based traffic anomaly detection.* Internet Measurement Conference, ACM-SIGCOMM (pp. 151-156).

Paninski, L. (2003). Estimation of entropy and mutual information. *Neural Computation, 15*, 1191–1253. doi:10.1162/089976603321780272

Roesch, M. (1999). *Snort - Lightweight intrusion detection for networks.* Paper presented in 13th USENIX Conference on System Administration (pp. 229-238). Retrieved from http://www.snort.org/

Shannon, C. (1948). A mathematical theory of communication. *Bell System Technical Journal, 27*, 379-423, & 623-656.

Thottan, M., & Ji, C. (2003). Anomaly detection in IP networks. *IEEE Transactions on Signal Processing, 51*(8), 2191–2204. doi:10.1109/TSP.2003.814797

Trac Project. (2003). *Libtrace*. Retrieved December 11, 2010, from http://www.wand.net.nz/trac/libtrace

Tukey, J. W. (1977). *Exploratory data analysis*. Addison-Wesley Series in Behavioral Science.

Velarde-Alvarado, P., Vargas-Rosales, C., Torres-Román, D., & Martinez-Herrera, A. (2008). Entropy-based profiles for intrusion detection in LAN traffic. *Advances in Artificial Intelligence: Algorithms and Applications. Research in Computing Science, 40*, 119–130.

Velarde-Alvarado, P., Vargas-Rosales, C., Torres-Roman, D., & Martinez-Herrera, A. (2009). Detecting anomalies in network traffic using the method of remaining elements. *IEEE Communications Letters, 13*(6), 462–464. doi:10.1109/LCOMM.2009.090689

Velarde-Alvarado, P., Vargas-Rosales, C., Torres-Roman, D., & Martinez-Herrera, A. (in press). IP traffic anomaly exposure, an information theoretic-based approach. *Journal of Applied Research and Technology*.

Velarde-Alvarado, P., Vargas-Rosales, C., Torres-Román, D., & Muñoz-Rodríguez, D. (2008). Entropy based analysis of worm attacks in a local network. *Research in Computing Science, 34*, 225–235.

Wagner, A., & Plattner, B. (2005). Entropy based worm and anomaly detection in fast IP networks. In *Proceedimgs of the 14th IEEE International WorksShop on Enabling Tech.: Infrastructure for Collaborative Enterprise* (pp. 172 – 177).

Wang, K., & Stolfo, S. (2004). Anomalous payload-based network intrusion detection. In E. Jonsson, A. Valdes, & M. Almgren (Eds.), *Recent Advances in Intrusion Detection* [REMOVED HYPERLINK FIELD](LNCS 3224, pp. 203 – 222). Berlin/Heidelberg, Germany: Springer-Verlag.

Wang, Y. (2009). *Statistical techniques for network security. Modern statistically-based intrusion detection and protection*. Hershey, PA: IGI Global.

Xu, K., Zhang, Z., & Bhattacharyya, S. (2008). Internet traffic behavior profiling for network security monitoring. *Transactions on Networking, IEEE/ACM, 16*(3), 1241 – 1252.

Ye, N., Newman, C., & Farley, T. (2006). A system-fault-risk framework for cyber attack classification. *Information Knowledge System Management*, 2(5), 135–151.

Ziviani, A., Gomes, A., & Monsores, M. (2007). Network anomaly detection using nonextensive entropy. *IEEE Communications Letters*, *11*(12), 1034–1036. doi:10.1109/LCOMM.2007.070761

KEY TERMS AND DEFINITIONS

Anomaly Level Exposure: This index is employed by our method to determine the type of approach required to set the status (i.e., abnormal or benign) of a traffic slot under analysis.

Exposure Threshold: Characterizes the maximum randomness that is reached through the process of extraction of significant elements for a given period of time and a traffic feature.

Flood: Access an asset repeatedly in order to overload the asset's capacity.

Long Time Traffic Slot (LTTS): This slot has a duration not exceeding 60 seconds. This larger slot has the ability to detect attacks with malicious traffic that contains very limited number of packets in each slot and is temporarily dispersed.

Probe: Access an asset in order to determine its characteristics.

Proportional Uncertainty: It is a measure of randomness based on the balanced entropy estimator II.

Residual Sequence: It is the sequence resulting from a process of extraction of its significant elements according to a threshold of exposure.

Scan: Access a set of assets sequentially in order to identify which assets have a specific characteristic.

Short Time Traffic Slot (STTS): This slot has a duration not exceeding 0.5 seconds and its purpose is to detect attacks with high volume of traffic in short and continuous periods. The size of this slot is sufficient to process and respond quickly to the existence of malicious traffic.

Chapter 5
Botnet Behavior Detection using Network Synchronism

Sebastián García
Universidad Nacional del Centro University, Argentina

Alejandro Zunino
Universidad Nacional del Centro University, Argentina

Marcelo Campo
Universidad Nacional del Centro University, Argentina

ABSTRACT

Botnets' diversity and dynamism challenge detection and classification algorithms depend heavily on static or protocol-dependant features. Several methods showing promising results were proposed using behavioral-based approaches. The authors conducted an analysis of botnets' and bots' most inherent characteristics such as synchronism and network load within specific time windows to detect them more efficiently. By not relying on any specific protocol, our proposed approach detects infected computers by clustering bots' network behavioral characteristics using the Expectation-Maximization algorithm. An encouraging false positive error rate of 0.7% shows that bots' traffic can be accurately separated by our approach by analyzing several bots and non-botnet network captures and applying a detailed analysis of error rates.

DOI: 10.4018/978-1-60960-836-1.ch005

Copyright ©2012, IGI Global. Copying or distributing in print or electronic forms without written permission of IGI Global is prohibited.

INTRODUCTION

In the last decade botnets have evolved from being used as a personal activity platform to becoming a financially aimed structure controlled by malicious groups (Wilson, 2007). A botnet is a network of remotely controlled, compromised computers, used for malicious purposes. Hosts in a botnet are called 'Bots' and the owner of a botnet is called 'Botmaster'. From small DDoS (Distributed Denial of Service attacks) to world wide spam campaigns, botnets have become the technological backbone of a growing community of malicious activities (Clinton, 2008) and remain as the most significant threat to the Internet today.

Technology to control malicious programs remotely first surfaced in late 1999 and since then their primary goal has been to obtain financial gain. This situation forced the development of several botnet detection technologies trying to cope with the attacks, but botnets resisted besiege security measures resting on their home based client attacks, circumventing security methods (Stone-Gross, Cova, Cavallaro, Gilbert, Szydlowski, Kemmerer, Kruegel & Vigna, 2009), encryption and anti-reverse engineering techniques. Although the IRC (Internet Chat Relay) protocol has been the most used means of communication among bots, in the last couple of years the trend towards decentralized networks, like P2P (Peer to Peer) (Yan, Eidenbenz & Nago, 2009) (Kang, Zhang, Li & Li, 2009) and Fast-Flux (Ssac, 2008), has made more difficult to shut botnets down.

Several botnet detection methods have been proposed to cope with this problem. A general classification schema includes signature-based methods, protocol-dependant feature analysis and some more recent techniques based on network behavior, but most of these approaches only detect a subset of botnets, limiting their applicability. Signature-based approaches (like looking for certain IRC messages or certain DNS names) only detect what they were configured to. Most of these approaches do not have a correct error rate analysis because they did not propose a testing environment that includes non-botnet data.

To detect every botnet, we find out what botnets and bots have in common. A thorough analysis was performed to learn their most inherent characteristics. Our proposal works under the assumption that botnets most typical characteristics are maliciousness (attacking and infecting, sending SPAM, DDoS, etc.), being remotely managed and synchronization. We also found that bots might synchronize differently when scanning new victims, downloading binary updates, attacking sites, asking for orders or receiving orders, among others situations.

This chapter proposes a new method for bots detection based on network behavioral patterns. We aim at detecting bots in a general practical manner regardless of its connection protocol.

Our work use clustering algorithms (Baeza-Yates, 1999) to group network flows, revealing the relationships between the number of IP addresses and ports among time intervals. These relationships may characterize the most inherent botnet activities. It is known that during some botnet life cycle phases, a single bot computer generates high network flow rates within very short time periods (Gu, 2008), for example, during Spam sending, DDoS attacks, network scanning and botnet distribution. We propose to extract TCP (Transport Control Protocol) flows from the network, aggregating three TCP features within a predefined time window. These features are the amount of unique source IP address (referred hereafter as *sips*), the amount of unique destination IP address (referred hereafter as *dips*) and the amount of unique destination ports (referred hereafter as *dports*). These features had been used to detect manual network attacks before (Onut & Ghorbani, 2007). Our first hypothesis is that these features can also be used to identify bots network behaviors. The algorithm has been validated by using labeled data from real botnets in the wild and labeled data from real non-botnet computers. This data set allowed us to achieve a verified and robust algorithm.

Some advantages of our method include bots detection independent of encrypted traffic and protocol details and that bots detection within the first stages of infection. Our second hypothesis is that a bot could be detected because of the high amount of connections generated in a time window. The preliminary experimental results reported, suggest that this detection can be accomplished successfully under certain conditions. Bots and non-botnet traffic showed different network characteristics that helped to separate them in clusters.

This chapter makes two contributions. First the separation of aggregated network flows in time windows using non-protocol dependant bots features, and second the clustering of them using the Expectation-Maximization algorithm with labeled data.

The rest of the chapter is organized as follows: Section Background describes previous work in the area; Section Proposed Technique shows details about our approach; Section Validation explains corroboration procedures; Section Data Acquisition shows how network data has been obtained; in subsection Data Processing the data preparation steps are explained; Section Results discusses the experiment outcomes; Section Future Research Directions refers to future work we are planning and finally Conclusions are presented.

BACKGROUND

Some approaches have been proposed to detect botnets in recent years using network features, including the study of anomalous DNS (Domain Name System) usage (Villamarin-Salomon & Brustoloni, 2008), IRC protocol analysis (Mazzariello,

2008) and P2P network features (Kang et al., 2009) among others (Shahrestani, Ramadass & Feily, 2009) (Zhu, Lu, Chen, Fu, Roberts & Han, 2008), but the variability of botnets and their rapid mutation have forced researchers from different security domains to consider the analysis of behavioral patterns as a solid foundation for botnet detection.

Particularly, network behavior detection has been studied from different perspectives: traffic classification based on flow characteristics (Strayer, Lapsely, Walsh & Livadas, 2007), protocol analysis based on temporal-frequent features (Lu, Tavallaee, Rammidi & Ghorbani, 2009) and network analysis based on spatial-temporal correlation (Gu, 2008), where activity response crowds on IRC botnets are grouped together by destination IP address-port pairs and time windows.

Behavior analysis of bots, based on protocol-dependent features, has proved to be successful only under certain conditions. There seems to be three main problems with behavioral protocol-dependant approaches. First, only a subset of botnets can be detected analyzing protocol dependent characteristics, e.g., analyzing IRC messages behavior is not enough to detect P2P botnets. Second, new unseen botnets are unlikely to be detected if a new protocol is used. Finally, botmasters can change their current malware protocol characteristics used to detect their botnet (Stinson & Mitchell, 2008).

Addressing the aforementioned problems, botnets invariants were sought in order to detect them independently of protocol changes and implementation details. Botnet correlation was proposed (Gu, Perdisci, Zhang & Lee, 2008) among other techniques (Liu, Chan, Yan & Zhang, 2008), based on the fact that every bot in a botnet normally act at the same time. However, synchronization has not been deeply studied, and temporal correlation approaches were found to be evadable under certain circumstances (Chen, Chen & Wang, 2009), for example, proposing a time delay in bot responses before applying commands.

Our feature set was selected based on a previous work of the best network features for intrusion detection (Onut & Ghorbani, 2007). They defined a time window based detection schema, where some features related to the number of TCP connections were used. We extended these paper ideas to the botnet detection problem. Detection of botnets using groups of source IP address and groups of destination of IP address was also proposed by (Li, Goyal, & Chen, 2007). They used a honeypot to analyze this *Sips/Dip* relationship.

PROPOSED TECHNIQUE

Detecting botnets behavior and bots behavior are two quite different problems. Bot detection can be accomplished by the distinguishable behavior of one host. Botnet behavior can be detected, for example, based on the synchronization of its individual bots, regardless of the amount of flows per second. Our technique focuses on differentiating bot behavior among non-botnet traffic.

The first step of our methodology consists in capturing network data from infected computers. This could be done by using the tcpdump tool (Lawrence Berkeley National Labs, 2010) on any machine in the wired network, taking care of not losing packets and that no other traffic is captured.

The second step entails extracting information from captures files and TCP flow separation. A tool called tcptrace (Shawn Ostermann, 2010) is used to find out every TCP flow, including its start time and network characteristics. Flow information is used because botnets tend to generate new flows almost constantly and use them for a short time period, where a non-botnet computer tends to generate few flows per second but use each one of them for long time periods.

As we aim at detecting synchronization, the third step of our approach involves dividing flows in one-second time windows, allowing us to monitor and identify bots behavior. Each time window contains aggregated information about every TCP flow within it. Then, for every TCP flow in that time window, we calculate the amount of unique source IP addresses, unique destination IP addresses and unique destination ports. This information is summarized in an attempt to reduce data processing complexity and only save useful information for further analysis. A time window can then be represented by a four dimensional vector containing the window Id, amount of unique source IP addresses in that time window, amount of unique destination IP addresses in that time windows and amount of unique destination TCP ports in that time window. An example vector should look like this: [23, 1, 10, 1].

The fourth step involves clustering these vectors using the EM (Expectation-Maximization) algorithm (Dempster, Laird & Rubin, 1977). Expectation-maximization is a method for finding maximum likelihood estimates of parameters in statistical models with incomplete data, and has been used successfully before in traffic flow analysis for characterizing communication connectivity patterns (Chen, Li & Cao, 2009), botnet detection (Masud, Gao, Khan, Han, & Thuraisingham, 2008) and spam detection (Zhang, 2009).

A basic introduction to the algorithm follows. We have a density function $p(x|\Theta)$ that is defined by a set of parameters Θ. We also have a known dataset $X=\{x1, ..., xn\}$, of size N, extracted from this distribution. The resulting density for the samples can be seen in Equation (1).

$$p(X \mid \Theta) = \prod_{i=1}^{N} p(x_i \mid \Theta) = L(\Theta \mid X) \tag{1}$$

This function L is called the likelihood of the parameters given the known data. The likelihood is a function of the parameters Θ where the known data X is fixed. In the maximum likelihood problem, represented by Equation (2), the goal is to find the Θ parameter that maximizes L.

$$\Theta' = \arg \max_{\Theta} L\left(\Theta \mid X\right) \tag{2}$$

The EM algorithm is a technique to solve the maximum likelihood problem. In our proposal, the windows vectors are the known data, coming from different statistical distributions (botnets). How many distributions and which vectors correspond to each one are the hidden variables to be found. Each botnet generates packets given a unique statistical distribution with unknown parameters Θ and our goal is to maximize the a-posteriori probability of these parameters given the known data (vectors) in the presence of hidden data.

The intuition of EM is to alternate between estimating the unknowns Θ and the hidden variables. The idea is to start with a guess of these parameters Θ and to determine for each vector which underlying distribution is more likely to have generated the observed data (using the current parameters estimates). Then, assume these guessed assignments to be correct and apply the regular maximum likelihood estimation procedure to get next Θ. The procedure iterates until convergence to a local maximum. The algorithm computes the models parameters and assigns the cluster number with highest probability to each window vector (McGregor, Hall, Lorier & Brunskill, 2004).

Our already captured and labeled data allow us to verify the proposed detection method error rates later. Expectation-maximization algorithm provides a simple, easy-to-implement and efficient tool for learning parameters of a model. Weka's (Hall, Frank, Holmes, Pfahringer, Reutemann & Witten, 2009) implementation of this algorithm was used because of the independence assumption of the attributes in the model, making it suitable for our purposes.

In this chapter we do not work with the concept of *normal* traffic, instead our algorithm focuses on differentiating bots behavior from non-botnet behavior. What our algorithm classifies as non-botnet could be normal traffic or manual attacks, that is why we use the term non-botnet. It can not find the difference between bots behaviors and *normal* behavior, because *normal* traffic varies greatly. This also forces us to carefully analyze non-botnet traffic, looking for manual attacks or misconfigurations.

It was important to consider the distinction between bot traffic and intrusion attempts, because non-botnet traffic could consist of both normal traffic and

Table 1. Labeled network data captures details

Name	Duration	Unique Flows
Botnet1	11h:12m:29s	37389
Botnet2	00h:20m:30s	21124
Botnet3	10h:11m:33s	34117
Non-botnet1	00h:10m:18s	45148
Non-botnet2	03h:28m:14s	1517
Non-botnet3	04h:19m:36s	976

manual or automatic attacks. Network attacks are often done manually and using automatic tools. Manual attacks have low traffic rates and do not have synchronous characteristics, while automatic attacks tend to have high traffic rates and could be misdetected by our method as bot traffic. One of the most traffic consuming attacks is the port scanning activity, which is often an essential part of the attack process. To cope with this problem we propose some experiments in the Results Section to accurately separate bots traffic and port scanning activity.

DATA ACQUISITION

Three different test beds were used to acquire the 92.630 unique botnet flows and more than 47500 non-botnet flows, against witch our algorithm was verified. We considered a TCP flow as the group of packets exchanged between two hosts and two ports in a single connection. Table 1 shows details about captures.

The first test bed, used for botnet1 and botnet3 captures, is composed of a Linux computer virtualizing a Microsoft Windows XP sp3 operating system using VirtualBox. The VM (Virtual Machine) connects to the Internet through a DHCP (Dynamic Host Configuration Protocol) enabled home DSL router. Packet sniffing is performed in the Linux box with certain filters applied; assuring that only Windows packets were caught. Current botnets usually target this type of home computers, looking for its high bandwidth and personal sensitive information (Corrons, PandaLabs, 2010), (Nazario, 2006). Botnet1 capture corresponds to a 'Virut' malware variant called 'Virut.n' and botnet3 capture corresponds to an 'Agobot' family member called 'Rbot'.

Botnet2 was captured with a second test bed composed of 18 hosts in an internal sub-network of a university campus. The network was monitored while five hosts were infected. The botnet2 malware is a spam sending 'Agobot' variant called 'eldorado'.

The third test bed used for non-botnet2 and non-botnet3 traffic captures is composed of one Linux computer connected to a University Campus WiFi Network. We ensure that the traffic was non-botnet by manually inspecting traffic and scanning it with Snort NIDS. Non-botnet traffic includes SMTP mail, web sites with AJAX updates, edonkey like protocols, torrent protocols, operating system updates, and web traffic using several Google online tools.

The non-botnet1 capture used the third test bed to perform an nmap port scanning activity, representing one of the most common network attacks. Using nmap version 5.35DC18, we performed a TCP SYN scan of the 65536 remote ports of one destination computer without changing nmaps default timing behavior.

Botnet1 malware, called 'Virut', is an IRC-based variant capable of giving total control of the computer to the remote botmaster. Botnet3 malware, called 'Rbot', is a highly configurable IRC controlled bot used to gain access to infected computers in several different ways, including password cracking, SMB (Server Message Block) shares access and exploiting software vulnerabilities. This bot can be instructed to download and execute files, perform denial of service (DoS) attacks or log keystrokes among other attacks. Botnet2 bot variant, called 'eldorado', is a web controlled bot designed to send spam, self update and perform malicious actions. These bots do not recognize the VirtualBox setup and consequently the infection was performed successfully. Newer bots with the ability to detect virtual environments were used, but its analysis was left for future work.

Data Processing

Data processing is a fundamental part of the analysis as it determines which characteristics will be taken into account. Processing steps include data verification, data labeling, data preprocessing and feature extraction among others. The first phase of data processing involves the extraction of TCP flows from the captured pcap data using the tcptrace tool (using the command *tcptrace -nl <pcap-file>*). Tcptrace generates a text file with every TCP flow characteristic.

The second phase is performed with a specially developed tool, called tcptrace-reader.py, to process the tcptrace output file. As a result of this phase, a text file is generated with the following information per flow: start timestamp in UNIX time format, source IP address in decimal format, destination IP address in decimal format and destination port. Each of these lines is called an instance. In this phase we also assign 'botnet' and 'non-botnet' labels to every instance of both types of traffic by hand.

Phase three uses the tcptrace-reader.py tool to perform time windows aggregation of instances, creating vectors in an Arff (Attribute-Relation File Format) file.

This Arff file will be used for clustering in Weka. This phase also generates a text file with the relation of instances and vectors for future back reference. When the algorithm assigns a certain vector to a cluster, we need to know which IP addresses were included on it.

The fourth phase consists in the processing of the Arff file using the Weka toolset. We apply the EM clustering algorithm to this data set. After clustering is done, a complete Arff file is also saved from Weka, adding the clusters assignments to each vector.

Once the clustering phase is finished, we compute the percentage of botnet and non-botnet instances in each cluster. This is done in the fifth phase using another specially developed tool called analysis.sh. For each cluster in the complete Arff file, this tool retrieves every vector on it and for each vector it retrieves every instance on it with its label. We can then compute how many botnets and non-botnets instances were assigned to each cluster.

VALIDATION

Validation of every phase was conducted to prove the practical soundness of our method. Following the methodology steps described in Proposed Technique section, in the first step, validation procedures included ensuring a clean experimental setting. For the first test bed, a Virtualized Windows XP SP3 was freshly installed, scanned with antivirus products and its traffic analyzed both with Snort NIDS (Network Intrusion Detection System) (Roesch, 1999) and by hand.

This configuration was used to create Virtual Machines for computers that were later infected. Confirmation of malware binaries was conducted using VirusTotal (Hispasec Sistemas, 2010) and the EUREKA! automated Malware Binary Analysis Service (Yegneswaran, Saidi, Porras, Sharif, Mark & President, 2008). Also a manual packet analysis was done to verify malware activity of botnet1 and botnet3 captures.

Validation in the third step was conducted through window counting, e.g., a one-hour capture must have almost 3600 one-second windows. Windows with a high amount of flows were manually verified.

The clustering step was verified by labeling data. Trustworthy botnet and non-botnet experiments were performed, building an accurate cluster compare base. Once available, this information allowed interpretation of the resulting clusters and experiments improvement. Labeling was performed by manually analyzing every flow using Wireshark (Wireshark, 2010).

Finally, an experimental validation was conducted on the hypothesis about the bot behavior detection methodology. Our hypothesis, based on the time window and network load concept proved in (Gu, 2008), states that bots can be detected analyzing the correlation of the time window *timestamp*, the amount of unique source IP addresses within the time window, the amount of unique destination IP addresses within the time window and the amount of unique destination ports within the time window. For example, finding 1 *sips*, 20 *dips* and 1 *dports* within a one second time frame might mean that we have detected a bot looking for vulnerabilities. This validation step generated next section Results.

RESULTS

Several experiments were conducted to analyze botnet behavior. Every experiment included a combination of one botnet and one non-botnet capture, because in this type of statistical experiments it is paramount to have a realistic setup. This combination was done concatenating both text files at tcptrace level and modifying captures start time. This approach proved easier than modifying and mixing pcap traces.

Non-botnet computers with normal data have continuous low traffic generation rates most of the time, whereas bots tend to have bursts of high traffic rates (Yen & Lee, 2009). This difference can make bots flow generation rate roughly three times faster than a non-botnet computer. Clustering experiments, then, tend to have an uneven number of packets, resulting in natural unbalanced experiments. If we have a balanced data set (the number of samples in botnet and non-botnet classes is almost equal), classifier error rates could be correctly interpreted because each instance will belong to one class with 50% probability. If we have an unbalanced data set (the number of samples in different classes varies greatly) the error rate of a classical statistics classifier *could not* represent the true effectiveness of the classifier. Some studies had to modify the EM clustering method to deal with unbalanced data sets (Wu, 1995). Both types of experiments were conducted to analyze this situation.

Selection criteria of both captures for each experiment had two steps. In the first step we selected captures based on how much representative of its own class they were. Captures with more non-botnet applications were preferred and botnets with more traffic rates were preferred. In the second step we decided how to mix both captures based on the assumption that superimposed traffic is more difficult to differentiate. When non-botnet and botnet traffic was only concatenated but not superimposed, separation of both classes was straight forward. Mixture was done trying to insert the smaller traffic into the larger one.

Our approach proposes to differentiate bot traffic from non-botnet traffic, but the latter can include normal traffic as well as manual attacks attempts and automatic penetration testing. It is very important that our algorithm does not confuse botnets

Table 2. Detection percentages of 45148 Non-botnet1 flows mixed with 21124 Botnet2 flows

Cluster Number	Botnet Flows	Non-botnet Flows	Botnet %	Non-botnet %
0	2128	0	100%	0%
1	7129	0	100%	0%
2	5633	0	100%	0%
3	0	7971	0%	100%
4	480	0	100%	0%
5	240	0	100%	0%
6	3322	0	100%	0%
7	2192	0	100%	0%
8	0	37177	0%	100%

with these intrusion attempts. One of the most common phases in every network attack is the port scanning activity, which generates high traffic rates. Clustering of concatenated port scanning and bot traffic is analyzed in the first experiment (Table 2), where the higher traffic rate of the port scan results in a very clear traffic separation. This experiment suggests that botnet traffic and network scans have different network behaviors.

The aim of the second experiment (Table 3) was to analyze the Rbot malware within the traffic of one non-botnet computer. Assuming that a computer behaves almost identically during fourteen days of office work, the original four-hour non-botnet capture was copied twenty times, making each copy start in a different day at the same hour. We finally had 19443 non-botnet flows from September 13 to October 2 and 34118 botnets flows from September 14 to September 15. After aggregating flows into one-second time windows, we generate the Arff file for this traffic and processed it with the EM algorithm, which generated four clusters.

Table 3. Detection percentages of 19443 Non-botnet3 flows mixed with 34118 Botnet3 flows

Cluster Number	Botnet Flows	Non-botnet Flows	Botnet %	Non-botnet %
0	14433	24	99.83%	0.16%
1	1517	18721	7.49%	92.50%
2	3539	14	99.60%	0.39%
3	14629	684	95.53%	4.46%

Table 4. Detection percentages of 1517 Non-botnet2 flows mixed with 34118 Botnet3 flows

Cluster Number	Botnet Flows	Non-botnet Flows	Botnet %	Non-botnet %
0	2147	1358	61.25%	38.74%
1	3539	12	99.66%	0.33%
2	14469	81	99.44%	0.55%
3	13963	66	99.52%	0.47%

This experiment tried to differentiate between 19 days of low rate non-botnet traffic and ten hours of a high rate bot burst in the middle of it. The second experiment also analyzed how the algorithm performed with an almost even number of packets in both classes.

The aim of the third experiment (Table 4) was to analyze an unbalanced and more realistic situation, where three hours of non-botnet traffic from one computer was mixed with ten hours of bots traffic. Non-botnet capture was modified to start on September 15, in the middle of botnet traffic. These capture files were selected with the goal of analyzing an IRC bot along side with a normal computer.

The aim of experiment four (Table 5) was to analyze one infected computer among a network of non-botnet computers. The five hour non-botnet capture was modified to start on September 15, in the middle of the ten-hour botnet traffic. Non-botnet traffic was composed of more than 40 office computers. This is a very realistic setup, where a lot of computers generate very low traffic rates.

False Positives and False Negatives

We analyzed error rates from two points of view. From the first point of view, false positives are accounted each time a non-botnet flow is detected as botnet. Thus, false negatives are accounted each time a botnet flow is detected as non-botnet. This is

Table 5. Detection percentages of 977 Non-botnet3 flows mixed with 34118 Botnet3 flows

Cluster Number	Botnet Flows	Non-botnet Flows	Botnet %	Non-botnet %
0	2147	916	70.09%	29.90%
1	13918	22	99.84%	0.15%
2	3539	14	99.60%	0.39%
3	14469	25	99.82%	0.17%
4	45	0	100%	0%

the most simple and theoretical point of view. From the second point of view, false positives are accounted each time a non-botnet IP address is detected as botnet at least once in a predefined period of time and false negatives are accounted each time a botnet IP address is detected as non-botnet during the whole same predefined period of time. Both points of view are discussed next.

From the first point of view, a quick analysis of our algorithm effectiveness could be done estimating false positives and false negatives regarding each IP address. Table 6 summarizes this information, where calculation about a certain IP address is made against the total number of times its flows where detected as botnet or non-botnet. We also found that IP addresses in this table are representative of the most active computers in the experiments. First experiment was not included in this calculation because its goal was to prove that botnet traffic and intrusion attempts could be successfully separated.

The second experiment false positives error rates, where a non-botnet IP address is detected as botnet, are reasonably low. There is only one false negative, where one IP address is detected as non-botnet 6.45% of the time. A detailed manual analysis showed that non-botnet label was assigned to this botnet when a single flow per second was generated. This was an example of a botnet behaving like a non-botnet computer. From a practical point of view, if we consider that IP address 10.1.1.1 was the network web proxy and that it can be white-listed by the administrator, perhaps we could achieve a better error rate.

The third experiment has, comparatively, higher false positive error rates. An analysis of these errors shows that both botnet and non-botnet computers were

Table 6. IP addresses error evaluation

Experiment	Error Type	IP address	Actually is	#Detected as Non-botnet	#Detected as Botnet	Error %
2	FP	10.1.1.1	Non-botnet	10570	180	1.67%
2	FP	192.168.2.79	Non-botnet	18697	542	2.81%
3	FP	10.1.1.1	Non-botnet	466	1	0.21%
3	FP	192.168.2.71	Non-botnet	5	1	16.66%
3	FP	192.168.2.74	Non-botnet	783	89	10.20%
3	FP	192.168.2.76	Non-botnet	235	31	11.65%
4	FP	192.168.2.79	Non-botnet	910	60	6.18%
2	FN	192.168.3.104	Botnet	1103	15978	6.45%
3	FN	192.168.3.104	Botnet	1563	15518	9.15%
4	FN	192.168.3.104	Botnet	1563	15518	9.15%

clustered together because they generated several connections at the same time. This situation is not uncommon and we are planning to analyze it carefully in future work.

The fourth experiment shows an increment in false negatives values and its false positive error rate is notably higher because fewer instances were used. In the worse case, 6.18% of the time a non-botnet computer is detected as botnet.

From Table 6 we can conclude that the most challenging problem is to classify a non-botnet computer traffic that behaves like a botnet as *non-botnet*.

After analyzing Table 6, a confusion matrix is shown in Table 7 to better analyze error rates meanings. A confusion matrix is a visualization tool commonly used in supervised learning, where each row represents how each instance was detected and each column what it actually was.

We have 124,291 different instances that the algorithm has to classify. The False Positive Rate (FPR) is the proportion of non-botnet flows that yield a botnet outcome (904 in our results) among all the tests performed. *FPR = 0.7%*. The False Negative Rate (FNR) is the proportion of botnet flows that yield a non-botnet outcome (4229 in our results) among all the tests performed. *FNR = 3.4%*.

Some technical results can also be extracted from Table 7, for example, *0.91%* is the proportion of *non-botnet* flows that were detected as *botnet* among the presumed botnets, i.e., from the total amount of infection alerts that the network administrator receives from our algorithm, only *0.91%* were not infected.

From Table 7 we can also conclude that *16.74%* is the proportion of botnet flows that were detected as *non-botnet* among the presumed non-botnet computers. This would be the proportion of infected flows that the administrator will not see. Note that we are talking about flows and not computers. An analysis from the computer point of view is done later.

Still from a technical perspective, if this algorithm was used in real botnet shut-down campaigns, 4.13% of the bots will not be detected and will remain active. Finally, we are going to bother 4.12% of our internal users trying to clean their non-infected computers.

Table 7. Confusion flow matrix

		Actual		
Detected		Botnet	Non-Botnet	
	Botnet	98125	FP=904	0.91%
	Non-Botnet	FN=4229	21033	16.74%
		4.13%	4.12%	

Figure 1. Error Analysis

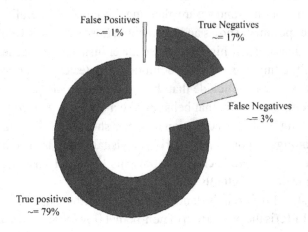

A graphical analysis of the confusion matrix showing approximate percentages can be seen in Figure 1. It shows the relation between errors and true detections.

Until now we have discussed error rate analysis when trying to detect every bot network flow. We are going to analyze results now from a different point of view; the need to detect infected computers in a real environment. A network administrator wants to disinfect computers and to detect bots in the traffic. This, more practical, point of view analyze error rates taking into account the problem domain and scope.

It is infeasible to classify every botnet flow as *botnet* because their dynamic and evolving nature generates traffic with different characteristics. An infected computer behaves like a non-botnet computer most of the time and during some of its life cycle phases it does not generate traffic like a botnet at all. Following this reasoning, if we can detect the botnet at least once during the one-hour time frame, it will be enough to stop it. If we consider a time frame of, for example, one hour, during which it will be enough to detect a bot at least once, we can define the following errors.

On the one hand, a real positive is considered now when a bot IP address is classified as bot at least once within this time frame. On the other hand, a real negative is considered when a non-botnet computer IP address is classified as non-botnet *always* within this time frame. False positives are accounted only when a non-botnet IP address is considered bot at least once within this time frame and false negatives, then, are accounted only when a bot IP addresses is classified as non-botnet *every* time within the same time frame. This is enough for most practical detection scenarios, and it shows the true impact of the algorithm in real scenarios clearly.

CONCLUSION

Botnet detection is still an ongoing research topic. In this chapter we presented a new approach for bot network behavior detection using the Expectation-Maximization clustering algorithm. Our work is based on the hypothesis that bots behave different than non-botnets computers. To analyze this situation, we captured several network flows with botnet and non-botnet traffic using three different test beds. This traffic included single and network captures of both current malware and not infected computers. After proper traffic pre-processing, we separated the traffic flows in time windows and studied the relationship between unique source IP addresses, unique destination IP addresses and unique destination ports within these time windows.

Error rates were analyzed closely to understand the needs of a network administrator and to know how our algorithm performed. Two points of view were proposed, one from the flow perspective and the other from the computer perspective. Results are encouraging, showing that bots can be differentiated from non-botnet traffic with a FPR of 0.7% and a FNR of 3.4%.

FUTURE RESEARCH DIRECTIONS

Several improvements are planned for future research. First of all, UDP (User Datagram Protocol) traffic will be considered in our captures, because plenty of botnet traffic is performed using this protocol, most notably DNS queries, that can be up to 40% of the total traffic. Another improvement will be to analyze the total amount of transferred bytes within a single flow, in order to capture long lived botnet connections with their C&C server. In the clustering area, we are currently working on analyzing cluster assignments to synthesize classification rules that later allows us to automatically classify clusters. In the network capture area, several one-week long LAN (Local Area Network) non-botnet capture are planned, during which different botnets will be executed from time to time. An extension in the number of captured botnets is planned too. To better analyze the difference between bot traffic and intrusion attempts, new experiments are planned, like an experiment with botnet, non-botnet and port scanning captures. Finally an important improvement will be done in the data set production and processing, creating a methodology for flow capture, publication, labeling, comparison and verification.

ACKNOWLEDGMENT

We thank the editor and anonymous reviewers for their helpful comments and suggestions to improve the quality of this paper. Also, thanks to ANPCyT for supporting this research through grants PAE-PICT 2007-02311 and PAE-PICT 2007-02312.

REFERENCES

Baeza-Yates, R. A., & Riberiro-Neto, B. A. (1999). *Modern information retrieval.* Boston, MA: ACM-Press / Addison-Wesley Longman Publishing Co., Inc.

Chen, A., Li, L., & Cao, J. (2009). Tracking cardinality distributions in network traffic. In *Proceedings of IEEE 28th Conference on Computer Comunications (INFOCOM 2009)* (pp. 819-827).

Chen, Z., Chen, C., & Wang, Q. (2009). Delay-tolerant botnets. In *Proceedings of 18th International Conference on Computer Communications and Networks (ICCCN 2009)* (pp. 1-6).

Corrons, L. (PandaLabs). (2010). *Mariposa botnet.* Retrieved August 17, 2010 from http://pandalabs.pandasecurity.com/mariposa-botnet/

Dempster, A. P., Laird, N. M., & Rubin, D. B. (1977). Maximum likelihood from incomplete data via the em algorithm. *Journal of the Royal Statistical Society. Series B. Methodological, 39*(1), 1–38.

Gu, G. (2008). *Correlation-based botnet detection in enterprise networks* (Doctoral dissertation, Georgia Institute of Technology).

Gu, G., Perdisci, R., Zhang, J., & Lee, W. (2008). BotMiner: Clustering analysis of network traffic for protocol-and structure-independent botnet detection. In *Proceedings of the 17th Conference on Security symposium* (pp. 139-154). Berkeley, CA: USENIX Association.

Gu, G., Zhang, J., & Lee, W. (2008). BotSniffer: Detecting botnet command and control channels in network traffic. In *Proceedings of the 15th Network and Distributed System Security Symposium (NDSS)*, San Diego, CA.

Ha, D., Yan, G., Eidenbenz, S., & Ngo, H. (2009). On the effectiveness of structural detection and defense against p2p-based botnets. In *IEEE/IFIP International Conference on Dependable Systems & Networks (DSN '09)* (pp. 297-306).

Hall, M., Frank, E., Holmes, G., Pfahringer, B., Reutemann, P., & Witten, H. I. (2009). The weka data mining software: An update. *ACM SIGKDD Explorations Newsletter, 11*(1), 10–18. doi:10.1145/1656274.1656278

Hispasec Sistemas. (2010). *Virus Total*. Retrieved March 30, 2010, from http://www.virustotal.com/es/

Kang, J., Zhang, J.-Y., Li, Q., & Li, Z. (2009). Detecting new p2p botnet with multi-chart cusum. In *Proceedings of the International Conference on Networks Security, Wireless Communications and Trusted Computing (NSWCTC '09)* (vol. 1, pp. 688-691).

LBNL. (2010). *TCPDUMP & LiBPCAP*. Retrieved March 30, 2010 from http://www.tcpdump.org/

Li, Z., Goyal, A., & Chen, Y. (2007). Honeynet-based botnet scan traffic analysis. *Botnet Detection, 36*, 25–44. New York, NY: Springer.

Liu, L., Chen, S., Yan, G., & Zhang, Z. (2008). Execution-based bot-like malware detection. *Information Security* (LNCS 5222, pp. 97-113). Berlin/Heidelberg, Germany: Springer-Verlag.

Lu, W., Tavallaee, M., Rammidi, G., & Ghorbani, A. A. (2009). Botcop: An online botnet traffic classifier. In *7th Annual Communication Networks and Services Research Conference (CNSR '09)* (pp. 70-77).

Masud, M. M., Gao, J., Khan, L., Han, J., & Thuraisingham, B. (2008). A practical approach to classify evolving data streams: Training with limited amount of labeled data. In *8th IEEE International Conference on Data Mining (ICDM '08)* (pp. 929–934).

Mazzariello, C. (2008). Irc traffic analysis for botnet detection. In *4th International Conference on Information Assurance and Security (ISIAS '08)* (pp. 318-323).

McGregor, A., Hall, M., Lorier, P., & Brunskill, J. (2004). Flow clustering using machine learning techniques. In *Passive and Active Network Measurement* (LNCS, pp. 205-214). Berlin/Heidelberg, Germany: Springer-Verlag.

Mielke, C., & Chen, H. (2008). Botnets, and the cybercriminal underground. In *IEEE International Conference on Intelligence and Security Informatics (ISI 2008)* (pp. 206-211).

Nazario, J. (2006). *Botnet tracking: Tools, techniques, and lessons learned (Tech. Rep.)*. Chemsford, MA: Arbor Networks.

Onut, I. V., & Ghorbani, A. A. (2007). A feature classification scheme for network intrusion detection. *International Journal of Network Security, 5*, 1–15.

Roesch, M. (1999). Snort-lightweight intrusion detection for networks. In *13th Systems Administration Conference (LISA '99)* (pp. 229-238).

Shahrestani, A., Ramadass, S., & Feily, M. (2009). A survey of botnet and botnet detection. In *3rd International Conference on Emerging Security Information, Systems and Technologies (SECURWARE '09)* (pp. 268-273).

Shawn, O. (2010). *Tcptrace*. Retrieved March 30, 2010 from http://www.tcptrace.org/

SSAC. (2008). *Ssac advisory on fast flux hosting and dns* (Tech. Rep.). ICANN Security and Stability Advisory Committee. Retrieved on March, 2008 from http://www.icann.org/en/committees/security/ssac-documents.htm.

Stinson, E., & Mitchell, J. (2008). Towards systematic evaluation of the evadability of bot/botnet detection methods. In *Proceedings of the 2nd Conference on USENIX Workshop on Offensive Technologies (WOOT '08)* (pp. 1-9). Berkeley, CA: USENIX Association.

Stone-Gross, B., Cova, M., Cavallaro, L., Gilbert, B., Szydlowski, M., & Kemmerer, R. ...Vigna, G. (2009). Your botnet is my botnet: Analysis of a botnet takeover. In *Proceedings of the 16th ACM Conference on Computer and Communications Security (CCS '09)* (pp. 635-647). New York, NY: ACM.

Strayer, W., Lapsely, D., Walsh, R., & Livadas, C. (2007). Botnet detection based on network behavior. *Advances in Information Security, 36*, 1-24. New York, NY: Springer.

Villamarin-Salomon, R., & Brustoloni, J. (2008). Identifying botnets using anomaly detection techniques applied to dns traffic. In *Proceedings of the 5th IEEE Consumer Communications and Networking Conference (CCNC 2008)* (pp. 476–481).

Wilson, C. (2007). *Botnets, cybercrime, and cyberterrorism: Vulnerabilities and policy issues for congress* (Tech. Rep.). Washington, DC: Library of Congress Congressional Research Service.

Wireshark. (2010). *Wireshark: The world's foremost network protocol analyzer*. Retrieved March 30, 2010, from http://www.wireshark.org/

Wu, J. M. (1995). *Maximum likelihood estimation in the random coefficient regression model via the EM algorithm*. Phd Thesis, Texas Tech University, Lubbock.

Yegneswaran, V., Saidi, H., Porras, P., Sharif, M., Mark, W., & President, V. (2008). *Eureka: A framework for enabling static analysis on malware* (Tech. Rep.). Atlanta, Gerogia: Georgia Institute of Technology.

Yen, S.-J., & Lee, Y. (2009). Cluster-based under-sampling approaches for imbalanced data distributions (LNCS). *Expert Systems with Applications, 36*, 5718–5727. doi:10.1016/j.eswa.2008.06.108

Zhang, L. (2009). A *sublexical unit based hash model approach for SPAM detection*. PhD Thesis, the University of Texas at San Antonio.

Zhu, Z., Lu, G., Chen, Y., Fu, Z., Roberts, P., & Han, K. (2008). Botnet research survey. In *32nd Annual IEEE International Computer Software and Applications (COMPSAC'08)* (pp. 967-972).

ADDITIONAL READING

Akiyama, M., Kawamoto, T., Shimamura, M., Yokoyama, T., Kadobayashi, Y., & Yamaguchi, S. (2007). A proposal of metrics for botnet detection based on its cooperative behavior. In *International Symposium on Applications and the Internet Workshops*. SAINT Workshops, (pp. 82-82). IEEE Computer Society.

Bächer, P., Holz, T., Kötter, M., & Wicherski, G. (2008). *Know your enemy: Tracking botnets*. Retrieved March 17, 2010 from HoneyNet Web site: http://www.honeynet.org/papers/bots/.

Barford, P., & Blodgett, M. (2007). Toward botnet mesocosms. In Proceedings of the first Workshop on *Hot Topics in Understanding Botnets, HotBots'07*, (pp. 6-6), Berkeley, CA, USA. USENIX Association.

Barford, P., & Yegneswaran, V. (2006). An Inside Look at Botnets. In *Special Workshop on Malware Detection*, Advances in Information Security, Springer Verlag.

Bayer, U., Comparetti, P., Hlauschek, C., Kruegel, C., & Kirda, E. (2009). Scalable, Behavior-Based Malware Clustering. In *Network and Distributed System Security Symposium* (NDSS).

Binkley, J. R., & Singh, S. (2006). An algorithm for anomaly-based botnet detection. In Proceedings of the 2nd conference on *Steps to Reducing Unwanted Traffic on the Internet,* SRUTI'06, (pp. 7-7), Berkeley, CA, USA. USENIX Association.

Caglayan, A., Toothaker, M., Drapaeau, D., Burke, D., & Eaton, G. (2009). Behavioral analysis of fast flux service networks. In Proceedings of the 5th Annual Workshop on *Cyber Security and Information Intelligence Research, CSIIRW '09,* (pp. 1-4), New York, NY: ACM.

Castle, I., & Buckley, E. (2008). The automatic discovery, identification and measurement of botnets. In Second International Conference on *Emerging Security Information, Systems and Technologies*, SECURWARE '08. (pp. 127-132).

Casullo, G. A., Fink, S. A., Jaime, J. M., & Tami, L. R. (2009). Webbotnets, la amenaza fantasma. In Proceedings of the *38 JAIIO, WSegI '09*, Buenos Aires, Argentina.

Chang, S., Zhang, L., Guan, Y., & Daniels, T. (2009). A framework for p2p botnets. In *WRI International Conference* on Communications and Mobile Computing. *CMC '09*, volume 3, (pp. 594-599).

Christodorescu, M., Jha, S., & Kruegel, C. (2008). Mining specifications of malicious behavior. In Proceedings of the *1st conference on India software engineering conference, ISEC '08,* (pp. 5-14), Hyderabad, India. ACM Press New York, NY: ACM.

Christodorescu, M., & Rubin, S. (2007). Can cooperative intrusion detectors challenge the base-rate fallacy? In *US, S., (Ed), Malware Detection, Advances in Information Security*, (pp. 193-209). Springer US.

Cooke, E., Jahanian, F., & McPherson, D. (2005). The Zombie Roundup: Understanding, Detecting, and Disrupting Botnets. In [USENIX Association.]. *Proceedings of the Steps to Reducing Unwanted Traffic on the Internet Workshop, SRUTI, 05,* 6–6.

Dagon, D., Gu, G., Zou, C., Grizzard, J., Dwivedi, S., Lee, W., & Lipton, R. (2007). A Taxonomy of Botnet Structures. In *IEEE Computer Security Applications Conference. ACSAC 2007.*

Dittrich, D. & Dietrich, S. (2007). Command and control structures in malware: From Handler/Agent to P2P. *USENIX*, 32(6).

Duan, Z. (2006). Behavioral characteristics of spammers and their network reachability properties. In Proceedings of *IEEE International Conference on Communications, ICC 2007, (pp 164-171).*

Erbacher, R., Cutler, A., Banerjee, P., & Marshall, J. (2008). A Multi-Layered Approach to Botnet Detection. In Proceedings of the *2008 World congress in computer science, computer engineering and applied computing, The 2008 International Conference on Security and Management.*

Erman, J., Arlitt, M., & Mahanti, A. (2006). Traffic classification using clustering algorithms. In Proceedings of *the 2006 SIGCOMM workshop on Mining network data, MineNet '06,* (pp. 281-286), New York, NY, USA. ACM.

Gao, Y., Zhao, Y., Schweller, R., Venkataraman, S., Chen, Y., Song, D., & Kao, M.-Y. (2007). Detecting stealthy spreaders using online outdegree histograms. In Proceedings of the *Fifteenth IEEE International Workshop on Quality of Service,* (pp. 145-153).

Gu, G., Sharif, M., Qin, X., Dagon, D., Lee, W., & Riley, G. (2004). Worm Detection, Early Warning and Response Based on Local Victim Information. In *Proceedings of the AnnualComputer Security Applications Conference*, (pp. 136-145).

Husna, H., Phithakkitnukoon, S., Palla, S., & Dantu, R. (2008). Behavior analysis of spam botnets. In Proceedings of the *3rd International Conference on Communication Systems Software and Middleware and Workshops, 2008. COMSWARE 2008.* (pp. 246-253).

Jacob, G., Debar, H., & Filiol, E. (2008). Behavioral detection of malware: from a survey towards an established taxonomy. *Journal in Computer Virology*, *4*(3), 251–266. doi:10.1007/s11416-008-0086-0

Kiayias, A., Neumann, J., Walluck, D., & McCusker, O. (2009). A combined fusion and data mining framework for the detection of botnets. In Proceedings of the *Conference For Homeland Security*. CATCH '09. Cybersecurity Applications & Technology, (pp. 273-284).

Kugisaki, Y., Kasahara, Y., Hori, Y., & Sakurai, K. (2007). Bot detection based on traffic analysis. In Proceeding of the *2007 International Conference on Intelligent Pervasive Computing. IPC.* (pp. 303-306).

Lim, S., & Jones, A. (2008). Network anomaly detection system: The state of art of network behaviour analysis. In Proceedings of the *International Conference on Convergence and Hybrid Information Technology. ICHIT '08* (pp. 459-465).

Lu, W., & Ghorbani, A. (2008). Detecting IRC Botnets on Network Application Communities. In *Fifth Annual Research Exposition* (pp. 57–57). Fredericton, New Brunswick, Canada: Faculty of Computer Science UNB.

Passerini, E., Paleari, R., Martignoni, L., & Bruschi, D. (2008). Fluxor: Detecting and monitoring fast-flux service networks. In *Detection of Intrusions and Malware, and Vulnerability Assessment*, Lecture Notes in Computer Science, (pp. 186-206). Springer Berlin / Heidelberg.

Strayer, W. T., Walsh, R., Livadas, C., & Lapsley, D. (2006). Detecting botnets with tight command and control. In Proceedings of *the 31st IEEE Conference on Local Computer Networks*, LCN, (pp. 15-16).

Sung, A., & Mukkamala, S. (2003). Identifying important features for intrusion detection using support vector machines and neural networks. In Proceedings of the *Symposium on Applications and the Internet, 2003.* (pp. 209-216).

Wang, B., Li, Z., Tu, H., Hu, Z., & Hu, J. (2009). Actively measuring bots in peer-to-peer networks. In Proceedings of the *International Conference on Networks Security, Wireless Communications and Trusted Computing. NSWCTC '09*, volume 1, (pp. 603-607).

Wang, P., Wu, L., Aslam, B., & Zou, C. (2009). A systematic study on peer-to-peer botnets. In Proceedings of *18th Internatonal Conference on Computer Communications and Networks. ICCCN 2009.*(pp. 1-8).

Yu, J., Li, Z., Hu, J., Liu, F., & Zhou, L. (2009a). Structural robustness in peer to peer botnets. In Proceedings of the *International Conference on Networks Security, Wireless Communications and Trusted Computing, NSWCTC '09*, volume 2, (pp. 860-863).

Yu, J., Li, Z., Hu, J., Liu, F., & Zhou, L. (2009b). Using simulation to characterize topology of peer to peer botnets. In Proceedings of the *International Conference on Computer Modeling and Simulation, ICCMS '09.*, (pp. 78-83).

KEY TERMS AND DEFINITIONS

Bot: Infected computer, member of a botnet.

Botnet: Coordinated group of infected computers externally managed by an attacker.

Command and Control (C&C) Server: These are the servers used by the botmaster to communicate and remotely control bots, who report back to these servers periodically.

Dips: Amount of unique destination IP address seen in a time frame.

Dports: Amount of unique destination ports seen in a time frame.

Network Behavior: Group of periodic patterns extracted from different network characteristics.

Sips: Amount of unique source IP address seen in a time frame.

Time Window: Period of time in which TCP flows characteristics are aggregated. This information is stored in a four dimensional vector.

Chapter 6

Detecting Denial of Service Attacks on SIP Based Services and Proposing Solutions

Zoha Asgharian
Iran University of Science and Technology, Iran

Hassan Asgharian
Iran University of Science and Technology, Iran

Ahmad Akbari
Iran University of Science and Technology, Iran

Bijan Raahemi
University of Ottawa, Canada

ABSTRACT

One of the main goals of employing Next Generation Networks (NGN) is an integrated access to the multimedia services like Voice over IP (VoIP), and IPTV. The primary signaling protocol in these multimedia services is Session Initiation Protocol (SIP). This protocol, however, is vulnerable to attacks, which may impact the Quality of Service (QoS), which is an important feature in NGN. One of the most frequent attacks is Denial of Service (DoS) attack, which is generated easily, but its detection is not trivial. In this chapter, a framework is proposed to detect Denial of Service attacks and a few other forms of intrusions, and then we react accordingly. The proposed detection engine combines the specification- and anomaly-based intrusion detection techniques. The authors set up a test-bed and generate a labeled dataset.

DOI: 10.4018/978-1-60960-836-1.ch006

Copyright ©2012, IGI Global. Copying or distributing in print or electronic forms without written permission of IGI Global is prohibited.

The traffic generated for the test-bed is composed of two types of SIP packets: at-tack and normal. They then record the detection rates and false alarms based on the labeled dataset. The experimental results demonstrate that the proposed approach can successfully detect intruders and limit their accesses. The results also confirm that the framework is scalable and robust.

INTRODUCTION

The Session Initiation Protocol (SIP) is an application layer protocol standardized by the Internet Engineering Task Force (IETF) for creating, modifying and terminat-ing sessions (Rosenberg et al, 2002, Ehlert, Geneiatakis & Magedanz, 2009). SIP is structured as a layered protocol, meaning that its behavior is described in terms of a set of independent processing stages with only a loose coupling between each stage (Ehlert, Geneiatakis & Magedanz, 2009).

The lowest layer of SIP is the syntax parsing and encoding layer and the sec-ond one is the transport layer. It defines how a client sends requests and receives responses, and also, how a server receives requests and sends responses over the network. The third layer is the transaction layer. Transactions are a fundamental component of SIP. A transaction is a request sent by the client transaction layer to the server transaction layer, along with all responses to that request which are sent from the server transaction layer back to the client transaction layer. The transac-tion layer handles application-layer re-transmissions, matching of responses to requests, and application-layer timeouts. The layer above the transaction layer is called the transaction user (TU). When a TU wishes to send a request, it creates a client transaction instance, and passes the request along with the destination IP address, its port, and its transport layer information (Figure 1).

In 2005, the US National Institute of Standards and Technology declared DoS attacks to be a serious threat for the SIP infrastructures (Ahson & Ilyas, 2009). A DoS attack makes a particular network node unavailable by flooding it with ille-gitimate packets in order to seize its bandwidth, memory and CPU processing power. DoS attacks can be classified as illustrated in Figure 2. The attacks catego-rized into two broad groups: intentional attacks and non-intentional attacks. Non-intentional attacks are usually the result of implementation bugs or configuration errors. However, intentional or malicious attacks are initiated purposefully by in-truders. Intentional attacks can be further subdivided into flooding and protocol misuse attacks. Flooding attacks are also referred to as exhaustion or depletion at-tacks because of their goal of depleting one or more resources of the victim and making it incapable of conducting its regular tasks, and processing the incoming requests (Sisalem, Floroiu, Kuthan, Abend & Schulzrinne, 2009).

Figure 1. SIP protocol layers

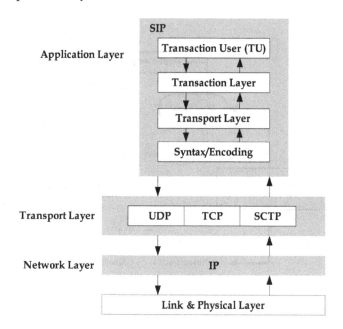

This chapter focuses on detecting some of the important intentional attacks indicated in Figure 2. These selected attacks deplete memory or bandwidth. The various scenarios of generating each attack are explained below.

(I) Bandwidth Depletion Attacks (INVITE flooding): In this scenario, the attacker generates a large number of INVITE packets and sends them in a short period of time to SIP server in order to deplete its bandwidth. This scenario is similar to overloading the SIP proxy with a significant difference: the generated messages in this scenario are not valid messages (Sisalem, Floroiu, Kuthan, Abend & Schulzrinne, 2009) (Figure 3).

(II) Brute Force Attacks (INVITE flooding): A SIP session is identified mainly by the FROM and TO tags, as well as the Call-ID and the VIA's BRANCH fields. Hence, the simplest methods for mounting an attack on the memory of a SIP server are to initiate a large number of SIP sessions with different session identities, i.e. with different TO, FROM tags, Call-ID or BRANCH fields. If the number of generated calls is greater than the threshold for which the memory of the SIP proxy was designed, then the proxy memory will be depleted eventually, and the SIP server will start dropping the incoming requests due to the lack of memory without any consideration on the behavior (normal or attack) of incoming packets (Sisalem, Floroiu, Kuthan, Abend & Schulzrinne, 2009) (Figure 3).

Figure 2. Classification of DoS Attack on SIP-based services

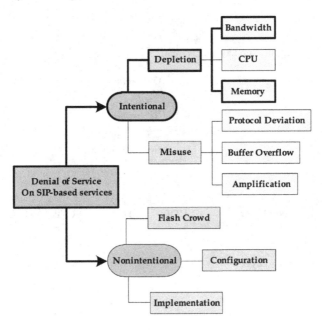

Figure 3. INVITE flooding

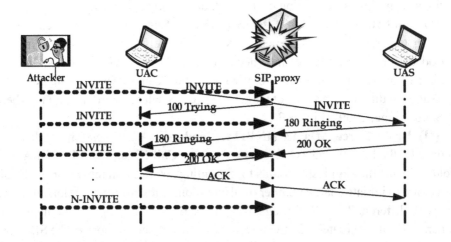

(III) Incomplete Transactions with Host Cooperation (Ringing Attacks): By sending provisional responses, e.g. 1xx replies, to INVITE requests, a receiving user agent can prolong the lifetime of a transaction to several minutes. In this attack scenario, the attacker sends INVITE requests to destinations that reply with 1xx

Figure 4. Incomplete transactions with cooperating hosts

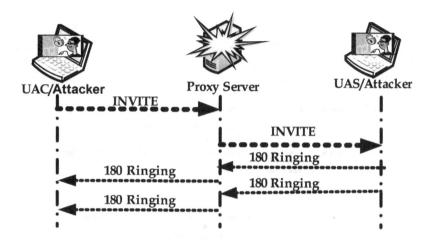

messages but do not send final responses. With this approach, the attacker needs to send even fewer requests to deplete the memory of the SIP server. For further prolonging the lifetime of the transactions, the used destinations have to cooperate and reply with provisional responses to the received requests (Sisalem, Floroiu, Kuthan, Abend & Schulzrinne, 2009) (Figure 4).

(IV) Attacks Using SIP Authentication (REGISTER Flooding): Using digest authentication, the authenticating server generates a nonce and adds it to a 401 Unauthorized or 407 Proxy Authentication Required responses in a WWW-Authenticate or Proxy-Authenticate header. The user agent then abandons the first transaction and generates a new request with its credentials calculated based on the shared secret with the provider and the nonce. While generating the 407 response and receiving the new request from the user, the server usually maintains a copy of the nonce. Attacker generates a request, and includes it in the FROM header of the identity of a subscriber of the attacked proxy or registrar server. Once asked to verify his identity, the attacker just ignores the challenge and starts a new request with another session identity. The attacked server keeps the allocated memory for a certain period of time. The memory of the attacked server is, hence, consumed by the saved nonce and the transaction data. This comes in addition to the wasted CPU resources for calculating the no (Sisalem, Floroiu, Kuthan, Abend & Schulzrinne, 2009) (Figure 5).

The main contributions of this study are (a) proposing an integrated framework for detecting important flooding attacks (including REGISTER, RINGING and INVITE); (b) responding to the attacks in the form of notification and prevention; (c) defining and generating normal SIP traffic based on its known parameters inspired

Figure 5. REGISTER flooding

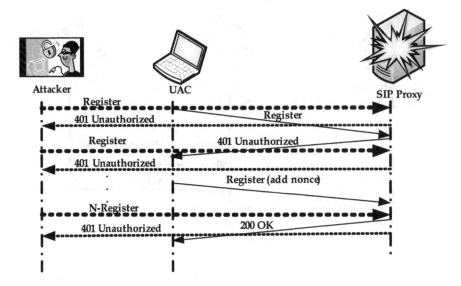

by practical considerations; (d) developing a tool to generate flooding attacks to SIP servers ; and (e) setting up a test-bed including both types of the traffics (normal and attacks).

The rest of this chapter is organized as follows. Section 2 briefly reviews the related works. In Section 3, we discuss our proposed framework for securing SIP proxies. Then, we discuss the architecture of the traffic generators in section 4. The setup of the experiments and analysis of the results are presented in Section 5. Finally, we conclude this chapter with an outlook to the future research.

BACKGROUND

The SIP DoS countermeasure systems can be seen as an additional layer of security. Multiple countermeasure schemes have been proposed to target the new SIP-related DoS attacks (Ahson & Ilyas, 2009). In (EY, 2006), the authors proposed a method to detect INVITE flooding attacks, where the primary finite-state machine of the SIP transactions are modified in such a way that anomalies can be detected in a stateful manner. The authors, however, did not present the experimental results. In (Ehlert, Wang, Magedanz & Sisalem, 2008), the authors proposed a specification-based intrusion detection framework based on the SIP finite-state machine to distinguish deviation from its normal or expected behavior. They also proposed a method for mitigation of detected attacks. Although they presented their experimental results, they did not compare their solutions with similar published works.

VoIP firewalls and more specifically those that address the security of the SIP protocol are still in early stages, and there is limited work published on this topic in (YS, Bagchi, Garg, Singh & Tsai, 2004), (Lahmadi & Festor, 2009), (Fiedler, Kupka, Ehlert, Magedanz & Sisalem, 2007). The authors of (YS, Bagchi, Garg, Singh & Tsai, 2004) proposed a solution for stateful intrusion detection called SCIDIVE. The system relies on a stateful engine that determines the current state from multiple packets involved in the same session. The system also uses cross-protocol detection to verify the consistency between two protocols involved in the same VoIP session, mainly SIP and RTP. The goal of their work is similar to that of SecSip (Lahmadi & Festor, 2009), sharing the idea of using the stateful features. VoIP defender (Fiedler, Kupka, Ehlert, Magedanz & Sisalem, 2007) is a SIP-based security architecture designed to monitor, detect, analyze and counter attack. The nature of the employed detection scheme (stateful or stateless) is not clearly stated. In addition, no details are provided about the language they used to build defense rules and how it can be used for SIP.

Despite many efforts in detecting intrusions on SIP based applications (Zhang, Gu, Liu & Jie, 2009)(Geneiatakis, Vrakas & Lambrinoudakis, 2009)(Ali Akbar, Tariq & Farooq, 2009). There is no common labeled dataset available to test these various solutions and compare them against each other. Also, for evaluation of these intrusion detection techniques, the SIP traffic is generated with specific assumptions which cannot be applied to all of them. For this reason, evaluation of these detection techniques is very hard, and also the comparison between them is almost impossible.

PROPOSED FRAMEWORK

A Security Operation Center (SOC) is made up of five distinct modules: *event generators, event collectors, message database, analysis engines and reaction management software* (Karim Ganame, Bourgeois, Bidou & Spies, 2007). The main problem encountered when building a SOC is the integration of all these modules, usually built as autonomous parts, while matching availability, integrity and security of data and their transmission channels. In this paper, we propose a framework for securing a SIP server based on the architecture of SOC. Our proposed solution is shown in Figure 6.

The relevance of the proposed modules with the ones defined in the SOC architecture are as follows:

Figure 6. Intrusion detection and response framework for securing SIP server

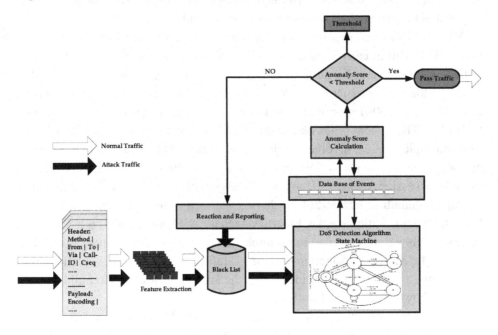

1. **Event generators**, the detection module acts as the event generator in the proposed framework.
2. **Event collectors and message database**, all important generated events are added to a database, managed by the event collector module.
3. **Analysis engines,** in this module, an anomaly score is computed using the records in the database. This score is then compared with a predefined threshold, and a status is determined for the traffic.
4. **Reaction management software**, after determining the traffic status, the detected intruders are added to the black list, and their access is then limited by the system. The intruders are identified by the main attributes of the SIP header.

Detection Mechanism

Keeping the status of active and in-progress transactions in the SIP server consumes both memory and CPU processing power. Therefore, attackers can degrade performance of the SIP server using two approaches:

1. To send a large number of transactions to the server within a short time to deplete its memory, bandwidth and CPU processing power.

2.   To extend the time of each transaction in the SIP server to seize its memory.

Intrusion detection approaches can be divided into misuse detection, anomaly detection and specification-based detection. Using this terminology, our approach is a combination of specification- with anomaly-based detection techniques (Sekar et al, 2002). We combine the attributes of the SIP messages with information about statistics that need to be maintained to detect anomalies. As such, the proposed approach mitigates the weaknesses of the two approaches while magnifying their strengths. We introduce a state machine for detecting the DoS attacks as shown in Figure 9. The states are derived from the definition of transactions of different SIP messages. The transitions are formed according to the different headers of the incoming SIP messages. Each packet raises an event in the state machine. In each state, and with the arrival of a new packet, the SIP security engine extracts and parses the SIP header, then makes a decision about the next state (transition) based on the METHOD field. INVITE and REGISTER are two essential methods in SIP transactions. Each transaction adds a new entry in a specific table in the database, while its related transaction response deletes a corresponding line from the database. We predefine four thresholds on the size of the database to distinguish the status of the input traffic (these values are shown with Tx in Figure 7). The complete state machine is shown in Figure 7.

Reaction Mechanism

The proposed security engine is equipped with a reporting module. After detecting new intrusion, we add specific information (SIP URI: FROM, TO) to the run-time hash table (this table is used to maintain black list), and also, append the alert log file to appropriate notification. Using the terminology of response systems, this is the notification and prevention stage. The "alert generation" acts as the notification response that administrators can use to take proper actions. The "black list" can be used to prevent the access of intruders temporally. It works independent of any existing firewalls in the system.

Labeled Dataset

The configuration of our test-bed, the traffic generation models, and the selected components of the SIP packets which are used as features in the dataset are described here in three subsections.

153

Figure 7. The proposed state machine for detecting flooding attck (INVITE, REG-ISTER, RINGING)

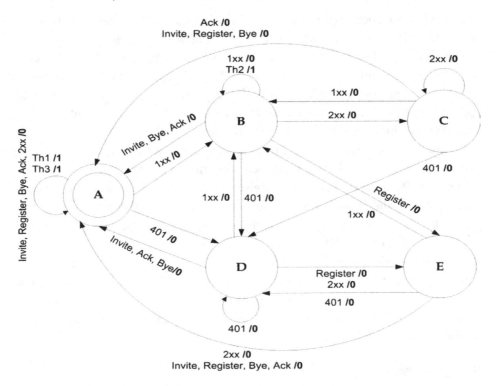

Figure 8. Our Test Bed

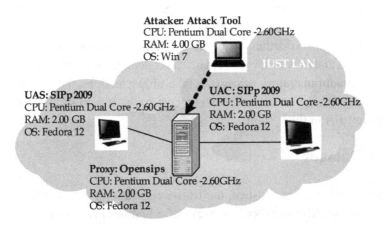

Figure 9. Screenshot of the attack tool developped in our work

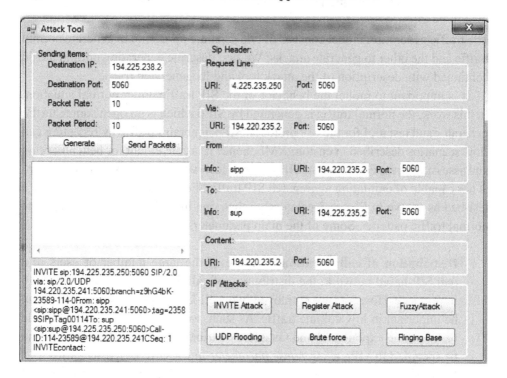

Test-Bed Configuration

A platform for experimentation of large development projects, test-bed allows for rigorous, transparent, and replicable testing of scientific theories, computational tools, and new technologies. A typical test-bed includes software, hardware, and networking components. Figure 8 shows the architecture and the main components of our test-bed. The test-bed is implemented on separate machines in a LAN.

Note that the clients – the caller and the called parties – are instantiated on separate machines. The User Agent Clients (UACs) initiate the calls; while the User Agent Servers (UASs) are the SIP clients that receive the call from UACs (with or without proxy) and start the dialogue. Attacks are separately launched from an attacker node. The UAS and UAC machines can represent the arbitrary number of SIP users. The detail of implementation is described in the following sections.

Traffic Generation Model

The traffic generation model consists of two separate parts, one to generate normal traffic and the other to generate attacks. We first describe generating normal traffic continued with description of the attack tool and its generated traffic.

It is important to model the behavior of the SIP traffic under normal situation. In this work, the normal traffic is generated by SIPp which is an open source traffic generator and test tool for the SIP protocol. SIPp generates traffic by repeating call flow scenarios described in custom XML, hence it is convenient for benchmarking and assessing stress conditions at SIP servers. However SIPp -in its current version- is not capable of emulating aggregated SIP traffic. For this reason, we configure a test-bed as shown in Figure 8 using more than one instance of SIPp to aggregate normal traffic patterns. Some of the main parameters are as follows:

1. **Distribution of call duration:** because of the large number of users in a real SIP-based network, the distribution of call duration may not be of high importance. However, we employed two well-known distributions which can be important in low volume traffic. As such, we generated the normal traffic based on the exponential and Gaussian distributions. These distributions can be specified in SIPp using *pause parameter* in its XML based scenarios.
2. **Calls per second:** this parameter has a direct relationship with the number of active users which is a fraction of the maximum number of users. Therefore, we assumed three types of networks (with low-, medium- and high-volume traffic) with different number of users, and collected information about their normal behavior. Since SIPp recognizes only call per second, we derived call per second based on the number of users as shown in the following formula:

$$a \ x \ N = \lambda \ x \ T \rightarrow \lambda = \frac{axN}{T} \tag{1}$$

Where, α is the percentage of active users in the network based on the normal activities in the network, N represents the maximum number of users (a known parameter in the network), T is call duration which is described next, and λ is the call per second ratio which is calculated based on the above mentioned parameters.

1. **Call duration:** call duration plays an important role in generating a comprehensive dataset for evaluation of intrusion detection systems. As such, more than 50% of active users (active calls) are completed in less than 60 seconds

Table 1. Low Volume Normal Traffic (10 call per sec)

Request	N	T (sec)	λ-(cps)
INVITE	2000	300	1
	5000	60	5
	3000	180	1
REGISTER	10000	3600	3
Number of Users: 10000, α = 0.05			

Table 2. Medium Volume Normal Traffic (18 call per sec)

Request	N	T (sec)	λ-(cps)
INVITE	4000	300	1
	10000	60	9
	6000	180	2
REGISTER	20000	3600	6
Number of Users: 20000, α = 0.05			

Table 3. High Volume Normal Traffic (82 call per sec)

Request	N	T (sec)	λ-(cps)
INVITE	20000	300	4
	50000	60	41
	30000	180	9
REGISTER	100000	3600	28
Number of Users: 100000, α = 0.05			

and about 20% of them are lasted more than 300 seconds and the others are done between 60 to 300 seconds. To generate normal traffic, we take two approaches into consideration: I) generate traffic with normal (Gaussian) distribution with a large standard deviation and an average of 300 seconds or II) generate three separate traffic flows and aggregate their outputs. We opted for the second approach as we believe it is more accurate than the first one. In addition to the active requests (INVITE, BYE, ACK, CANCEL) and their respected responses (1xx to 6xx), the REGISTER request is an important SIP request which is generated periodically for each user. The period of REGISTER requests are about 3600 seconds.

Table 4. Sample Values considered in an Attacker Node

Type	INVITE (pkt/sec)	1xx (pkt/sec)	REGISTER (pkt/sec)
Scenario I	1000	0	0
Scenario II	500	0	0
Scenario III	1	50	0
Scenario IV	0	0	200

2. **Random selection of the SIP message fields**: the SIP packets should be generated with different SIP URIs (different FROM and TO fields in SIP message). As such, we generate the SIP URIs with random TO and FROM fields.

Considering the above parameters, the characteristics of the normal traffic generated for our test-bed are summarized in Table1, Table2, and Table3.

The attacker entity is implemented as an attacker node running on a separate machine. Then an attacker node, implemented in C#, is capable of launching DoS attacks on a SIP proxy server. It generates some basic DoS attack scenarios selected from the attack classification.

In this work, we developed one attack tool that can generate all of the above mentioned types of attacks. It is implemented in C# and its main GUI is shown in Figure 9.

The final aggregated traffic is composed of the traffic generated by the attack tool (whose behavior is summarized in Table 4) and the normal traffic (whose behavior is summarized in Tables 1, 2, 3). The values in Table4 are the typical values we used randomly in each iteration.

Selected Features for Labeled Dataset

We filtered the network traffic according to its port number on the primary SIP server in the test-bed, and dumped the SIP traffic to file for further analysis. The raw traffic data collected from the test-bed using tcpdump [16] is not ready to use. Therefore, a transformation function, which transforms the raw traffic into attributes records, is used to generate well-formatted data for further analysis. Table 5 summarizes the selected features in the dataset. These features are typical attributes that can be found in existing SIP-based intrusion detection systems.

Table 5. Selected Attribute list of the dataset

Attribute	Description
Method	Indicates the type of the SIP message, its value is derived from the first line of the SIP header.
From	Corresponds to the logical initiator of the request, and is derived from the FROM header field.
To	Corresponds to the logical recipient of the request, and is derived from the TO header field. It is used to follow a dialog between two UAs.
Branch	Via field in SIP header contains a branch parameter that is unique in each transaction and is used for transaction signature.
Call-ID	Contains a globally unique identifier for each dialog. It is generated by the combination of a random string and the softphone's host name or IP address. This feature is derived from Call-ID field in SIP header.

The Dataset

We devised a set of normal and attack scenarios in the test-bed introduced in the previous sections. The scenarios are constrained by an execution time of 5 to 20 minutes for each experiment, and the processing power supported by the SIP server machine such that the SIP server is capable of responding to all of the calls during execution of the test scenarios. The resulting traces of all experiments are available in (http://nrg.iust.ac.ir/sip-security, 2011), where there is a folder for each experiment including at least three files: a file containing the network traces in tcpdump format, a text file (in .xlsx format) representing the features as listed in Table5, as well as a comma separated values (CSV) format of these files. Since we already knew the IP addresses of the attacker nodes in the test-bed, we were able to label each packet accordingly in the final dataset. Doing so, the attribute files also contain one separated column representing the type of each packet (attack or normal).

Other resources including SIPp scenario files, attack tool application, transformation module, and feature extraction tool that can be used to generate traffic, aggregate and collect them are also available by request. The following table summarizes the traffic generated for the test.

SIP Security Engine Evaluation

The SIP security engine is the heart of our proposed solution for detecting and mitigating attacks. It is implemented in C# as an extension module to be placed at the network ingress point. We implemented the engine in an NIDS placed in front of the SIP proxy of the network. For attack mitigation (prevention and response), the hash tables have a connection to the SIP proxy to communicate when it should

Table 6. Summary of Prepared Labeled Dataset

Name	Attack Type	Attack Intensity (pps)	Attack Applied Time (second)	Trace Duration (min)	Normal Active Calls (cps)
S1,S2, S3	None	None	None	5	10, 18, 82
S4, S5, S6	INVITE	1000	Random	5	10, 18, 82
		500*			
	REGISTER	200			
	RINGING	50			
S7, S8, S9	INVITE	1000	Random	10	10, 18, 82
		500*			
	REGISTER	200			
	RINGING	50			
S10,S11,S12	INVITE	1000	Random	20	10, 18, 82
		500*			
	REGISTER	200			
	RINGING	50			
S13	INVITE	1000	Random	5	10
		500*			
S14	REGISTER	200	Random	5	10
S15	RINGING	50	Random	5	10

* Brute force INVITE flooding

Figure 10. Placement of SIP security engine in the network

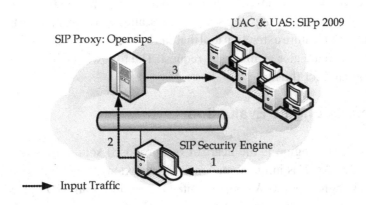

Figure 11. Logical block diagram of the Proposed SIP Security Engine

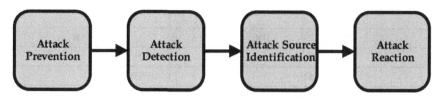

throttle the requests or block them temporarily (see Figure 10). It features a multi-layered approach that can be deployed on multiple machines. This makes the solution scalable, and capable of dealing with high volume of messages.

As explained before, the proposed SIP security engine requires four thresholds. To obtain the best values for these thresholds, the ROC (Receiver Operating Characteristic) analysis was performed. We repeated the experiments on the labeled dataset with different values. The best values were then selected using scenarios (S4, S5, S6), and the derived thresholds were used in the next experiments (S7 to S15). Figure 12 shows a sample of the ROC graph.

The detection rates and false alarms were calculated using the following equations:

$$detection\ rate\ (DR) = \frac{True\ Positive}{True\ Positive + False\ Negative} \qquad (2)$$

Figure 12. Sample of the ROC graph for dataset 4

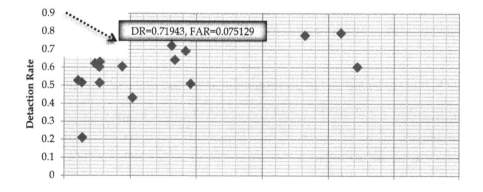

Table 7. the detection rate and false alarm of the SIP Security Engine in different scenarioes

Name	DR	FAR
S7	0. 7719834	0.0900595
S8	0.8695826	0. 01495126
S9	0.6897099	0.07307112
S10	0.869971	0.1168597
S11	0.878754	0.03447238
S12	0.7319137	0.09860304
S13	0.8284615	0.1554773
S14	0.9985185	0.02035793
S15	0.9810175	0.02692051

$$false\ alarm\ (FAR) = \frac{False\ Positive}{False\ Positive + True\ Negative} \tag{3}$$

We validated the proposed mechanism using normal traffic scenarios (S1, S2, and S3) and verified that the security engine doesn't report FAR. The results of other scenarios are summarized in Table 7.

If the characteristics of the input traffic do not follow a normal distribution, we may observe some periods of burst of traffic. As such, we simulated the effects of the other traffic distributions (Poisson and exponential) by inserting some periods of burst of traffic. The specifications of the generated traffic and the corresponding detection rate and false alarm are listed in Table 8.

As shown in Table 8, the false alarm rate increases when burst of traffics are added to the input. This is expected as it means our proposed solution labels some benign traffic as an attack because its traffic behavior is abnormal.

Table 8. Burst of traffic and its corresponding detection rate and false alarm

Traffic Spec.	DR	FAR
10 cps, 10 min	0.7719	0.0900
200 cps, 20 sec (repeated each 100 sec)	0.7499	0.2126
100 cps, 20 sec (repeated each 100 sec)	0.8666	0.1910
82 cps, 20 sec (repeated each 100 sec)	0.7737	0.0672
50 cps, 20 sec (repeated each 100 sec)	0.8297	0.0662

Table 9. Effective of response mechanisim

Name	Response	DR	FAR
S4	No	0. 1838996	0.0315256
	Yes	0.810192	0.06548638
S5	No	0.6365387	0.344387
	Yes	0.7734718	0.01797855
S6	No	0.529954	0.3896613
	Yes	0.7194296	0.07512894

Table 9 shows the detection rate and false alarm rate of the proposed solution before and after a response module is considered for the system. After adding the response module to the system, we used an access control list (i.e black list) to control the access of the known intruders. As expected, by adding the response mechanism, the detection and false alarm rates are improved. This is due to the fact that the response module blocks the intruders' packets for a specific duration that is usually set by the network administrator.

FUTURE RESEARCH DIRECTIONS

In the BYE attack the attacker tries to terminate the communication session of the victim prematurely. Eavesdropping on the user's communications once a session is established, the attacker can issue a BYE request to one of the parties involved in the session. With the CANCEL attack, the attacker can prevent a caller from establishing a communication session. After eavesdropping on a user's INVITE request, the attacker sends directly a CANCEL request to the callee afterwards. We will investigate other SIP attacks, and specifically BYE and CANCEL attacks in our future work.

CONCLUSION

We presented a security framework for Session Initiation Protocol based on the Security Operation Center (SOC) architecture. The proposed framework can detect the most frequent attacks (INVITE, REGISTER and RINGING) on SIP-based services, and accordingly, generate appropriate responses to the detected intrusions. Two approaches are considered in responding to attacks: notification and prevention. The framework generates appropriate notifications after detecting intrusions. It also employs an access control list (black list) to limit the access of the intruders. The proposed detection mechanism was implemented in the form of state machines; we first analyzed the SIP state machines, and accordingly, introduced a detection state in the SIP state machine which is capable of detecting and reporting attacks. In the process of design and implementation of the framework, our main focus was on the scalability, robustness and performance. For the purpose of testing the proposed security framework, we also generated a SIP dataset for the evaluation (and also comparison) of intrusion detection systems. The dataset is publically available in (SIP Security page in NRG site: http://nrg.iust.ac.ir/sip-security).

REFERENCES

Ahson, A., & Ilyas, M. (2009). *SIP handbook* (pp. 3–173). New York: Taylor & Francis Group.

Akbar, M. A., Tariq, Z., & Farooq, M. (2009). *A comparative study of anomaly detection algorithms for detection of SIP flooding in IMS*, 2nd International Conference on Internet Multimedia Services Architecture and Applications (pp. 1-6).

Asgharian, Z., Asgharian, H., Akbari, A., & Raahemi, B. (2011). *A framework for SIP intrusion detection and response systems*, IEEE International Symposium on Computer Networks and Distributed Systems, Tehran, Iran.

Chen, E. Y. (2006). *Detecting DoS attacks on SIP systems*, In 1st IEEE Workshop on VoIP Management and Security (pp. 53- 58).

Ehlert, S., Geneiatakis, D., & Magedanz, T. (2009). *Survey of network security systems to counter SIP-based denial-of-service attacks*. Amsterdam, The Netherlands: Elsevier.

Ehlert, S., Wang, C., Magedanz, T., & Sisalem, D. (2008). *Specification-based denial-of-service detection for SIP voice-over-IP networks*, 3rd International Conference on Internet Monitoring and Protection (pp. 59-66).

Fiedler, J., Kupka, T., Ehlert, S., Magedanz, T., & Sisalem, D. (2007). VoIP defender: Highly scalable SIP-based security architecture. In *Proceedings of the 1st International Conference on Principles, Systems and Applications of IP Telecommunications* (pp. 11-17).

Ganame, A. K., Bourgeois, J., Bidou, R., & Spies, F. (2007). *A global security architecture for intrusion detection on computer networks*. IEEE International Parallel and Distributed Processing Symposium (IPDPS '07) (pp. 1-8).

Geneiatakis, D., Vrakas, N., & Lambrinoudakis, C. (2009). Utilizing bloom filters for detecting flooding attacks against SIP based services. *Elsevier Journal on Computers and Security, 28*(7), 578–591.

Invent, H. P. (2010). *SIPp*. Retrieved February 2011, from http://sipp.sourceforge.net/

Lahmadi, A., & Festor, O. (2009). *SecSip: A stateful firewall for SIP-based networks*, 11th IFIP/IEEE International Symposium on Integrated Network Management (pp.172-179).

NRG. (2011). *NRG Lab*. Retrieved February 2011, from http://nrg.iust.ac.ir/sip-security

Rosenberg, J., Schulzrinne, H., Camarillo, G., Johnston, A., Peterson, J., & Spark, R. ...Schooler, E. (2002). *RFC 3261, Session Initiation Protocol.* Retrieved from http://www.ietf.org/rfc/rfc3261.txt

Sekar, R., Gupta, A., Frullo, J., Shanbhag, T., Tiwari, A., Yang, H., & Zhou, S. (2002). Specification-based anomaly detection: A new approach for detecting network intrusions, In *Proceedings of the 9th ACM Conference on Computer and Communications Security* (pp. 265-274).

Sisalem, D., Floroiu, J., Kuthan, J., Abend, U., & Schulzrinne, H. (2009). *SIP Security* (pp. 225–290). Hoboken, NJ: John Wiley & Sons. doi:10.1002/9780470516997.ch8

TCPDUMP. (2010). TCPDUMP & LibCAP. Retrieved February 2011, from http://www.tcpdump.org/

Wu, Y.-S., Bagchi, S., Garg, S., Singh, N., & Tsai, T. (2004). *SCIDIVE: A stateful and cross protocol intrusion detection architecture for voice-over-IP environments*, International Conference on Dependable Systems and Networks (pp. 433- 442).

Zhang, H., Gu, Z., Liu, C., & Jie, T. (2009). *Detecting VoIP-specific denial-of-service using change-point method*, 11th International Conference on Advanced Communication Technology (vol. 2, pp.1059-1064).

ADDITIONAL READING

Ehlert, S. (2009). *Denial-of-Service Detection and Mitigation for SIP Communication Networks,* Dissertation thesis, Technische Universität Berlin, Telecommunication and Network Group.

Fokus. (2011). Retrieved February 2011, from http://www.fokus.fraunhofer.de

SNOCER European research project documentation. (2004-2006). *Low Cost Tools for Secure and Highly Available VoIP Communication Services*, 2004-2006.

KEY TERMS AND DEFINITIONS

Denial of Service Attack (DoS): An attempt to make a computer resource unavailable to its intended users.

Distributed DoS (DDoS): An attack which a multitude of compromised systems attack a single target, thereby causing denial of service for users of the targeted system.

Flooding Attack: An attack that attempts to cause a failure in a computer system or other data processing entity by providing more input than the entity can process properly.

Intrusion Detection System (IDS): A type of security management system for computers and networks. An IDS gathers and analyzes information from various areas within a computer or a network to identify possible security breaches, which include both intrusions (attacks from outside the organization) and misuse (attacks from within the organization).

IP Television (IPTV): Defined as the secure and reliable delivery to subscribers of entertainment video and related services. These services may include, for example, Live TV, Video On Demand (VOD) and Interactive TV (iTV). These services are delivered across an access agnostic, packet switched network that employs the IP protocol to transport the audio, video and control signals. In contrast to video over the public Internet, with IPTV deployments, network security and performance are tightly managed to ensure a superior entertainment experience, resulting in a compelling business environment for content providers, advertisers and customers alike.

Next Generation Network (NGN): A packet-based network which can provide services including Telecommunication Services and able to make use of multiple broadband, Quality of Service-enabled transport technologies and in which service-related functions are *independent* from underlying *transport-related* technologies. It offers unrestricted access by users to different service providers.

Session Initiation Protocol (SIP): An IETF-defined signaling protocol widely used for controlling multimedia communication sessions such as voice and video calls over Internet Protocol (IP). The protocol can be used for creating, modifying and terminating two-party (unicast) or multiparty (multicast) sessions consisting of one or several media streams.

SIP Uniform Resource Identifier (URI): The SIP addressing schema to call another person via SIP. In other words, a SIP URI is a user's SIP phone number.

The SIP URI resembles an e-mail address and is written in the following format: SIP URI = sip:x@y:Port (Where x=Username and y=host (domain or IP))

Transaction User (TU): The layer above the transaction layer in SIP is called the transaction user (TU). Each of the SIP entities, except the stateless proxy, is a transaction user.

User Agent Server (UAS): A term in the SIP based VOIP system, is a server application that contacts the user when a SIP request is received, and then returns a response on behalf of the user. The response accepts, rejects, or redirects the request.

User Agent Client (UAC): A term in the SIP based VOIP system, is a client application that initiates the SIP request.

Voice Over Internet Protocol (VoIP): A technology that allows you to make voice calls using a broadband Internet connection instead of a regular (or analog) phone line. Some VoIP services may only allow you to call other people using the same service, but others may allow you to call anyone who has a telephone number - including local, long distance, mobile, and international numbers. Also, while some VoIP services only work over your computer or a special VoIP phone, other services allow you to use a traditional phone connected to a VoIP adapter.

Section 2

Chapter 7
Dimension Reduction and its Effects on Clustering for Intrusion Detection

Peyman Kabiri
Iran University of Science and Technology, Iran

Ali A. Ghorbani
University of New Brunswick, Canada

ABSTRACT

With recent advances in network based technology and the increased dependency of our every day life on this technology, assuring reliable operation of network based systems is very important. During recent years, a number of attacks on networks have dramatically increased and consequently interest in network intrusion detection has increased among the researchers. During the past few years, different approaches for collecting a dataset of network features, each with its own assumptions, have been proposed to detect network intrusions. Recently, many research works have been focused on better understanding of the network feature space so that they can come up with a better detection method. The curse of dimensionality is still a big obstacle in front of the researchers in network intrusion detection. In this chapter, DARPA'99 dataset is used for the study. Features in that dataset are analyzed with respect to their information value. Using the information value of the features, the number of dimensions in the data is reduced. Later on, using several clustering algorithms, effects of the dimension reduction on the dataset are studied and the results are reported.

DOI: 10.4018/978-1-60960-836-1.ch007

Copyright ©2012, IGI Global. Copying or distributing in print or electronic forms without written permission of IGI Global is prohibited.

INTRODUCTION

In the past two decades with the rapid progress in the Internet based technology, new application areas for computer network have emerged. At the same time, wide spread progress in the Local Area Network (LAN) and Wide Area Network (WAN) application areas in business, finance, industry, security and healthcare sectors made us more dependent on the computer networks. All of these application areas made the network an attractive target for the abuse and a big vulnerability for the community. A fun to do job or a challenge to win action for some people became a nightmare for the others. In many cases malicious acts made this nightmare to become a reality.

In addition to the hacking, new entities like worms, Trojans and viruses introduced more panic into the networked society. As the current situation is a relatively new phenomenon, network defenses are weak. However, due to the popularity of the computer networks, their connectivity and our ever growing dependency on them, realization of the threat can have devastating consequences. Securing such an important infrastructure has become the priority one research area for many researchers.

One of the major concerns is to make sure that in case of an intrusion attempt, the system is able to detect and to report it. Once the detection is reliable, next step would be to protect and defend the network (response). In other words, the IDS will be upgraded to an Intrusion Detection and Response System (IDRS).

However, no part of the IDS is currently at a fully reliable level. Even though researchers are concurrently engaged in working on both detection and respond sides of the system. A major problem in the IDS is the guarantee for the intrusion detection. This is the reason why in many cases IDSs are used together with a human expert. In this way, IDS is actually helping the network security officer and it is not reliable enough to be trusted on its own. The reason is the inability of IDS to detect the new or altered attack patterns. Although the latest generation of the detection techniques has significantly improved the detection rate, still there is a long way to go.

There are two major approaches for detecting intrusions, signature-based and anomaly-based intrusion detection. In the first approach, attack patterns or the behavior of the intruder is modeled (attack signature is modeled). Here the system will signal the intrusion once a match is detected. However, in the second approach normal behavior of the network is modeled. In this approach, the system will raise the alarm once the behavior of the network does not match with its normal behavior. There is another Intrusion Detection (ID) approach that is called specification-based intrusion detection. In this approach, the normal behavior (expected behavior) of the host is specified and consequently modeled. In this approach, as a direct price for the security, freedom of operation for the host is limited.

Another major problem in this research area is the speed of detection. Computer networks have a dynamic nature in a sense that information and data within them are continuously changing. Therefore, to accurately and promptly detect an intrusion into the network, the system has to operate in real time. Operating in real time is not just to perform the detection in real time, but is to adapt to the new dynamics in the network. Real time operating IDS is an active research area pursued by many researchers. Most of the research works are aimed to introduce the most time efficient methodologies. The goal is to make the implemented methods suitable for the real time implementation.

The real time requirement for implementation of an IDS asks for a short processing time. However, large number of parameters makes it very difficult to achieve such a speed. In other words, curse of dimensionality is one of the greatest obstacles in front of the IDS technology. Work presented in this paper aims to study this problem and will try to help to break this curse. It is clear that not all the selected parameters are as effective and as influential as the rest. Some features in the feature space may have more influence on the final result than the others.

Authors of this paper have briefly studied the current literature in the field of intrusion detection (Kabiri and Ghorbani, 2005) and noticed that curse of dimensionality is one of the major problems in the intrusion detection. Evaluation of the features with respect to their importance in the intrusion detection process is an important issue that requires further research.

The following sections of this paper are organized as follows. In Section 2 several intrusion detection approaches that might be related to the proposed approach are explained. In Section 3 our proposed dimension reduction technique based on the Principal Component Analysis (PCA) concept and its implication on both dimension reduction and feature evaluation are explained. Section 4 will explain the effects of the proposed dimension reduction method on a subset of DARPA'99 dataset with respect to a number of different clustering techniques. In this section we will provide some important information to understand the behavior of these methods with respect to the reduced number of dimensions and some experimental results are presented. Subsequently the last two sections are future work and conclusion, respectively, some ideas will be provided to expand the current research and where results will be analyzed.

INTRUSION DETECTION BASED ON ARTIFICIAL INTELLIGENCE AND STATISTICS

There are several approaches to tackle the intrusion detection problem area. Two of the most popular fields are Artificial Intelligence (AI) and Statistical approaches. It is not unusual to see that researchers use a combination of these methods to tackle real world problems. Nowadays many fields of science have converged so that they can be used to support each other. Bridging the gap between the sciences is a very attractive and yet effective approach to solve multidisciplinary real world problems.

Application of the AI is widely used for the ID purpose. Researchers have proposed several approaches in this regard. Some of the researchers are more interested in applying rule-based methods to detect the intrusion. Data mining using the association rule is also one of the approaches used by some researchers to tackle this problem (Barbara et al., 2001b, a; Yoshida, 2003; Lee et al., 1998).

Others have proposed application of the fuzzy logic concept into the intrusion detection problem area (Dickerson and Dickerson, 2000; Bridges and Rayford, 2000; Botha and von Solms, 2003). Some researchers even used a multidisciplinary approach, for example, they have combined fuzzy logic, genetic algorithm and association rule techniques in their work (Gomez and Dasgupta, 2001). Cho (Cho, 2002) reports a work where fuzzy logic and Hidden Markov Model (HMM) have been deployed together to detect intrusions. In this approach, HMM is used for the dimensionality reduction. Due to its nature, the data mining approach is widely appreciated in this field of research.

Another group of researchers have chosen to use the Bayesian methodology to solve the intrusion detection problem. The main idea behind this approach is the unique feature of the Bayesian methodology. For a given consequence, using the probability calculations Bayesian methodology can move back in time and find the cause of the events. This feature is suitable for finding the reason for a particular anomaly in the network behavior. Using Bayesian algorithm, system can somehow move back in time and find the cause of the events. This algorithm is sometimes used for the clustering purposes as well (Bulatovic and Velasevic, 1999; Barbara et al., 2001b; Bilodeau and Brenner, 1999).

Although using the Bayesian approach for the intrusion detection or intruder behavior prediction can be very appealing, there are some issues that one should be concerned about them. Since the accuracy of this method is dependent on certain assumptions, distancing from those presumptions will decrease its accuracy. Usually these assumptions are based on the behavioral model of the target system. Selecting an inaccurate model may lead to an inaccurate detection system. Therefore, selecting an accurate model is the first step towards solving the problem. Unfortunately due to the complexity of the behavioral model within this system, finding such a model is a very difficult task. This paper will address the system modeling in the following section. Reader should also note that unknown interdependencies among the network features, makes it very difficult to find a good model for the system.

Some researchers find the Artificial Neural Network (ANN) approach more appealing (Zanero and Savaresi, 2004; Kayacik et al., 2003; Lei and Ghorbani, 2004).

These researchers had to overcome the curse of dimensionality for the complex systems problem. One of the proposed methods is the Kohonen's Self Organizing features Map (SOM). Hu reports an improvement to the SOM approach that was originally used by Kayacik et al. (Kayacik et al., 2003), where the Support Vector Machine (SVM) method has been implemented to improve SOM (Hu and Heywood, 2003). Using SOM will significantly improve the sensitivity of the model to the population of the input features. Zanero et al., use the SOM to compress payload of every packet into one byte (Zanero and Savaresi, 2004).

The main goal of using the ANN approach is to provide an unsupervised classification method to overcome the curse of dimensionality for a large number of input features. Since the system is complex and input features are numerous, clustering the events can be a very time consuming task. Using the Principal Component Analysis (PCA) or Singular Value Decomposition (SVD) methods can be an alternative solution (Analoui et al., 2005). However, if not used properly, both of these methods can become computationally expensive algorithms. At the same time, reducing the number of features will lead to a less accurate model and consequently it will reduce the detection accuracy.

In the computer networks intrusion detection problem area, the size of the feature space is obviously very large. Once the dimensions of the feature space are multiplied by the number of samples in the feature space, the result will surely present a very large number. This is why some researchers either select a small sampling time window, reduce the dimensionality of the feature space or both. Since the processing time is an important factor in timely detection of the intrusion, efficiency of the deployed algorithms is very important. Time constraint may sometimes force us to have the less important features pruned (dimensionality reduction). However, the pruning approach is not always possible. Implementing data mining methodology, some researchers have proposed new data reduction approaches. Data compression can be considered to be an alternative approach to solve the high dimensionality problem. Generation of association rules as it was proposed by Lee et al. is an alternative to reduce the size of the input data (Rule-based approach) (Lee et al., 1998, 2000).

Size and dimensionality of the feature space are two major problems in IDS development. At the same time, methods such as Bayesian and HMM that use statistical or probability calculations can be time consuming. Dimensionality reduction and data compression methods are two major methods that can help us with the problem of computation time. A PCA-based dimensionality reduction approach is proposed and explained in the following sections.

It should be noted that sometimes features that are labeled as important using quantitative analysis, may not necessarily prove to be as effective as it was originally expected. Therefore, it is required to analyze them with respect to their role in the intrusion process as well. Nevertheless, simply knowing the importance of the features without any further qualitative analysis will still provide valuable information about the dataset that is being studied.

FEATURE EVALUATION AND DIMENSION REDUCTION

In the reported work, the Principal Component Analysis (PCA) approach is selected as the tool for the dimensionality reduction. PCA is a strong dimensionality reduction tool that is based on the variance of the components. In this approach, intension is to find a linear transfer function such that the n dimensional y data is transferred into a z in a new dimension (Equation 1).

$$z = A^T y \tag{1}$$

Whose variance is $A^T \Sigma A$, where A^T is the transpose of A and Σ is the covariance matrix. Let A to be with $n \times n$ dimensions, at the most, then z can be in A's n dimensional space. This means that each column of the eigenvector matrix A will map the given vector of data onto a new axis in a new space such that the new axes are all orthogonal on each other and are uncorrelated. Here the covariance matrix Σ or even sometimes correlation matrix R are used to calculate the eigenvector matrix A. The eigenvector matrix is also referred to as the weights matrix or the loading matrix.

Let $A = (a_1, a_2 \cdots a_n)$ be a $n \times n$ matrix (eigenvector matrix) and assume y to be a column vector, intension is to maximize the $A_T SA$ and consequently to calculate a restricted A (Rencher, 2002). Achieving this goal, one can write equations 2 and 3:

$$\lambda = \frac{a^T S a}{a^T a} \tag{2}$$

$$(S - \lambda I) a = 0 \tag{3}$$

Where λ is a number that represents an eigenvalue or characteristics value, S is the sample covariance matrix and a is called an eigenvector or characteristics vector. A is an orthogonal matrix (Rencher, 2002). For each eigenvalue there is a corresponding eigenvector. Characteristic equation is derived from the Equation 3. Equation 4 presents the characteristic equation.

$$\det (S - \lambda I) = 0 \tag{4}$$

The resulted new dimensions are all orthogonal on one another and are uncorrelated. This feature of the resulted feature space is a source of improvement in the detection process. In the current approach, values of the cells from the eigenvector (weights) matrix are considered to be the information value of their corresponding principal component associated with that column in the matrix. This text will use the term weights for calling the eigenvector's cell values. This approach seems logical as well, because the larger this value is the larger will be its effect on the outcome of the process. In the proposed approach, no dimensions are discarded and therefore lose of information is minimized.

It should be reminded that data should be first normalized (white data). In a book by Hyvarinen et al. it is explained that once the value for the mean is calculated to be zero, covariance and correlation matrices will become the same (Hyvarinen et al., 2001). Here it will be worth noting that this feature is a source of problem in the calculations for the clustering. This subject will be further discussed in the conclusion section. It is obvious that the accuracy of this approach will be dependent on the stability of the mean and variance of the input variables in the training dataset. The book describes the whiteness property of a random dataset by saying that random vectors having zero mean and unit variance (or constant variance for all the rows) are said to be white (Hyvarinen et al., 2001). Considering the mean vector equal to zero, will make the covariance matrix the same as the correlation matrix. The whiteness property implies that both the covariance and correlation matrices are going to be a unity matrix. This also indicates that a preprocess is required to calculate the mean and the variance of the variables in the training dataset. However, the sensitivity of the process is manageable as it will be explained in the conclusion section.

Figure 1 depicts a result of calculation for the weights matrix 40×40. It is a common knowledge that DARPA'99 dataset has 41 features. A subset of 311029 records each with 42 features where selected. The last feature in DARPA'99 dataset is actually the attack category and, therefore, is not among the input features to the system (it is the outcome). Consequently, 41 input features remain to be processed. A preprocessor can process the dataset looking for the redundancy in the records and can then eliminate the redundant records if any exists. At the same time, system will check to see if there exists a feature whose value is not changing. If such a feature was detected then that feature is worthless and should be deleted.

Analyzing these features, it was noticed that feature number 20 has a constant value. Name of this feature is "num outbound cmds". After reporting the situation, system eliminated the component and finally 40 features are left for the PCA to be applied on. Therefore, the weights matrix is a 40×40 matrix. A sample calculated weights matrix is depicted in Figure 1 (top left corner). Later on, for a better understanding of the information value of the components, their values were sorted and normalized. Figure 1 depicts the result of the process. Figure 1 is merely used for

Figure 1. Original and processed weights matrix for a subset of DARPA'99 dataset

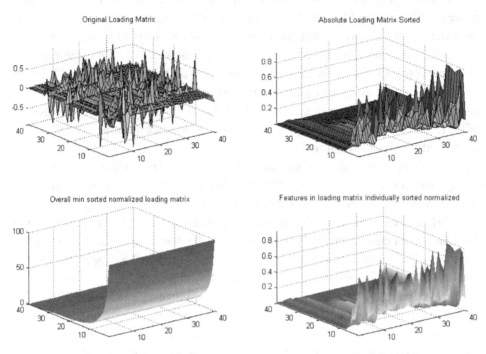

the visualization purposes. This result can be compared with the information reported in Table 1.

In order to understand the information presented in Table 1, reader must understand the way information value column is calculated. The idea is to show the influence of the weight factor on the new variable that is created in the target space with reduced number of dimensions. To do so, since weights can be both positive and negative it was decided to just use their absolute values. This is because regardless of their sign, their absolute value indicates how effective they are. Their sign will only show the direction of their effects.

Considering the last paragraph, values in the information value column in Table 1 are calculated in the following way: First their absolute values are calculated. Then each column of the resulted matrix is sorted. To help with the visualization, at the final stage, sorted columns are normalized (scaled) to the [0 100] boundary. It should be noted that Table 1 only presents the first column of the weights matrix after being processed in the aforementioned way. Complete DARPA'99 dataset is used for calculating the Table 1.

Also it should be noted that in the current presentation, the absolute value of the weights are important. Regardless of the different presentations, only the original weights matrix will be used for the dimensionality reduction.

Table 1. The result reported for a subset of DARPA '99 dataset, using values (absolute values are sorted and normalized) in the first column of the weights matrix (PC1).

Order	Component column	Component label	Information Value
1	5	src_bytes	100
2	31	srv_diff_host_rate	58.863164
3	23	num_outbound_cmds3	40.216154
4	6	dst_bytes	30.642976
5	3	service	24.32323
6	22	num_outbound_cmds2	20.199406
7	32	dst_host_count	15.943834
8	4	flag	12.369222
9	2	protocol_type	10.250081
10	1	duration	8.692573
11	40	dst_host_rerror_rate	7.718143
12	26	num_outbound_cmds6	6.702952
13	27	rerror_rate	5.849946
14	39	dst_host_srv_serror_rate	5.123684
15	24	num_outbound_cmds4	4.597225
16	25	num_outbound_cmds5	4.173682
17	38	dst_host_serror_rate	3.935441
18	37	dst_host_srv_diff_host_rate	3.728027
19	12	logged_in	3.585549
20	29	same_srv_rate	3.440618
21	34	dst_host_same_srv_rate	3.301319
22	28	srv_rerror_rate	3.064928
23	30	diff_srv_rate	2.882241
24	11	num_failed_logins	2.814118
25	10	hot	2.670513
26	21	num_outbound_cmds1	2.479703
27	36	dst_host_same_src_port_rate	2.317742
28	8	wrong_fragment	2.09239
29	7	land	1.826742
30	19	num_access_files	1.521224
31	13	num_compromised	1.261154
32	16	num_root	0.847263
33	17	num_file_creations	0.514439
34	20	num_outbound_cmds	0.446425
35	14	root_shell	0.367598
36	18	num_shells	0.279533
37	9	urgent_13	0.255997
38	15	su_attempted	0.194672
39	33	dst_host_srv_count	0.104623
40	35	dst_host_diff_srv_rate	0

Weights of the features presented in the weights matrix are merely a measure of their importance with respect to their variances. These values are by no means a sign of their analytical importance or effectiveness. Weights only show the importance of the features from the data analysis point of view.

There are many techniques for handling the n dimensional random vectors as several of them are explained in a book by Hyvarinen et al. (Hyvarinen et al., 2001). However, two closer ones to our approach is to either use all the variables as one random vector or to divide them into two different random vectors. It was decided to use a single random vector in this work.

Considering the weights presented in the weights matrix, three strategies are applicable for the dimension reduction using these values. Please note that in any case dimension reduction will lead to loss of accuracy, however, the magnitude of this loss will depend on choice of the approach. Three considered approaches are explained in below:

1. Eliminating the less important features, only use those that are at the top of the sorted list. This approach will cause a major loss of information and consequently it is expected to reduce the accuracy significantly. A benefit for this approach is the increased processing speed, considering the cost of lower accuracy is acceptable. In the current work this approach was not selected.

2. As a second approach, although some of the less important features can be eliminated this number is not equal to the maximum number of the end dimensions (variables). The dimensionality of the outcome is a number less than the number of original dimensions. Here a numerical constraint can be applied, so that, for example only features that hold more than 80 or 90 percent of the total information are used for the dimensionality reduction and the rest are eliminated. In comparison with the previous approach, this approach will provide a better accuracy but will be slower in processing time. Dimension reduction will need to process more features in this approach.

3. The final approach is to use all the features and let the weights extracted from the weights matrix decide how much each feature can be effective on the output variables. This approach will make the most out of the available information and the highest accuracy is expected from it. However, it will require more processing power than all the previous ones and will be slower in execution. This approach is implemented in the reported work.

In the reported work, the dimension reduction operation is explained in Equation 5.

for $i = 1 : ND$

$\quad ReducedDataSet =$

$\quad \left[\mathrm{Re}\, ducedDataSet, DataSet^{T}(:,:) * WeightsMatrix(:,i) \right];$ (5)

end

Where the ReducedDataSet is made of transposed DataSet (columns/features transposed) multiplied by the appropriate columns from the WeightsMatrix. At the end of the loop, ReducedDataSet matrix contains the reduced version of the DataSet matrix. ND stands for Number of Dimensions and it is smaller than or equal to the number of columns in DataSet matrix.

Questions such as: which approach is better and which clustering algorithm with how many number of dimensions will have a better performance, will easily occupy mind of any researcher that works in this area. Authors of this paper were inspired by these questions. Feeding the clustering methods with data that is produced by the dimensionality reduction process, it was decided to setup a framework to test the performance of these methods. Clustering methods based on the following techniques are currently implemented in the reported framework: K-means, Self-Organizing Map (SOM), Competitive Learning Network (CLN) and Improved Competitive Learning Network (ICLN). Proposed by Lei and Ghorbani, ICLN is an extension on the CLN method (Lei and Ghorbani, 2004).

A comparison between different clustering techniques is reported in the following section. In this report, performance of these clustering techniques are studied and compared. To do so, clustering engines are fed with the same data and with different dimensionality reduction rates.

Feature Analysis for the DARPA'99 Dataset

Although it is not the main intension of this paper to relate the calculated importance of the features to their real world value, a short discussion around this subject seems to be necessary. Table 1 clearly shows that most of the information in the system is embedded in the top 25% of the features. The last 25% of the features in the list present no significance for consideration.

It might be the case that these features might be a clue for some rare conditions, but this has to be studied using real attack scenarios. At the same time, frequency of these attacks and the significance of these features in comparison to other features that constitute signs of those attacks should be studied. To do the analysis, information extracted from a reported work by Salvatore J. Stolfo et al. and presented in the "http://kdd.ics.uci.edu/databases/kddcup99/" website is used. Before considering features individually, it is interesting to note that the first four top ranking features in Table 1 are of the continuous type. This shows the significance of this type of data in the detection process. Only 3 features out of ten top features are of the discrete type, i.e. "protocol_type", "service" and "flag". Considering these features from another angle, basic features category holds most of the significant features. This is an indication for the importance of the basic features.

To start with, at the top of the list in Table 1, the "src_bytes" feature is noted as the most valuable feature in the DARPA99 dataset. The definition provided by the aforementioned site for this feature says that this feature presents number of data bytes that is transferred from source to destination. Considering this feature together with another high ranking feature in Table 1, i.e. "dst_bytes", proves the importance of the traffic volume in the detection process. It is also an indication of the importance of direction of the traffic (incoming versus outgoing traffic). It is interesting to see the difference in the information value between the first and the second top features in the list and compare it with other items in Table 1. Difference between values for the first and the second feature in comparison to the rest of the features is significant.

"srv_diff_host_rate" that is defined to be in the group of traffic features, is another high ranking feature in Table 1. This feature indicates the number of connections to different hosts. This traffic measure can be an indication of a port scan. For a better analysis, it is necessary to study several attack scenarios. This work is left for future work. Similarly, "dst_host_count" (is defined under the name "count" and belongs to the traffic features category) is the number of connections to the same host as the current connection in the past two seconds; is yet another traffic related feature.

"Service" feature is another significant feature that is among the high ranking features presented in Table1. This is a logical conclusion that the type of the service used for the connection is an important factor in detecting an intrusion. Even some attacks are specifically service oriented. Number of outbound commands in an ftp session is another important features highlighted in this ranking. Two features: "num_outbound_cmds3" and "num_outbound_cmds2" respectively with the value of 40.21 and 20.20 show the significance of these types of features in the intrusion detection.

Two discrete features named in Table 1 are "flag" and "protocol_type'. These features are respectively an indication of normal or error status of the connection and type of protocol, e.g. TCP, that is used for the connection. These features can indicate attacks that are either protocol oriented or those that try to crash the system by sending faulty packets.

Finally, "duration" feature is an indication of the duration of the connection in seconds. Value of this feature is important in detecting irregularities in the connection time. Longer than usual connection time for a system can be due to a DoS attack. Nevertheless, this paper is not dedicated to studying these types of relations between features and attacks. This a different research work, that has to be followed.

EFFECTS OF DIMENSION REDUCTION ON SOME CLUSTERING TECHNIQUES

In this section, effects of dimensionality reduction on four different clustering techniques are studied. In this study, the quality of clustering is compared versus the speed and the number of dimensions for the data fed into the system. In this way, it will be possible to understand and analyze effects of the dimension reduction on quality and speed of different clustering techniques.

Features used as a measure for the quality in the experiments are False Positive (FP), Detection Rate (DR), Execution Time (ET) and Number of Dimensions (ND). The comparison is made between the first three features versus the ND where all three graphs are plotted in a single diagram. Plotting them on a single diagram makes it possible to see effects of the change in ND feature on other features and to compare them. ND feature is associated with the horizontal axis and the rest of the features are associated with the vertical axis.

Due to the fact that applying these techniques will produce different results for each execution cycle, it was decided to run the test scenario several times and then calculate an average value. Consequently, it is required to have the calculations within an iteration loop where the resultant values are added together and once out of loop, an average is calculated. ET is the averaged execution time.

Initially, following this approach and during the execution of the experiments, there were some instances showing anomalous results that in turn could affect the total overall average for the results. This anomaly in the result will appear as a larger than usual FP or DR values. It was obvious that this effect was due to the poor training. Some instances of the trained clustering system do not provide an optimum result and therefore they will affect the overall quality of the result.

In order to improve the outcome, it was decided to set a threshold value and to discard inappropriate training results. The threshold values are selected manually dependent on the results out of the majority of the training instances. Once the training result is detected to be larger than these threshold values, system will ignore that training instance and will repeat it. In this way, system will somehow produce an enhanced result. It should be kept in mind that poor training results are not good options anyway, and it would be a better choice to ignore them and look for a better result.

Finally, it seems necessary to explain that once the dimensionality of data is reduced (by means of the proposed approach) all the original feature set is moved into a new feature space where number of features is smaller. Having this new feature space in mind, one should note new intrinsic properties of the new features in this space. Due to the effects of the PCA method, each new feature is a combination of all of the original features and is normal to all the other features in the new features space (orthonormal/orthogonal property). This property of the new generation of the features will provide us with a valuable opportunity to use it in statistical and probability based calculations. Applying these two approaches guarantee that features are completely separated and independent from one another.

It should be also noted that the reported FP and DR values are variable. This means that each clustering/labeling attempt will produce new FP and DR values. The reported numbers are sampled averaged values in series of experiments.

Enhanced Solution

In this approach, any outcome will not be acceptable training result for the clustering method. There is a threshold assigned to the FP to omit those results with FP larger than the threshold value. Applying the threshold value will help us to prevent anomalies that affect our judgment on the overall performance of the system. Updating the code with respect to the aforementioned thresholds, experiments were repeated. There can be different thresholds for different clustering techniques and even there can be some clustering algorithms with no thresholds assigned to them. Threshold values are selected with respect to the past experiments and they are based on the judgment of the people who perform the experiment.

In the new experiments, only those results with FP values not larger than FP-threshold will be counted for and the rest will be ignored. In other words, if value of the FP for a result is greater than FP-threshold, then that result will be ignored and the trial counter will not increase. This approach will guarantee that the FP values will not appear to be significantly larger than their value in previous trials.

In this approach, there is a drawback regarding the processing time. This is because the processing time is variable and it depends on the way that large FP values are generated during the experiments. If no large values are generated, then experiment will be completed in the shortest period of time. However, if some trials produce FP with large values, then the execution time will be dependent on the number of instances that generate large FP values.

Considering the overall execution time will make it impossible to analyze and compare the FP, DR and ET features versus the ND feature. Goal is to find a solution for this problem and to calculate the time in such a way that it makes sense.

Table 2. The data resulted from the K means clustering method

ND	FP	DR	ET(Sec)	ET(Hours)
9	0.0078	0.9	11	0.00306
18	0.0028	0.95	13.645	0.00379
27	0.0028	0.95	19.206	0.00534
36	0.0071	0.95	24.366	0.0067
40	0.003	0.96	16.579	0.00461

Table 3. The data resulted from the CLN clustering method

ND	FP	DR	ET(Sec)	ET(Hours)
9	0.0043	0.66	1486.3	0.41286
18	0.0048	0.83	1531.5	0.42542
27	0.0037	0.84	1617.1	0.44919
36	0.006	0.87	1668.4	0.46344
40	0.005	0.84	1680.6	0.46683

Therefore, it was decided to only consider the execution time for the final trial on which FP is not greater than FP-threshold and therefore it can be used for the calculations. For all the implemented methods that need training, e.g. CLN, ICLN and SOM, the number of epochs for the training phase is selected to be 500 epochs.

EXPERIMENTAL RESULTS

The result of the aforementioned approach is presented in this section. As it was mentioned earlier in the text, there are 4 experiments carried out using 4 different clustering methods. Result of each experiment is presented using a table together with its corresponding diagram. Reader should note that during all of the work reported in this paper, the same subset of DARPA'99 dataset is used for all the experiments. This will make the results comparable versus one another.

Before starting with the experiments, it should be noted that goal of these experiments is to analyze and understand the influence and the effects of the ND parameter with respect to the accuracy and quality of the selected clustering methodology. Reader should keep in mind that all the values for the FP and DR are calculated after the labeling process. Thus, they present the worst case scenario. It should be also noted that these values indicate average values for the new feature values out of at

Figure 2. The plotted FP, DR and ET features versus ND using the K-means clustering method

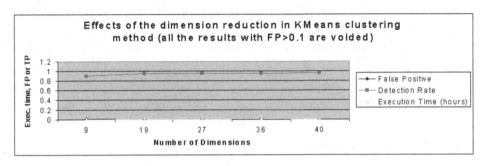

least 10 successful experiments. All the tables presented in the following present the data for at least 10 trials of running the selected clustering method.

To start with, K-means clustering technique is used to calculate average values of its associated features in 10 iterations. Table 2 presents the calculated averaged values for the selected features and Figure 2 depicts its corresponding diagram. As it is depicted in Figure 2, K-means clustering method is very fast and experiences only small variations with respect to its selected features. All together K-means displays small sensitivity to changes in ND. K-means is least dependent on the dimension reduction than the other clustering methods. However, its execution time is affected by the changes in the ND value. Generally speaking, with ND in the range of [18 ... 40] K-means shows a better performance on both FP and DR values than any other ND values with the exception of the ND=36 that shows a small rise in the FP parameter (Table 2).

CLN clustering method is the second studied clustering technique. Table 3 presents the averaged value for the selected features calculated after implementing the CLN clustering technique on a subset of DARPA'99 dataset. Figure 3 depicts

Figure 3. The plotted FP, DR and ET features versus ND using the CLN clustering method

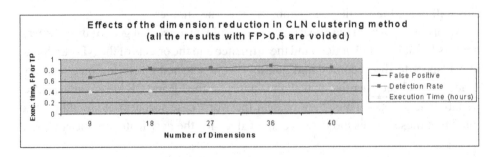

Figure 4. The plotted FP, DR and ET features versus ND using the ICLN clustering method

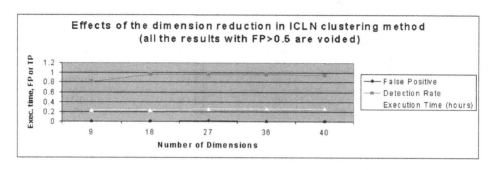

the diagram plotted using the data from Table 3. In Figure 3, as the ND increases, graph associated with DR ascents and then becomes nearly a straight line with only a minor variation at ND = 36. Surprisingly, graphs associated with FP and ET ascent. The graph is self explanatory and proves that the higher ND will not necessarily mean a better result. Anomalous behaviors are the sudden rise in DR at ND = 18 and a small variation on ND = 36. The DR parameter has a small variation once ND is higher than 18 dimensions (Figure3). On the other hand, there is a sudden rise in the FP value once the ND becomes larger than 27 dimensions (Table 3).

After presenting results from the CLN, naturally ICLN would be the next choice for the discussion. The calculated average values are presented in Table 4 and the resulted diagram is depicted in Figure 4. As it is illustrated in Figure 4, for the ICLN method, after the ND = 18 the overall trend for DR is very close to constant. However, between the ND = 9 and ND = 18, DR increases. As for the rest of the features, i.e. FP, the best value is 0.0045 at ND = 18. The variation in the values of FP, DR and the ET with respect to the ND suggests that one can be better off with a smaller number of dimensions while enjoying a better execution time and accuracy.

As the last clustering technique to analyze, the subset of the DARPA'99 dataset is fed into the SOM clustering technique. As a result of the SOM clustering with

Table 4. The data resulted from the ICLN clustering method

ND	FP	DR	ET(Sec)	ET(Hours)
9	0.0054	0.81	818.77	0.22744
18	00.045	0.96	851.75	0.2366
27	0.0058	0.96	898.37	0.24955
36	0.0053	0.96	963.24	0.26757
40	0.005	0.95	963.41	0.26761

Table 5. The data resulted from the SOM clustering method

ND	FP	DR	ET(Sec)	ET(Hours)
9	0.0058	0.88	1242.5	0.34513889
18	0.0039	0.93	1299.1	0.36086111
27	0.0036	0.94	1396.5	0.38791667
36	0.0029	0.94	1453.3	0.40369444
40	0.0029	0.94	1476.4	0.41011111

respect to different ND values, Table 5 denotes the calculated average values. Figure 5 depicts these values using three different graphs. Again other than the interval between the ND 9 and 18, value for the DR stays unchanged for different values of ND. However, FP constantly declines as the ND value increases. However, the decline in the FP value is very small.

Considering aforementioned examples, one can gain an understanding of how the value of ND together with the choice of the clustering algorithm affects the quality of the result. Generally, authors of this paper believe that a carefully planned dimension reduction can decrease the execution time of the process and at the same time keep the FP and DR factors close to their optimum values.

A sample execution of the CLN clustering with 500 epochs for training, ND=27, FP=0.0037 and DR=0.84 (both after labeling) is depicted in Figure 6.

As another sample, the same subset of the DARPA'99 dataset is used for clustering the attacks with ND = 36, using the K-means clustering method. The result is depicted in Figure 7 where FP = 0.0071 and DR = 0.95.

In both Figures 6 and 7, the first two images on the top row are the true representation of the training and the testing datasets. Normal operating conditions are presented with light color. Two images on the lower row represent the result of the

Figure 5. The plotted FP, DR and ET features versus ND using the SOM clustering method

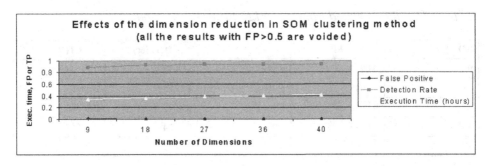

clustering technique after the binary labeling process. As a result of the binary labeling process, the output result of the system will be either normal or attack condition. Points in light color are an indication of the normal operation and those in dark color show the attack condition.

FUTURE WORK

In an attempt to increase the accuracy of anomaly detection, number of labels in Figure 6 was increased to 25 and the result is depicted in Figure 8. In this approach, some clusters have to be merged into one cluster so that their group can represent a certain type of attack.

As it is previously mentioned in this report, significance of the features with respect to their information value should be compared versus their importance with respect to different attack scenarios. This study will provide important information on how one can relate the information value of a feature to the appropriate attack scenarios. Although current results seem to be reasonable, studying features with respect to different attack scenarios will verify the results derived from the Table 1.

Figure 6. The reported result of the training using a sampled subset of DARPA'99 dataset (CLN clustering method). New feature 1 is plotted against new feature 2.

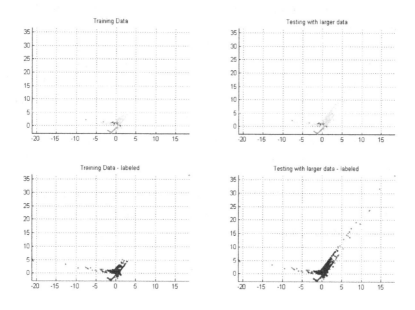

Figure 7. The second sampled training using the same subset of DARPA'99 dataset (K-means). New feature 1 is plotted against new feature 2.

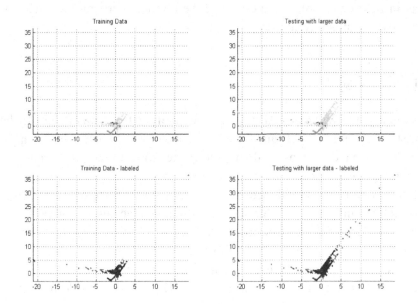

As an alternative for the normalization and as it was explained in previous section, normalization between 0 and 1 (scaling) can be an alternative. The approach can be easily adapted to the current setup of the system but it is left as a future work to be implemented and to study its effects.

The possibility of having some features not well presented in the training data but becoming active during the execution is an important issue related to the sampled data. For example, in the current work, feature 20 in the selected subset of DARPA'99 dataset can be a good example. It is absolutely vital to make sure that sampled dataset for the training holds all the requirements for a well selected training dataset that covers all the boundary values of the sampled feature space.

It should be noted that boundary and distribution of the attack samples in the training dataset play an important role in these experiments. In the aforementioned experiments, a raw dataset was used for the experiments. In future experiments, the training dataset will be carefully sampled and the boundary values for each feature will be included in the dataset.

Figure 8. The result of the training using a sampled subset of DARPA'99 dataset with 25 labels. New feature 1 is plotted against new feature 2

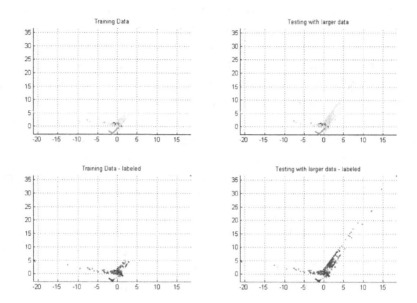

CONCLUSION

As for the enhanced solution, the following conclusions can be derived: Strange as it may sound, results of the experiments show that dependent on the clustering method used, somehow some ND values are exceptionally less favorable for the clustering methods than the others, e.g. ND=9. Experiments also show that despite our expectations, reducing the ND down to 18 will improve the ET value with minimum effect on the accuracy and the quality of the classification process. Generally speaking, ND has a negative effect on the ET. Considering DR and FP values versus ND, experiments show a complicated relation between them, dependent on the implemented algorithm. However, within the range of ND= [18 27] most of the experimented clustering techniques show a good performance.

One of the main objectives of this study was to understand the effects of the dimension reduction on the performance of different clustering techniques with respect to their quality measures. Intension was to see if it is possible to reduce the number of dimensions in order to improve the speed without significantly compromising the quality of the result. Even if the quality of the result is affected, knowing that how much is the cost will be of great help. The reported experiments provide us with answers to these questions. As a result of the experiments it can be derived that, a carefully selected ND will improve the ET while keeping the quality measures for the result, i.e. FP and DR, within an acceptable range.

It would be interesting to study this effect once some of the features are eliminated from the original dataset prior to the dimension reduction and to analyze the inaccuracy caused by ignoring these features.

Change in the mean and standard deviation of the feature space is one of the major sources of error in the detection system. This is because, before starting the dimension reduction process, input data is normalized to zero mean and standard deviation of one (white data). The normalization process is carried out for both the training and the test data. However, once the system start operating, it only has access to the training mean and standard deviation values.

Using values of the mean and standard deviation calculated during the training phase to normalize the test data will introduce inaccuracy to the detection process. In order to control and minimize effects of this problem, it is proposed to pay special attention to the collection of a suitable training data. It is very important to make sure that maximum and minimum values for every feature are included in the training dataset. Although there is no guarantee that this approach may have a big effect, considering the variable nature of the mean and standard deviation, this is the least that can be done. Although these two values can be considered to be constant, intension is to avoid having such assumptions that may lead to an inaccurate modeling of the network data.

ACKNOWLEDGMENT

This work was funded by the Atlantic Canada Opportunity Agency (ACOA) through the Atlantic Innovation Fund (AIF) to Dr. Ali A. Ghorbani.

REFERENCES

Analoui, M., Mirzaei, A., & Kabiri, P. (2005). Intrusion detection using multivariate analysis of variance algorithm. In *IEEE 3rd International Conference on Systems, Signals & Devices (SSD '05)* (vol. 3), Sousse, Tunisia.

Barbara, D., Couto, J., Jajodia, S., & Wu, N. (2001a). Special section on data mining for intrusion detection and threat analysis: Adam: A testbed for exploring the use of data mining in intrusion detection. In *Association for Computer Machinery Special Internet Group on Management of Data. SIGMOD Record, 30*(4), 15–24.

Barbara, D., Wu, N., & Jajodia, S. (2001b). Detecting novel network intrusions using bayes estimators. In *Proceedings of the 1ˢᵗ SIAM International Conference on Data Mining (SDM 2001),* Chicago, USA.

Bilodeau, M., & Brenner, D. (1999). *Theory of multivariate statistics.* New York, NY: Springer - Verlag, electronic edition at ebrary, Inc.

Botha, M., & von Solms, R. (2003). Utilising fuzzy logic and trend analysis for effective intrusion detection. *Journal of Computers & Security, 22*(5), 423–434. doi:10.1016/S0167-4048(03)00511-X

Bridges, S. M., & Rayford, M. V. (2000). Fuzzy data mining and genetic algorithms applied to intrusion detection. In *Proceedings of the 23ʳᵈ National Information Systems Security Conference.* Gathersburg, Maryland: National Institute of Standards and Technology.

Bulatovic, D., & Velasevic, D. (1999). *A distributed intrusion detection system based on Bayesian alarm networks* (. LNCS, 1740, 219–228.

Cho, S.-B. (2002). Incorporating soft computing techniques into a probabilistic intrusion detection system. *IEEE Transactions on Systems, Man and Cybernetics. Part C, Applications and Reviews, 32*(2), 154–160. doi:10.1109/TSMCC.2002.801356

Dickerson, J. E., & Dickerson, J. A. (2000). Fuzzy network profiling for intrusion detection. In *Proceedings of NAFIPS 19ᵗʰ International Conference of the North American Fuzzy Information Processing Society* (pp. 301–306), Atlanta, GA.

Gomez, J., & Dasgupta, D. (2001). Evolving fuzzy classifiers for intrusion detection. In *Proceedings of the 2002 IEEE Workshop on the Information Assurance,* West Point, NY.

Hu, P., & Heywood, M. I. (2003). Predicting intrusions with local linear model. In. *Proceedings of the IEEE International Joint Conference on Neural Networks, 3,* 1780–1785.

Hyvarinen, A., Krhunen, J., & Oja, E. (2001). *Independent component analysis.* Hoboken, NJ: Wiley Interscience, John Wiley & Sons Inc.doi:10.1002/0471221317

Kabiri, P., & Ghorbani, A. A. (2005). Research on intrusion detection and response: *A survey. International Journal of Network Security, 1*(2), 82–104.

Kayacik, H. G., Zincir-Heywood, A. N., & Heywood, M. I. (2003). On the capability of an SOM based intrusion detection system. In. *Proceedings of the IEEE International Joint Conference on Neural Networks, 3,* 1808–1813.

Lee, W., Stolfo, S. J., & Mok, K. W. (1998). Mining audit data to build intrusion detection models. In *Proceedings of the 4th International Conference on Knowledge Discovery and Data Mining (KDD '98),* New York, NY.

Lee, W., Stolfo, S. J., & Mok, K. W. (2000). Adaptive intrusion detection: A data mining approach. *Journal of Artificial Intelligence Research, 14*(6), 533–567. doi:10.1023/A:1006624031083

Lei, J. Z., & Ghorbani, A. (2004). Network intrusion detection using an improved competitive learning neural network. In *Proceedings of the IEEE 2nd Annual Conference on Communication Networks and Services Research (CNSR '04)* (pp.190–197). Washington, DC: IEEE-Computer Society.

Rencher, A. C. (2002). Methods of multivariate analysis (2nd ed.). *Wiley series in probability and mathematical statistics.* Hoboken, NJ: John Wiley & Sons Inc.

Yoshida, K. (2003). Entropy based intrusion detection. In *Proceedings of IEEE Pacific Rim Conference on Communications, Computers and signal Processing (PACRIM '03)* (vol. 2, pp. 840–843). IEEE Explore.

Zanero, S., & Savaresi, S. M. (2004). Unsupervised learning techniques for an intrusion detection system. In *Proceedings of the 2004 ACM symposium on Applied computing* (pp. 412–419). Nicosia, Cyprus: ACM Press.

Chapter 8

A Subspace-Based Analysis Method for Anomaly Detection in Large and High-Dimensional Network Connection Data Streams

Ji Zhang
University of Southern Queensland, Australia

ABSTRACT

A great deal of research attention has been paid to data mining on data streams in recent years. In this chapter, the authors carry out a case study of anomaly detection in large and high-dimensional network connection data streams using Stream Projected Outlier deTector (SPOT) that is proposed in (Zhang et al. 2009) to detect anomalies from data streams using subspace analysis. SPOT is deployed on the 1999 KDD CUP anomaly detection application. Innovative approaches for training data generation, anomaly classification, and false positive reduction are proposed in this chapter as well. Experimental results demonstrate that SPOT is effective and efficient in detecting anomalies from network data streams and outperforms existing anomaly detection methods.

DOI: 10.4018/978-1-60960-836-1.ch008

Copyright ©2012, IGI Global. Copying or distributing in print or electronic forms without written permission of IGI Global is prohibited.

INTRODUCTION

Great research efforts have been taken by researchers in recent years to study discovery of useful patterns from data streams. One important category of such data streams are the streams collected over the network. Analyzing these network data streams is quite critical in unveiling suspicious patterns that may indicate network intrusions. An intrusion into a computer network can compromise the stability and security of the network, leading to possible loss of privacy, information and revenue (Zhong et al. 2004). To safeguard network security, there are two major classes of approaches for detecting anomalies that may represent the manifestations of intrusions: misuse-based detection (or signature-based detection) and anomaly-based detection.

As far as data format representation is concerned, data streams collected in network environments can be typically, but not necessarily, modeled as continuously arriving high-dimensional connection oriented records. Each record contains a number of varied features to measure the quantitative behaviors of the network traffic. Such data representation is used in the 1999 KDD CUP anomaly detection application. In high-dimensional space, anomalies are embedded in some lower-dimensional subspaces (spaces consisting of a subset of attributes). These anomalies are termed projected anomalies in the high-dimensional space context. The underlying reason for this phenomenon is the Curse of Dimensionality. The increase in dimensionality will make data to be equally distant from each other. Consequently, the difference of data points' outlier-ness will become increasingly weak and thus undistinguishable. Only in moderate or low dimensional subspaces can significant outlier-ness of data be observed. This is the major motivation for detecting outliers in subspaces.

We can formulate the problem of detecting projected anomalies from high-dimensional data streams as follows: given a data stream D with ϕ-dimensional data points, each data point $pi = \{pi1, pi2,. . ., pi\phi\}$ in D will be labeled as either a projected anomaly if it is found abnormal in one or more subspaces. Otherwise, it will be flagged as a regular data. If pi is a projected anomaly, its associated outlying subspace(s) will be presented as well in the result.

Unfortunately, the existing outlier/anomaly detection techniques are mostly limited in identifying anomalies embedded in subspaces. Most are only capable of detecting anomalies in relatively low dimensional and static data sets (stored in databases without frequent changes) (Breuning et al., 2000; Knorr et al., 1998; Knorr et al., 1999; Ramaswamy et al, 2000; Tang et al., 2002). Recently, there are some emerging work in dealing with outlier detection either in high-dimensional data or data streams. However, there have not been any substantial research work so far for exploring the intersection of these two active research areas. For those methods in projected outlier detection in high-dimensional space (Aggarwal et al., 2001; Aggarwal et al., 2005; Boudjeloud et al., 2005; Zhu et al., 2005; Zhang et al., 2006; Guha et al., 2009), their measurements used for evaluating points' outlier-ness are not incrementally updatable and many of the methods involve multiple scans of data, making them incapable of handling fast data streams. The techniques for tackling outlier detection in data streams (Aggarwal, 2005; Palpanas et al, 2003;, Zhang et al., 2010) rely on full data space to detect outliers and thus the projected outliers cannot be discovered by these techniques.

To detect anomalies from high-dimensional data streams, a new technique, called Stream Projected Outlier deTector (SPOT), is proposed (Zhang et al, 2009). It utilizes a novel subspace analysis method to detect anomalies hidden in the sub-spaces of the full data space. In this paper, efforts are taken to carry out a real-life case study of SPOT to test its practical applicability. We apply in 1999 KDD CUP anomaly detection application. We have also tackled several important issues, including training data generation, anomaly categorization using outlying subspaces analysis and false positive reduction, for a successful deployment of SPOT in the case study. Experimental evaluates reveals that SPOT is efficient in this application for detecting anomalies.

Overview of SPOT

Before the case study is carried out, it is worthwhile presenting a short description of SPOT. SPOT performs anomaly detection into two stages: the learning and detection stages. SPOT can further support two types of learning, namely offline learning and online learning. In the offline learning, Sparse Subspace Template (SST) is constructed using either the unlabeled training data (e.g., some available historic data) and/or the labeled anomaly examples provided by domain experts. SST is a set of subspaces that feature higher data sparsity/outlier-ness than other subspaces. SST consists of three groups of subspaces, i.e., Fixed SST Subspaces (FS), Unsupervised SST Subspaces (US) and Supervised SST Subspaces (SS), where FS is a compulsory component of SST while US and SS are optional components. SST casts light on where projected anomalies are likely to be found in the high-dimensional space. SST is mainly constructed in an unsupervised manner where no labeled examples are required. However, it is possible to use the labeled anomaly exemplars to further improve SST. As such, SPOT is very flexible and is able to cater for different practical applications that may or may not have available labeled exemplars.

When SST is ready, SPOT enters the detection stage and starts to screen projected anomalies from constantly arriving data. The incoming data will be first used to update the data synopsis in each subspace of SST. This data will then be labeled as an anomaly if the values of the data synopsis are lower than some pre-specified thresholds. The detected anomalies are archived in the so-called Outlier Repository. Finally, all or only a specified number of the top anomalies in Outlier Repository will be returned to users when the detection stage is finished.

During the detection stage, SPOT can perform online training periodically. The online training involves updating SST with new sparse subspaces SPOT finds based on the current data characteristics and the newly detected anomalies. Online training improves SPOT's adaptability to dynamics of data streams. A system overview of SPOT is presented in Figure 1. Interested reader can refer to (Zhang et al. 2009) for more details on SPOT.

Case Study Description

The data streams in KDD-CUP'99 anomaly detection application contains a wide variety of intrusions simulated in a military network environment. Each instance in this data stream is a vector of extracted feature values from a connection record obtained from the raw network data gathered during the simulated intrusions. The TCP packets were assembled into connection records using the Bro program modified for use with MADAM/ID. Each connection was labeled as either normal or as

Figure 1. An overview of SPOT

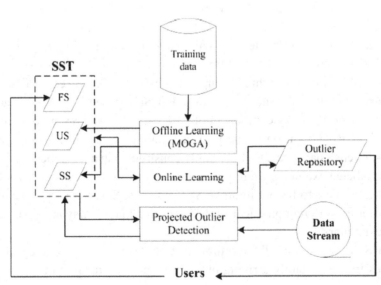

exactly one specific kind of attack. All labels are assumed to be correct. The attacks will be considered as anomalies in our study.

There are a total of four categories for the simulated attacks in this study: DoS: Denial of Service (e.g., a syn flood); R2L: unauthorized access from a remote machine (e.g., password guessing); U2R: unauthorized access to superuser or root functions (e.g., a buffer overflow attack); Probing: surveillance and other probing for vulnerabilities (e.g., port scanning). There are 42 features for this data stream. In addition, labeled training and test data sets are available in this application. They are the data collected in the first seven weeks of the DARPA experiments.

In this case study, identifying only anomalies from data streams is not sufficient. Given the inherently varying behaviors of different categories of anomalies, it is desirable that the anomalies we detect could be further categorized into one of known anomaly subtypes for a better understanding of their nature and characteristics. In this application, anomalous network connections may be manifestations of anomalies that can be divided into as many as 4 different classes. Different classes of attacks may distinguish themselves by anomalous connection behaviors exhibiting in different subspaces. Our task is to, by means of their different connection behaviors in outlying subspaces revealed by SPOT, classify anomalous connection records into one of the known attack classes (or the false-positive class).

Network Anomaly Detection using SPOT

When applying on KDD-CUP'99 anomaly Detection data stream, SPOT takes three major steps in its learning stage to detect anomalies, which are presented below:

- **Step 1:** SST is first generated. As a large number of labeled sample anomalies are available in this application, SST will contain SS besides FS and US. Supervised learning is performed to generate SS in SST. Since the sample anomalies have been assigned varied class labels, we can perform MOGA on all the sample anomalies belonging to the same class to produce the SS for that particular class, and the final SS in SST contains SS s for the four different classes. That is, $SST = FS \cup US \cup SS\,(OD)$, where OD is whole set of label anomaly samples in the data set. $SS\,(OD)$ is computed as $SS\,(OD) = \cup_{i=1}^{4} SS\,(OD_i)$, where OD_i is the set containing the anomaly samples that belong to the i_{th} attack class.
- **Step 2:** Once we have obtained SST, we need to generate PCS for each subspace in SST to detect anomalies from the data set. Because normal samples are available in the training data set, thus it is possible for us to use only the normal samples, rather than the whole training data, to construct PCS. This

ensures that PCS is constructed in a way to better reflect the normal behavior of data in the application.

- **Step 3:** All the sample anomalies in the training data will be evaluated in SST to find their outlying subspaces. Please note that, when we are evaluating each anomaly, we only retrieve, but do not update, the PCS of the cell it falls into. This is because the total number of anomaly samples is far larger than that of normal samples. Updating PCS using anomaly samples will therefore bias it towards anomalies, which will disable the ability of SPOT to accurately identify anomalies thereafter. When outlying subspaces of all anomaly samples are found, signature subspace lookup table will be built. Signature subspace lookup table records the outlying subspaces of anomalies that are used to categorize anomalies. We will discuss it later on in this subsection.

Training Data Generation

A major obstacle impeding the direct application of SPOT and other anomaly-based detectors is the high proportion of attack instances in this training data set; over 90% of the samples in this training data are attacks. Normal data behavior is needed in identifying anomalies from the data stream. As such, we need to construct new training data sets based on the original one to meet the distribution assumption that the number of normal connections is much larger than the number of attack connections.

In order to do this, all the normal instances are selected from the original training data set and uses sampling technique to sample the attack samples (Cui, 2002) (see Figure 2). In this way, a new training data satisfying the distribution assumption is obtained. In this new training data set, normal connections are dominating the whole data set with 98% of the samples being normal connections while the number of samples for the four attack classes combined amounts to 2%.

Nevertheless, since only a small number of attack instances are sampled, the new training data set may not be comprehensive enough for capturing sufficient

Figure 2. Generating single training data set for obtaining SS

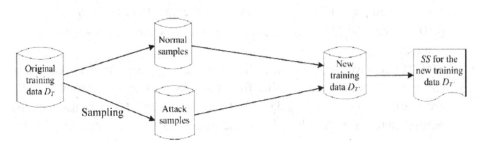

attack instances to generate accurate profiles for different attack classes. Another major limitation of the approach is that the training data set contains anomaly samples of different classes. Samples of one class may become noises for another class in the training. To minimize the effect of noises, it would be desired that the training data set contain only anomaly samples that belong to the same class. MOGA can be applied to cleaner training data sets to find outlying subspaces that are more relevant to different classes.

To curb the inherent drawbacks of the single training data set generation method, we adopt a strategy to generate multiple training data sets in order to meet the learning needs of SPOT, as presented in Figure 3. The basic idea of this strategy is that, for each anomaly class, multiple training data sets are generated and MOGA will be applied on each of them to produce for each class.

Mathematically, let D_T be the original training data set available. D_T consists of two parts, the normal and anomaly samples, denoted by D_N and D_I, respectively. D_T can be expressed as

$$D_T = D_N \cup D_I \tag{1}$$

where D_I consists of anomaly instances of up to four different classes, so we have

$$D_I = \cup_{i=1}^{4} D_I^i \tag{2}$$

Figure 3. Generating multiple training data sets for obtaining SS

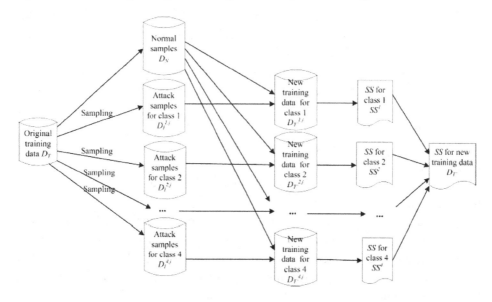

In our work, we generate multiple new training data sets with replacement from D_I^i for each class $i \in [1,4]$, each such training data set can be expressed as

$$D_{T'}^{i,j} = D_N \cup D_I^{i,j} \qquad (3)$$

where j is the number of data sets generated from D_I^i. The data distribution in each new training data set for different classes satisfies the requirement that the normal data dominate the whole training data set. By applying MOGA on $D_{T'}^{i,j}$, we can obtain SS for class i, denoted as SS^i, as

$$SS^i = \cup_j MOGA(D_{T'}^{i,j}) \qquad (4)$$

The complete SS is simply the union of SS^i for $i \in [1,4]$ as

$$SS = \cup i \, SS^i \qquad (5)$$

By including *FS* and *US*, the complete SST is finally constructed as

$$SST = FS \cup US \cup SS \qquad (6)$$

Redundant Outlying Subspace Removal

SPOT is able to find outlying subspaces for data in the stream. However, we may obtain a large number of resulting outlying subspaces even for a single data in the stream. Amongst these outlying subspaces, there are some dominating outlying subspaces that contribute to the outlier-ness of anomalies. Other outlying subspaces are considered as redundant ones. To facilitate the analysis of anomalies, we need to extract the dominating outlying subspaces for anomalies from their outlying subspaces detected by SPOT.

Definition 1. Dominating subspace: Let s and s' be two subspaces in the set of outlying subspaces of an anomaly o. If $s \subset s'$, then we call s a dominating subspace over s'. Here $s \subset s'$ (i.e., s is a proper subset of s') if for each dimension $d \in s$, we have $d \in s'$ and $\exists d \in s'$ that $d \notin s$.

In a space lattice where the low order subspaces are positioned in the bottom while the high order subspaces are put on the top, there exists a boundary between dominating outlying subspaces and non- dominating outlying subspace/non-outlying subspaces. In our work, we term this line as *Outlying Subspace Front*. Next, we present the definition of Outlying Subspace Front of an anomaly.

Definition 2. Outlying Subspace Front: Let OS(o) denote the set of outlying subspaces of an anomaly o. The Outlying Subspace Front of o is defined as the set of all its dominating subspaces in OS(o), *i.e.*, OSF (o) = {s, where s is a dominating subspace in OS(o)}

OSF has the following attributes:

- A subspace in OSF cannot dominate (or be dominated by) any other subspaces in OSF. They are all partial ordered subspaces;
- OSF is a subset of the corresponding OS and each subspace in OS will be dominated by one or a few subspaces in OSF;
- OSF is able to capture the subspaces that are truly contributing to the outlierness of anomalies. The existence of a large number of non-dominated (redundant) subspaces may adversely bias the weights of the underlying contributing subspaces in the classification analysis of anomalies.

Figure 4 presents an example of outlying subspaces of an anomaly and its corresponding Outlying Sub- space Front. The algorithm for finding OSF for an anomaly o is presented in Figure 5.

Anomaly Classification

Anomaly classification mainly involves categorizing detected anomalies into one of known anomaly classes or the class of false positive. We derive categorization functionality and incorporate it into SPOT for achieving this objective.

To achieve anomaly categorization, we generate signature subspaces for each anomaly class. The signature subspaces for a target class are those subspaces that can be used to identify anomalies for this particular class. To generate signature subspaces for a particular class, we collect the subspaces in OSF of those anomalies falling to this class and use them as the signature subspaces of this class. Mathematically speaking, the set of signature subspaces of class c is defined as

Figure 4. Example of outlying subspaces and its corresponding Outlying Subspace Front (OSF) for an anomaly

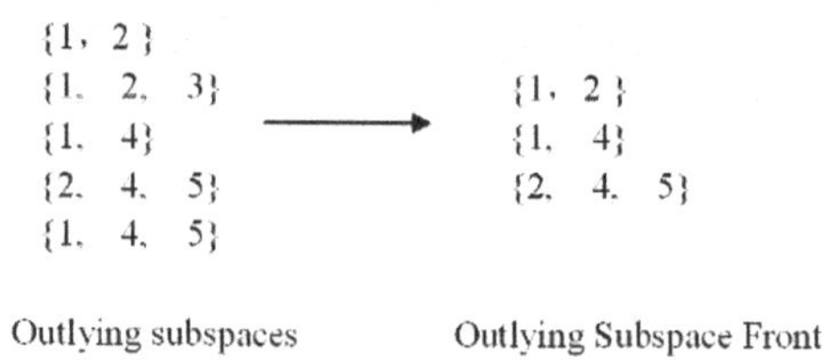

```
{1, 2 }
{1, 2, 3}                    {1, 2 }
{1, 4}        ------>        {1, 4}
{2, 4, 5}                    {2, 4, 5}
{1, 4, 5}

Outlying subspaces      Outlying Subspace Front
```

Figure 5. Algorithm for finding Outlying Subspace Front

Algorithm: Find_OSF

Input: $OS(o)$ (Outlying subspace set of o).
Output: $OSF(o)$ (Outlying Subspace Front of o).
1. $OSF(o) \leftarrow \emptyset$;
2. Sort subspaces in $OS(o)$ in an ascending order in terms of their dimensionalities;
3. FOR each existing subspace s in sorted $OS(o)$ DO {
4. $OSF(o) \leftarrow OSF(o) \cup s$;
5.   Delete s from $OS(o)$;
6.   FOR each existing subspace s' in sorted $OS(o)$ DO
7.   IF ($s \subseteq s'$) THEN delete s' from $OS(o)$;}

$$\text{Signature(c)} = \{s: \exists o \text{ belonging to c, } s \in \text{OSF (o)}\} \tag{7}$$

Within a class, different signature subspaces have varying weights to indicate their capability in correctly identifying anomalies for this class. The weighting scheme is necessary in the similarity measure used in the categorization process.

The weight of a signature subspace s with respect to a class represents the discriminating ability of s towards c. The higher the weight is, the stronger the discriminating power of this subspace is in identifying the instances of class c. Because OSF is by nature a bag of subspaces, we thus borrow the idea of tf-idf (*term frequency-inverse document frequency*) weighting method, a commonly used technique in the domain of information retrieval and text mining, to measure the weight of signature subspaces for each class. The tf-idf weight is a statistical measure used to evaluate how important a term is to a document in a collection or corpus. The importance increases proportionally to the number of times a term appears in the document but is offset by the frequency of the term in the whole corpus.

Term Frequency (TF)

The *term frequency* (tf) for a class is simply the number of times a given signature subspace appears in that class. This count is normalized to give a measure of importance for the signature subspace within the class. The normalization is performed to prevent a bias towards class with larger number of signature subspaces that may feature a higher term frequency regardless of the actual importance of those subspaces in the class. The tf for subspace s_i in class c_j is defined as

$$tf_{i,j} = \frac{N(s_i, c_j)}{N(c_j)} \tag{8}$$

where $N(s_i, c_j)$ denotes the number of occurrences of signature subspace s_i in class c_j and $N(c_j)$ is the number of occurrences of all signature subspaces in class c_j.

Inverse Document Frequency (IDF)

The *inverse document frequency* (idf) is a measure of the general importance of the term. The idf for signature subspace s_i in class c_j is defined as the inverse of percentage of the classes that contained s_i. Normally, the logarithmic form of this ratio is used for scaling purpose, *i.e.*,

$$idf_{i,j} = log \frac{|C|}{|\{c_j, \ where \ s_i \in c_j\}|} \tag{9}$$

where $|C|$ corresponds to the total number of classes and $|\{c_j, where \ s_i \in c_j\}|$ is the number of classes that contain s_i.

Finally, the tf-idf weight of signature subspace si with regard to class cj is the product of tfi,j and id fi,j, *i.e.*,

$$w_{s_i, c_j} = tfidf_{i,j} = tf_{i,j} \times idf_{i,j} \tag{10}$$

Similarity Measure

Similarity measure needs to be properly defined before the anomalies can be classified. The similarity between an anomaly o and class c is defined as their average inner product, which is the normalized sum of weight products of the outlying subspaces of o and the signature subspaces of class c, *i.e.*,

$$Sim(o, c) = \frac{o \cdot c}{|OSF(o)|} \tag{11}$$

where $|OS(o)|$ denotes the number of outlying subspaces of o. Let $w_{o,s}$ be the binary vector of o and $w_{c,s}$ be the weight vector of class c. Normally, we assign $w_{o,s} = 0$ if subspace s does not appear in OS(o), so the above similarity measurement can be written as

$$Sim(o, c) = \frac{\sum_{s \in Q} w_{s,o} \cdot w_{s,c}}{|OSF(o)|} \tag{12}$$

Signature Subspace Lookup Table

In order to compute the similarity between anomalies and classes efficiently, we need to have a mechanism to realize fast retrieval of tf-idf information for a give signature subspace. To this end, we construct a signature subspace lookup table to store all the signature subspaces, occurring in different classes, for efficient retrieval. Also, to render it suitable for handling data stream, we incorporate time stamp information to implement time model in this table. We term this table the *time-decayed signature subspace lookup table*, which is defined as follows.

Definition 3. Time-decayed signature subspace lookup table. Given the set of classes C and the signature subspaces for all the classes in C, the time-decayed signature subspace lookup table is a $(|S|+1) \times |C|)$ table, where $|S|$ and $|C|$ are the total number of signature subspaces and classes, respectively. C consists of the attack and false-positive classes. The entry of $a_{i,j}, 1 \leq i \leq |s|, 1 \leq j \leq |C|$ is a pair of $< N(s_i, c_j), T(s_i, c_j) >$, corresponding respectively to the count of s_i in c_j and the time stamp when this entry was last updated. The entry of $a_{|s|+1,j}, 1 \leq j \leq |C|$ is also a pair in the format of $<N(c_j), T(c_j)>$, recording the total number of signature subspaces in c_j and the time stamp when this entry was last updated.

An example of the time-decayed signature subspace lookup table is given in Table 1. It is worthwhile noting that, in time-decayed signature subspace lookup table, $T(s_i, c_j)$ needs to be updated every time when an anomaly that has outlying subspace s_i is classified into class c_j, and $T(c_j)$ needs to be updated when an anomaly is classified into c_j, regardless of its outlying subspaces.

Based upon the signature subspace lookup table, it will be very efficient to compute td-idf of each signature subspace. First, $tf_{i,j}$ can be computed as follows.

$$tf_{i,j} = \frac{weight(T', T(s_i, c_j)) \cdot N(s_i, c_j)}{weight(T', T(c_j)) \cdot N(c_j)} \tag{13}$$

Table 1. The time-decayed signature subspace lookup table

	c_1	c_2	...	c_m
s_1	$N(s_1,c_1),T(s_1,c_1)$	$N(s_1,c_2),T(s_1,c_2)$	...	$N(s_1,c_m),T(s_1,c_m)$
s_2	$N(s_2,c_1),T(s_2,c_1)$	$N(s_2,c_2),T(s_2,c_2)$	...	$N(s_2,c_m),T(s_2,c_m)$
...	...	...	...	...
s_n	$N(s_n,c_1),T(s_n,c_1)$	$N(s_n,c_2),T(s_n,c_2)$	...	$N(s_n, c_m),T(s_n,c_m)$

where T' is the time stamp when the data that has outlying subspace s_i is processed. The information of $N(s_i, c_j)$ and $N(c_j)$ can be directly retrieved for computation from the signature subspace lookup table. The weight coefficients are defined as

$$weight(T', T(s_i, c_j)) = e^{-\frac{\alpha(T' - T(s_i, c_j))}{\Delta t}} \tag{14}$$

$$weight(T', T(c_j)) = e^{-\frac{\alpha(T' - T(c_j))}{\Delta t}} \tag{15}$$

$idf_{i,j}$ can be computed as

$$idf_{i,j} = log \frac{|C|}{|c, \text{ where } s_i \in c \text{ at } T'|} \tag{16}$$

where $|c, \text{ where } s \in c \text{ at } T'|$ denotes the number of classes that contain s at time T'. This only involves counting from the lookup table the classes that contains s_i.

The time-decayed signature subspace lookup table is constructed in the training stage of SPOT using the labeled training data. To do so, we need to register signature subspaces of different classes into this lookup table. Specifically, for each anomaly o found in the labeled training data with its Outlying Subspace Front $OSF(o)$, class label c and time stamp T', we need to register all the subspaces of $OSF(o)$ into the lookup table. This mainly involves initializing and/or updating the counts and time stamps for classes and signature subspaces in the lookup table. Varying updating schemes are used in the following two cases

If $s_i \in OSF(o)$ has already existed in the signature subspace lookup table, then we update class count $N(c)$ and time stamp $T(c)$ of class c as

$$N(c) = weight(T', T(c)) \cdot N(c) + 1 \tag{17}$$

$$T(c) = T' \tag{18}$$

and update subspace count $N(s,c)$ and time stamp $T(s,c)$ as

$$N(s, c) = weight(T', T(s, c)) \cdot N(s, c) + 1 \tag{19}$$

$$T(s, c) = T' \tag{20}$$

If $s \in OSF(o)$ does not exist in the signature subspace lookup table, then we will update class count $N(c)$ and time stamp $T(c)$ of class c as

$$N(c) = weight(T', T(c)) \cdot N(c) + 1 \tag{21}$$

$$T(c) = T' \tag{22}$$

and initialize subspace count $N(s,c)$ and time stamp $T(s,c)$ as

$$N(s,c) = 1 \tag{23}$$

$$T(s,c) = T' \tag{24}$$

For each class $c' \neq c$, we perform the following initialization:

$$N(s,c') = 0 \tag{25}$$

$$T(s,c') = \text{Null (null time stamp)} \tag{26}$$

When constructed, the signature subspace lookup table can be used to classify anomalies in the data stream. Each anomaly is classified into one or more possible attack classes or the false-positive class based on the class membership probabilities of the anomaly. The class membership probability of an anomaly o with respect to class $c_i \in C$ is computed as

$$pr(o, c_i) = \frac{sim(o, c_i)}{\sum_i sim(o, c_i)} \times 100\%, \text{ where } c_i \in C \tag{27}$$

The higher the probability for a class is, the high chance that the anomaly falls into this class.

An anomaly o can be classified into a class c_i if $pr(o, c_i) \geq \tau$, where τ is the similarity threshold. As s result, under a given τ, it is possible that an anomaly o is classified into a few, instead of one, classes if their similarities are high enough. The set of classes that o may fall into, denoted as $class(o)$, is defined as

$$class(o) = \{c_i, \text{ where } pr(o, c_i) \geq \tau, c_i \in C\} \tag{28}$$

For each anomaly, we can further sort its membership classes based on the respective membership probabilities in a descending order. This facilitates users to pick up the top k ($k \in [1,|C|]$) most likely attack class(es) of the anomaly for further investigation.

After the classification of o is finished, we need to update the counts and time stamps for classes and signature subspaces in the lookup table. Such updates reflect the concept drift as the lookup table is updated accordingly in response to the data dynamics by adjusting the weights of signature subspace in the lookup table. A promising characteristic of signature subspace lookup table is that it can be updated incrementally, enabling the update of lookup table to be performed very efficiently in the detection process. For each detected anomaly, the steps of class membership probability computation, class classification and signature subspace lookup table updating are performed in an on-the-fly manner.

Handle False Positives

False positives, also called false alarms, are those anomalies that are erroneously detected as the attacks by the system. Even though they are benign in nature and not harmful as compared to real attacks, false positives consume a fair amount of human effort spent on investigating them whatsoever and thus making it almost impossible for security officers to really concentrate only on the real attacks. Generally, among all the anomalies detected, up to 90% of them may be false positives. It is much desirable to quickly screen out these false positives in order to allow closer attention to be paid towards the real harmful attacks.

The situation we are facing in the KDD-CUP'99 anomaly detection application is that there are no avail- able false-positive exemplars in the training data set. Therefore, unlike the attack classes, it is not easy to directly create the signature subspaces for the false-positive class. However, there are a fair amount of normal samples in the training data set. If any of them are found abnormal, *i.e.*, they have some outlying subspaces, then they will be considered as false positives. These false positives from the training data provide the basis for constructing the signature subspace for the false-positive class. Consequently, like other attack classes, the construction of signature subspaces of false-positive class can be started as early as in the learning stage of SPOT.

The set of signature subspaces of the false-positive class starts from an empty set. In the learning stage of SPOT, a normal data in the training data set will be considered as a false positive if it is found abnormal in some subspaces. Formally, a data point p is a false positive if we have

$$OS(p) = \varnothing \text{ and } label(p) = normal \tag{29}$$

The moment a data point p is identified as a false positive, the subspaces in its OSF will be properly registered into the current signature subspace lookup table. Ideally, the similarity between false positives and the false-positive class should be significantly higher than their similarities to other attack classes. However, this may not be true in the early stage due to the immatureness of the signature subspaces of the false-positive class. As an increasing number of false positives are continuously registered, the signature subspaces of the false-positive class will keep on growing. As a result, we will witness an continuously improved classification accuracy of false positives. We keep trace of the goodness of the signature subspaces we have constructed thus far at any time of the learning process. As a rule of thumb, the growing stage could be continued until the moment when satisfactory detection accuracy, say 90%, is achieved for false-positive class.

If the training data fail to establish a signature subspace lookup table for achieving a satisfactory classification accuracy, the construction of signature subspaces for the false-positive class will be continued to the detection stage of SPOT. Since the examination of false positives by domain experts during the detection stage is rather time-consuming, if it is not completely impossible, we thus employ an alternative automatic approximation method to expand the set of signature subspaces for the false-positive class. The basic idea for this automatic approach is that we collect the anomalies detected by SPOT and label those anomalies as false positives whose probability for falling into any known attack class is lower than a corresponding probability threshold. Given that the overwhelming majority of anomalies detected by SPOT are false positives, it is reasonable to consider all these anomalies that cannot be categorized into any attack classes as false-positives without significantly compromising its detection accuracy. This could save a lot of human efforts taken in anomaly examination.

When labeled samples are absent, we cannot rely on the detection rate to properly pinpoint the transition from the growing stage to the later mature stage. Alternatively, we depend on the changes in the membership probabilities of anomalies with regard to the false-positive class. The higher the membership probability is, the better identification is achieved for the false positives. Such membership probability value is relatively low at the beginning due to the immatureness of the signature subspaces of the false-positive class. When this set grows as time evolves, we gradually obtain a better detection performance of false positives and the similarity value will be increased. When the similarity value starts to converge (reaching a plateau stage), then we can consider the set of signature subspaces of the false-positive class to be mature. Figure 6 shows the change of the membership probabilities of anomalies with respect to the false-positive class. Please note that, after the set of signature subspace has reached the mature stage, we are in a better position to identify anomalies. One such example will be the 93th anomaly shown in Figure 6 that has remarkably low probability with respect to false-positive class compared to other anomalies. It is probably an attack instance, though its exact attack class is unknown by solely reading this figure.

Experimental Evaluation

In this section, we will conduct experimental evaluation on SPOT in 1999 KDD anomaly detection application in terms of its effectiveness and efficiency.

Effectiveness Study Results

We will first report the results of experimental evaluation on the effectiveness of SPOT in 1999 KDD CUP anomaly detection application.

Effect of Number of Training Data Sets

When applying SPOT to KDD-CUP'99 anomaly detection application, we need to generate multiple training data sets for each attack classes for training purpose. This

Figure 6. Change of the member probabilities of anomalies with regard to the false-positive class

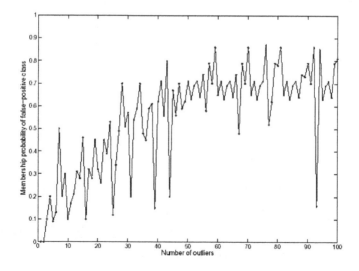

is to sample an enough amount of attack instances and at the same time satisfy the distribution requirement regarding normal and attack instances in each training data set. In this experiment, we investigate the effect of the number of training data sets generated for each class on the detection performance of SPOT. Recall that, due to the size limitation, each training data set is only able to contain a small portion of the labeled anomaly exemplars from the original training data set. Therefore, it is expected that, as the number of training data set for each class is increased, the detection accuracy will be enhanced accordingly and finally a kind of convergence phenomenon is expected to be observed. In this experiment, we evaluate the true positive rate and false positive rate of SPOT under varying number of training data sets. The result is presented in Figure 7. Besides the curve of true positive rate, two additional curves corresponding respectively to the cases of using and not using the false positive reduction are also presented for the false positive rate in the figure. We can see that, as the number of training data set increases, the true positive rate is indeed improved. However, a larger number of training data set tend to result in a higher false positive rate. Fortunately, we observe a noticeably lower false positive rate for SPOT thanks to the false positive categorization we introduced in SPOT to automatically screen out false positives through the anomaly categorization process.

Redundant Outlying Subspace Removal

We also investigate the existence of redundant outlying subspaces of anomalies. We first study the percent- age of anomalies that have redundant outlying subspaces

Figure 7. Effect of number of training data sets for each attack class

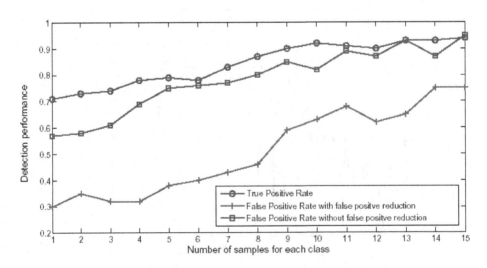

Table 2. Analysis on the redundant outlying subspaces of anomalies

	5.0	4.0	3.0	2.0	1.0
% of anomalies without redundant outlying subspaces	51%	54%	56%	59%	81%
Redundancy Ratio	55%	56%	57%	60%	66%

in KDD-CUP'99 anomaly detection data stream and other data sets. We can see from Table 2 that the majority of anomalies have redundant subspaces (ranging from 51% to 81%). We also study the Redundancy Ratio for these data sets. Here, the Redundancy Ratio (RR) of a data set D is defined as the ratio of the number of outlying subspaces (OS) of anomalies against the size of their outlying subspace front (OSF), *i.e.*

$$RR(D) = \frac{\sum |OS(o)|}{\sum |OSF(o)|},$$

(30)

for o being an anomaly in D

As also shown in Table 2, from the whole data set's perspective, the Redundancy Ratio of its outlying subspace set is between 55% and 66%, indicating a fairly high Redundancy Ratio for different data sets. As a result, using Outlying Subspace Front would help reduce the number of outlying subspaces by from 55% to 66%. Another important observation is that the values of these two measures are increased when the outlier-ness threshold goes down. This is because that, as the outlier-ness threshold become smaller, more subspaces will become outlying subspaces and they are likely to be dominated by some of their lower dimensional counterparts.

Signature Subspace Analysis

We are also interested in studying the diversity of signature subspaces of the false-positive class, as compared with those of the attack classes. We record the number of strong unique signature subspaces for different classes (including the false-positive class) as the number of data we evaluated increases. In this experiment, the strong signature subspaces we select are those signature subspaces whose tf-idf weight is 5 times higher than the average weight level. This definition of strong signature subspaces is of course subjective. We plot the results in Figure 8. Interestingly, we find that the number of unique strong signature subspaces for the false-positive class is significantly higher than any other attack classes by a factor of three or four. This

Table 3. Comparison of the manual and automatic methods for identifying false positives

	0.5	0.6	0.7	0.8	0.9
Difference of signature subspaces generated	23.5%	7.6%	13.7%	17.8%	28.5%
Accuracy in classifying false positives	87.2%	92.3%	88.5%	83.4%	72.1%

means that the strong signature subspaces for the false-positive class is far more diverse than those of the attack classes. This finding offers an important insight to us when we are creating the set of signature subspaces of the false-positive class. We need to collect a relatively large pool of signature subspaces in the detection process to achieve an accurate detection of false positives.

Comparative Study

Comparative study is also performed to investigate the detection accuracy and false positive rate between SPOT and other existing anomaly detection methods.

Competitive Methods

Since there is little research conducted in projected anomaly detection for high dimensional data streams, we cannot find the techniques tackling exactly the same problem as SPOT does for comparison. However, there are some related existing approaches for detecting anomalies from data streams that we can compare SPOT with. These methods can be broadly categorized as methods using *histogram, Kernel density function, distance-based function* and *clustering analysis*, respectively.

Histogram and Kernel density function are amongst the most commonly used statistical techniques in anomaly/intrusion detection. Histograms are created for each dimension of the data stream. The density (i.e., number of data points) falling into each bin of the histogram are recorded. The outlier-ness of a data point is computed feature-wise for multi-variate data as

$$outlier\_ness(p) = \sum_{f \in F} w_f \times (1 - p_f) / |F| \tag{31}$$

Figure 8. Number of strong signature subspaces for each attack class under varying number of data being processed

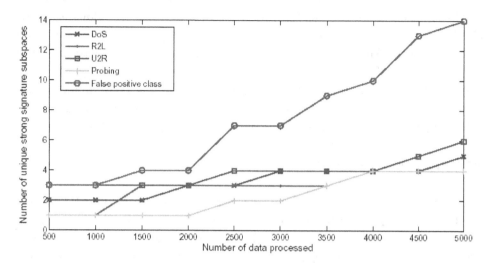

where pf is the probability that feature f takes the value of p, pf is calculated as the ratio of the density of the bin p belongs to against the total number of points arriving thus far. wf is the weight assigned to feature f. For simplicity, wf is set equal for all the attributes in the data stream. All attributes are considered in calculating the outlier-ness of data points of the stream in the histogram method. |F | denotes the total number of features in the data set. In this histogram-based anomaly detection method, a data point is an anomaly if its outlier- ness is above a threshold. Kernel density function models local data distribution in a single or multiple dimensions of space. One of the representative methods using Kernel function is proposed for detecting anomalies from sensor network (Palpanas et al., 2003). A point is detected as an anomaly if the number of values that have fallen into its neighborhood (delimited by a sphere of radius r) is less than an application-specific threshold. The number of values in the neighborhood can be computed by the Kernel density function. To facilitate the comparison, the functionalities of this Kernel function based method for dealing with distributed nodes are ignored. Anomaly detection from data stream is performed only in a single-node mode for this method. A major recent distance-based method for data stream is called *Incremental LOF* (Pokrajac et al., 2007). It is a variant of LOF method tailored for coping with frequent data updates (insertions and deletions) for dynamic databases. Clustering analysis can also be used to detect anomalies from those data that are located far apart from the data clusters. *HPStream* (Aggarwal et al., 2004) is the representative method for finding subspace clusters in high-dimensional data streams. In our experiments, a minor modification is needed to enable HPStream to detect anomalies. A data will be labeled abnormal if it is far apart from the so-called limiting radius of all the clusters. Here, the limiting radius of a cluster is typically a few times of the average radius of the data points in the cluster. We test four different possible sets of dimensions associated with each cluster, *i.e.*, 1, 2, 3 and 4, respectively. The exact number of dimension for a cluster is chosen from these four configurations such that the best F -measure can be achieved. This specification ensures that all the subspaces explored in HPStream are included in the 4-dimensional space lattice.

Effectiveness Measures

Appropriate performance metrics are needed in evaluating the detection performance of SPOT and other competitive detection methods. In the KDD-CUP'99 anomaly detection application, we will use *detection rate* (or called true positive rate) and *false positive rate* for performance evaluation. These two metrics are the most commonly used ones in detection systems. Detection rate refers to the percentage of hits (correctly identified anomalies) in the whole set of anomalies existing in the data set and false positive rate represents the percentage of erroneously labeled anomalies in the whole set of normal data.

Based on detection rate and false positive rate, Receiver Operating Characteristic (ROC) analysis is usually used. ROC is a commonly used technique for performance evaluation of detection methods by plotting its detection rate and false positive rate in the same ROC space. In a ROC curve, the detection rate is plotted in function of the false positive rate for different cut-offs. The closer the ROC curve of a method is from the left-upper corner in ROC space, the better the detection performance of this method will be.

Comparative Study Results

In this subsection, we will report the results of comparing the effectiveness of SPOT with other existing anomaly detection methods, including histogram method, Kernel function method, Incremental LOF and HPStream in KDD-CUP'99 anomaly detection application. ROC analysis is used in this comparative study. To conduct ROC analysis, we need to know in advance the true positives (anomalies) and true negatives (normal data). This is possible in KDD-CUP'99 anomaly detection application as labeled test data are available. As we know, any detection method can easily achieve a 100% detection rate by simply labeling all the connections as anomalies. However, this strategy will result in an extremely high false positive rate. Likewise,

Figure 9. ROC curves of different methods

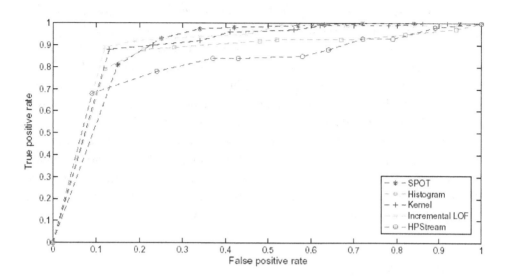

one can obtain a 0% false positive rate by claiming all the connections as normal, but this will lead to 0% true positive rate. Therefore, we need to consider these two rates simultaneously. In Figure 9, we plot the ROC curves for SPOT and other four competitive methods. We can see from this figure that the ROC curves of SPOT, Incremental LOF and Kernel function method progress much closer to the upper-left corner of the plot than the curves of histogram method and HPStream, indicating that SPOT, Incremental LOF and Kernel function method generally achieve a better detection performance. A closer examination of the figure suggests that Incremental LOF and Kernel function method perform better than SPOT when the false positive rate is relatively low (i.e., in the early stage of the ROC curves). However, SPOT starts to outperform Incremental LOF and Kernel function method as the false positive rate further increases. The false positive categorization that SPOT is equipped with enables it to identify false positives in an automated fashion while other competitive methods cannot. This helps SPOT to significantly reduce false positives and achieves a lower false positive rate under the same detection rate (or achieves a higher detection rate under the same false positive rate).

CONCLUSIONS AND FUTURE WORK

In this paper, we investigate anomaly detection problem in large and high-dimensional network data streams. By applying SPOT, we carry out a detailed case study using

1999 KDD CUP anomaly detection data stream. As the major contributions, several important issues, including training data generation, anomaly categorization using outlying subspaces analysis and false positive reduction, have been tackled in this paper for rendering SPOT applicable in this study. The experimental evaluations show that SPOT is not only more effective in detecting anomalies hidden in the subspaces of high-dimensional data streams but also produces a significantly lower level of false positives than the existing anomaly detection methods. Moreover, SPOT is efficient and scalable to large and high-dimensional data streams.

In the current stage, SPOT mainly relies on a static detection template to detect anomalies. In the future, we are interested in investigating the scenarios where the network traffic data feature frequent changes which requires our method to update the detection template dynamically. In addition, we will further explore the effect of the number of signature subspaces of the false positives on our method.

ACKNOWLEDGMENT

The author would like to thank Dr. Qigang Gao from Dalhousie University Canada, Dr. Hai Wang from St. Mary's University, Canada, Dr. Qing Liu and Dr. Kai Xu from CSIRO ICT Centre Australia, for their contribution to the development of SPOT.

REFERENCES

Aggarwal, C. C., Han, J., Wang, J., & Yu, P. S. (2004). A framework for projected clustering of high dimensional data streams. *International Conference on Very Large Data Base (VLDB)* (pp. 852-863), Toronto, Canada.

Aggarwal, C. C., & Yu, P. S. (2001). *Outlier detection in high dimensional data.* SIGMOD Conference (pp. 37-46), Santa Barbara, California.

Aggarwal, C. C., & Yu, P. S. (2005). An effective and efficient algorithm for high-dimensional outlier detection. *The VLDB Journal, 14*, 211–221. doi:10.1007/s00778-004-0125-5

Boudjeloud, L., & Poulet, F. (2005). Visual interactive evolutionary algorithm for high dimensional data clustering and outlier detection. In *Proceedings of the 9th Pacific-Asia Conference on Advances in Knowledge Discovery and Data Mining (PAKDD)* (pp. 426-431), Hanoi, Vietnam.

Breuning, M., Kriegel, H.-P., Ng, R., & Sander, J. (2000). *LOF: Identifying density-based local outliers.* SIGMOD Conference (pp. 93-104), Dallas, Texas.

Cui, H. (2002). *Online outlier detection over data streams*. Master thesis, Simon Fraser University, British Columbia, Canada.

Guha, A., Krishnamurthi, S., & Jim, T. (2009). *Using static analysis for ajax intrusion detection. International World Wide Web Conferences* (pp. 561–570). Madrid, Spain: WWW.

Knorr, E. M., & Ng, R. T. (1998). *Algorithms for mining distance-based outliers in large dataset*. International Conference on Very Large Data Base (VLDB) (pp. 392-403), New York, NY.

Knorr, E. M., & Ng, R. T. (1999). *Finding intentional knowledge of distance-based outliers*. International Conference on Very Large Data Base (VLDB) (pp. 211-222), Edinburgh, Scotland.

Palpanas, T., Papadopoulos, D., Kalogeraki, V., & Gunopulos, D. (2003). Distributed deviation detection in sensor networks. *SIGMOD Record, 32*(4), 77–82. doi:10.1145/959060.959074

Pokrajac, D., Lazarevic, A., & Latecki, L. (2007). Incremental local outlier detection for data streams, In *IEEE symposiums on computational Intelligence and Data Mining (CIDM'07)* (pp. 504-515), Honolulu, HI.

Ramaswamy, S., Rastogi, R., & Kyuseok, S. (2000). *Efficient algorithms for mining outliers from large data sets*. SIGMOD Conference (pp. 427-438), Dallas Texas.

Tang, J., Chen, Z., Fu, A., & Cheung, D. W. (2002). *Enhancing effectiveness of outlier detections for low density patterns*. Pacific-Asia Conference on Knowledge Discovery and Data Mining (PAKDD), Taipei, Taiwan.

Zhang, J., Gao, Q., & Wang, H. (2006). *A novel method for detecting outlying subspaces in high- dimensional databases using genetic algorithm*. IEEE International Conference on Data Mining (pp.731-740), Hong Kong, China.

Zhang, J., Gao, Q., Wang, H., Liu, Q., & Xu, X. (2009). Detecting projected outliers in high-dimensional data streams. *International Conference on Database and Expert Systems Applications* (pp. 629-644).

Zhang, J., Gao, Q., Wang, H., & Wang, H. (2010). Detecting anomalies from high-dimensional wireless net- work data streams: A case study. *Soft Computing - A Fusion of Foundations, Methodologies and Applications - Special Issue on Recent Advances on Machine Learning and Cybernetics, 15*(6).

Zhang, J., & Wang, H. (2006). Detecting outlying subspaces for high-dimensional data: The new task, algorithms and performance. [KAIS]. *Knowledge and Information Systems*, 333–355. doi:10.1007/s10115-006-0020-z

Zhong, S., Khoshgoftaar, T. M., & Nath, S. V. (2005). A clustering approach to wireless network intrusion detection. *IEEE International Conference on Tools with Artificial Intelligence (ICTAI)* (pp. 190-196).

Zhu, C. Kitagawa. H., & Faloutsos, C. (2005). *Example-based robust outlier detection in high dimensional datasets*. IEEE International Conference on Data Mining (pp. 829-832).

Zhu, C., Kitagawa, H., Papadimitriou, S., & Faloutsos, C. (2004). OBE: Outlier by example. *Pacific-Asia Conference on Knowledge Discovery and Data Mining (PAKDD)* (pp. 222-234).

ADDITIONAL READING

Aggarwal, C. C. (2005). On Abnormality Detection in Spuriously Populated Data Streams. *SIAM Conference on Data Mining*, Newport Beach, CA.

Aggarwal, C. C., Han, J., Wang, J., & Yu, P. S. (2003).A Framework for Clustering Evolving Data Streams. *International Conference on Very Large Data Base (VLDB)*, (pp. 81-92). Berlin, Germany.

Angiulli, F., & Pizzuti, C. (2002). Fast Outlier Detection in High Dimensional Spaces. *European Conference on Principles of Data Mining and Knowledge Discovery (PKDD)*, Helsinki, Finland, (pp. 15-26).

Barbara, D. (2002). Requirements for Clustering Data Streams. [ACM Press.]. *ACM SIGKDD Explorations Newsletter*, *3*(2), 23–27. doi:10.1145/507515.507519

Eskin, E., Arnold, A., Prerau, M., Portnoy, L., & Stolfo, S. (2002). *A Geometric Framework for Unsupervised Anomaly Detection: Detecting Intrusions in Unlabeled Data*. Applications of Data Mining in Computer Security.

Guttman, A. (1984). R-trees: a Dynamic Index Structure for Spatial Searching, *SIGMOD Conference*, (pp. 47-57). Boston, Massachusetts.

Han, J., & Kamber, M. (2000). *Data Mining: Concepts and Techniques*. Morgan Kaufman Publishers.

Zhang, J., Lou, M., Ling, T. W., & Wang, H. (2004). HOS-Miner: A System for Detecting Outlying Subspaces of High-dimensional Data. *International Conference on Very Large Data Base (VLDB)*, (pp. 1265-1268). Toronto, Canada.

KEY TERMS AND DEFINITIONS

Anomaly Classification: The classification process of the anomies into one or more known categories/classes.

Anomaly Detection: The process for detecting those data that are considered as inconsistent, abnormal when compared with the majority of the data in the databases or population.

Data Streams: A set of continuously arriving data generated from different application such as telecommunications, network, sensor networks, etc.

False Positive: The data that are detected the ones that satisfy a certain hypothesis but does not actually the case.

Genetic Algorithms: is a search heuristic that mimics the process of natural evolution. This heuristic is routinely used to generate useful solutions to optimization and search problems.

Subspaces: Data spaces that only contain a partial set of the attributes of the data under study.

ROC: The analysis of the relationship between the true positive fraction of test results and the false positive fraction for a diagnostic procedure that can take on multiple values.

Chapter 9
Applying Weighted PCA on Multiclass Classification for Intrusion Detection

Mohsen Moshki
Iran University of Science and Technology, Iran

Mehran Garmehi
Iran University of Science and Technology, Iran

Peyman Kabiri
Iran University of Science and Technology, Iran

ABSTRACT

In this chapter, application of Principal Component Analysis (PCA) and one of its extensions on intrusion detection is investigated. This extended version of PCA is modified to cover an important shortcoming of traditional PCA. In order to evaluate these modifications, it is mathematically proved that these modifications are beneficial and later on a known dataset such as the DARPA99 dataset is used to verify results experimentally. To verify this approach, initially the traditional PCA is used to preprocess the dataset. Later on, using a simple classifier such as KNN, the effectiveness of the multiclass classification is studied. In the reported work, instead of traditional PCA, a revised version of PCA named Weighted PCA (WPCA) will be used for feature extraction. The results from applying the aforementioned method to the DARPA99 dataset show that this approach results in better accuracy than the traditional PCA when a number of features are limited, a number of classes are large, and a population of classes is unbalanced. In some situations WPCA outperforms traditional PCA by more than 1% in accuracy.

DOI: 10.4018/978-1-60960-836-1.ch009

Copyright ©2012, IGI Global. Copying or distributing in print or electronic forms without written permission of IGI Global is prohibited.

INTRODUCTION

Feature selection and feature reduction techniques are two major approaches to increase the performance of pattern recognition systems. Processing power needed by supervised and unsupervised learning algorithms has a close and direct relation with the number of features within the dataset. If it was possible to eliminate some of the less informative features or to reduce the total number of features, then it would lead to a dramatic reduction in the processing power required by pattern recognition systems used for intrusion detection. The advantages of feature reduction are not limited to faster processing but in some cases it may result in more accuracy. When the size of dataset is small, large of number of the features may confuse the classifier. Some classifiers such as Multi Layer Perceptron (MLP) are sensitive to the ratio of the number of features to the number of database records. In these cases, feature reduction can be used as a solution to decrease this ratio for better classification.

Principal Component Analysis (PCA) is a well known feature extraction and reduction algorithm. PCA is an unsupervised algorithm and its transformation process is neither related to the population of the dataset nor number of the classes in the dataset. Although PCA extracts new features that make it possible to discriminate patterns more precisely, but there is no guarantee to increase class discrepancy. In this work, a simple modification to traditional PCA is used to remove this shortcoming. This version of PCA is a supervised extension that uses a weighting scheme by considering population of classes. After applying PCA to reduce the number of features, K-Nearest Neighbor (KNN) is used to classify samples. KNN is a simple instance-based method for object classification. Classification is a supervised task which tags new instances according to previously instances encountered by a classifier. KNN classifies each instance based on the learned pattern from its neighbors. In fact, this approach classifies each input based on the votes given by its neighbors.

First section of this paper is devoted to the related works in this area of research. After getting familiar with the scope of the problem, traditional PCA as a feature reduction method and KNN as a general purpose classifier will be introduced. In the following sections a simple and essential modification on PCA will be introduced. It will be proved that this modification is beneficial, and to do so, some practical studies will be presented. Finally, chapter will be concluded by presenting results and drawing the path to the future studies.

Related Works

One of the most challenging issues in intrusion detection and response is the necessary processing power. Most of the time the performance and accuracy are two sides of a coin. As a result of this fact the network security research communities pay more attention to approaches which can improve performance leading us to less decrease in the accuracy. There are several works on this area. One important category of these works is feature selection and reduction.

Some other related works are devoted to the improvement of feature selection and reduction using methods such as PCA. Koren and Karmel (Koren & Karmel, 2004) introduce a new approach for improving PCA which in addition to transforming and reducing the feature space, tries to keep the structure of input data. Forbes and Fiume (Forbes & Fiume, 2005) utilized a WPCA to represent the movement data in field of image processing.

There are some variations of PCA such as two dimensional PCA (Yang et al. 2004) and WPCA. Nhat and Lee (Nhat & Lee, 2005) proposed a method for face recognition based on two-dimensional WPCA. In 2D-PCA, PCA technique is applied directly on the original images without converting the two dimensional data to one dimension. They proposed a new version of 2D-PCA named two-dimensional WPCA which can improve the performance of 2D-PCA. Wang and Wu (Wang & Wu, 2005) proposed a new PCA-based approach for face recognition. They improved conventional PCA by weighting the extracted features from images. Xie and Li (2009) proposed a novel feature extraction method based on a combination of PCA and Independent Component Analysis (ICA) for network intrusion detection. They used extracted features as input to their classifier. Their experimental results show that the proposed method uses advantages of PCA and ICA in feature extraction. Sun and Liu (2010) proposed a robust method based on incremental PCA for visual object tracking. They used incremental Kernel PCA to find an object and represent the tracking target object. Kernel PCA does not transform original dataset directly. It first applies a kernel function to the original dataset and nonlinearly maps it onto new feature space and finally traditional PCA is applied on the resulted dataset. Van de Plas et al. (2007) used a PCA-based unsupervised method for Mass Spectral Imaging (MSI) decomposition of an organic tissue section into its underlying biochemical trends. They proposed a scalable method to control weights that affect the final decomposition model. Que et al. (2008) used a new PCA-based method named Modular Weighted PCA (MWPCA). This method combined WPCA and an image blocking technique. MWPCA is a 2D version of PCA for applying this feature reduction method to 2D signals like images. Zhao et al. (2008) proposed a new PCA-based method based on a new extension of PCA named wavelet transform weighted modular PCA. Their algorithm has four steps and uses wavelet transform and WPCA method together to reduce computational costs. Cheng (2006) proposed a PCA-based method to reduce number of the bands in remote sensing images in order to decrease processing costs. Traditional PCA does not consider spatial association and structural properties of the original images.

They proposed three methods to solve this problem and have successfully applied it on remote sensing images.

Alzate and Surkens (Alzate & Surkens, 2007) introduced a new image segmentation method based on weighted Kernel PCA. Using weighted kernel PCA the computation time for the segmentation was reduced.

Because of the effect of dimension reduction methods such as PCA in improving the performance of Intrusion Detection Systems (IDSs), their use is commonly considered in IDS. Kim et al. (Kim et al., 2005) proposed an optimized IDS using PCA and Back Propagation (BP) Artificial Neural Network (ANN). They used Genetic Algorithm (GA) to optimize the parameters determining how PCA and BP ANN should be combined together. Vladimir et al. (Vladimir et al., 2007) proposed an IDS-based the combination of PCA and MLP neural network. PCA was employed for feature reduction and MLP was employed to recognize attacks using reduced features instead of original data. Xiao and Song (2009) report a novel approach for intrusion detection based on Adaptive Resonance Theory (ART) and PCA. In their model, PCA was applied to extract features and multi-layered ART2 was used to subdivide the imprecise clustering. Zargar and Kabiri (2009) propose an effective PCA-based method to detect Smurf attacks. They used PCA as feature reduction method to reduce number of the input features for their classifier. Kabiri and Zargar (2009) also introduced another PCA-based method that is a category-based intrusion detection. They searched for the most effective features for each attack class instead of searching for the most effective features for all classes. Their proposed method is supervised because they needed to label classes before applying the PCA. Kuang and Zulkernine (2008 A) propose an intrusion tolerant mechanism for intrusion detection system. Their system used KNN classifier to detect attacks. Du et al. (2008) propose a novel method to detect abnormal behaviors and intrusions. They selected KNN algorithm as classifier with a new kernel method to calculate the deviation between normal and intrusion classes. Wang et al. (2009) reports several schemes for feature normalization to preprocess the data for anomaly-based intrusion detection. They applied KNN, PCA and SVM on normalized data to compare different normalization schemes. Their results show that feature normalization processes can significantly improve detection performance. Feng et al. (2009) propose an improved swarm intelligence clustering algorithm to optimize the topology of a Radial Basis Function Neural Network (RBFNN) and the optimized RBFNN was applied for intrusion detection. Also, Liao arid and Rao Vemuri (2002), Middlemiss and Dick (2003) and Kuang and Zulkernine (2008 B) used traditional KNN and some of its variations as the classifier for intrusion detection.

BACKGROUND

There are many techniques that can be used for monitoring the nodes, analyzing the network traffic and detecting intrusions. In the proposed method an improved version of PCA named WPCA is introduced. In this section, PCA and KNN classifier are described.

Principal Component Analysis

PCA transform is an unsupervised method for feature extraction and reduction (Jackson 1991; Jolliffe 2002). In this method the first goal is to represent the information in a less complicated feature space. This approach makes this simplification in the feature space with the least possible square error rate. In this way PCA calculates the eigenvectors of the data and then using these eigenvectors it transforms feature space of the input data into a new feature space.

As every eigenvector of the data contains a specific amount of the total variance of the raw data and the amplitude of these eigenvectors are directly dependant on the amount of the variance, it is possible to make decision on inclusion or exclusion of every feature in the dataset. In order to make this decision, the transformation matrix is calculated and the rows with less importance will be masked. After this step, vector of features will be mapped to a new space.

This conversion matrix is the core of PCA transform and can be calculated as follows. Consider a set of M instances of a stochastic variable with N features:

$$X_i = \{X_1, \quad X_2, \quad ..., \quad X_N\}^T \tag{1}$$

Dataset matrix is a M x N matrix consists of all vectors of the all instances. In the next step we calculate the covariance matrix using Equation 2.

$$C = \frac{1}{M} \sum_{i=1}^{M} (X_i - \mu)(X_i - \mu)^T \tag{2}$$

$$\mu = \frac{1}{M} \sum_{i=1}^{M} X_i \tag{3}$$

Now we can calculate eigenvalues and eigenvectors of this covariance matrix. As the covariance matrix is real and symmetric, it's possible to extract N real and nonzero eigenvalues like λ_i. Also, it is obvious that we have orthogonal eigenvectors. As mentioned before the importance of every eigenvector depends on the total variance of information along with its direction. Therefore, the importance of each eigenvector depends on the size of its eigenvalue. Eigenvectors and eigenvalues are calculated by Equation 4.

$$C. \ V_i = \ »_i.V_i \tag{4}$$

In order to calculate the conversion matrix, the eigenvectors are first put together with a decreasing order based on their eigenvalues. Having this matrix calculated and using this equation, the feature space can be transformed using Equation 5.

$$\hat{X} = T.\left(X - \mu_x\right) \tag{5}$$

As it can be seen one should adjust the average value for each feature in the data to zero prior to using this transformation. Knowing that the importance of the features decrease as traversing the matrix rows from top to the bottom, some lower rows which has less importance can be excluded and dimensionality of the dataset can be reduced.

KNN Classification

Learning methods in pattern recognition are dividing in to two major categories: supervised learning methods and unsupervised learning methods. In supervised learning methods, label of the samples are known while unsupervised methods do not consider sample label.

In pattern recognition, K-Nearest Neighbor (KNN) is a simple instance-based method for object classification. Classification is a supervised task that uses a trained classifier to tag new instances in accordance to previously seen instances. KNN classifies each instance based on the pattern learned from its neighbors. In fact, this approach classifies each input using the votes given by its neighbors. So, if we set K to 1 each instance will be classified as its nearest neighbor. KNN uses a distance metric such as Euclidean distance to find K nearest neighbors of an instance. However, KNN's distance matrix is not limited to Euclidean distance and other distance metrics such as hamming distance can be used as well. Euclidean distance between two vectors is given by Equation 6.

$$d(p,q) = \sqrt{(q_1 - p_1)^2 + (q_2 - p_2)^2 + ... + (q_n - p_n)^2}$$

$$= \sqrt{\sum_{i=1}^{n}(q_i - p_i)^2} \tag{6}$$

where p and q are two points in n-dimensional feature space and d(p, q) is Euclidean distance between these two points.

One common instance of KNN gives larger weights to closer neighbors. Most of the time, these weights are inversely related to Euclidean distance. This classifier has high sensitivity to local structure of the data distribution. Learning information in this algorithm is a labeled dataset in the feature space. This algorithm has no training phase and learning phase is just storing a labeled dataset as the training set. In classification phase, K is the only adjustable parameter by the user and test dataset using this variable will be examined to estimate the accuracy of the classifier. K is mostly selected using trial and error approach. Increasing K decreases the effect of noise on classifier and decreasing K increases the bias to major classes.

Proposed Method

As mentioned earlier, PCA is an unsupervised method. This simple fact means that it makes its transformation from one data space to another regardless of the class label of data instances presented in the dataset. Knowing this fact, it is reasonable to conclude that it is possible to have a high variance on one of the features in one of the classes which is harmful for classifiers. In other words, it is possible for PCA to generate features which are not useful for the classification. This situation is common when the population of the classes is not equal as it is common in network traffic traces.

In order to study the impact of including the class population factor in calculation of PCA we consider the covariance matrix which is the basis of PCA. As it is obvious, changing the order of rows in initial data matrix has no effect on the covariance matrix so we assume that the dataset is sorted such that the first portion of the matrix contains only instances of class a and instances that belong to class b occupy the remaining rows, so if initial dataset is called M, it consists of two derived matrices A and B. Population of M, A and B, are respectively equal to k, n and m. Matrix A is a sub-matrix of M that contains its first n rows and all its instances belong to class a. Matrix B is a sub-matrix of M that contains the next m rows and all the instances in B belong to class b.

Weighted covariance of M is defined using Equation 7:

$$COV_w(M) = \frac{n}{m+n}COV(A) + \frac{m}{m+n}COV(B) \qquad (7)$$

First question is to know if there is any difference between $COV(M)$ and $COV_w(M)$. Also, it can be questioned that if there is any difference between these matrices and which one of them is more suitable for this study.

Comparison of Two Covariance Matrices

It is obvious that in covariance matrix diagonal elements are variance of features, so:

$$COV(M)_{j,i} = \frac{\sum_{j=1}^{k}(M_{j,i} - \bar{M}_i)^2}{k} \qquad (8)$$

which $\bar{M}_i$ is the average of ith feature in the dataset and it can be calculated using Equation 9.

$$\bar{M}_i = \frac{n\bar{A}_i}{k} + \frac{m\bar{B}_i}{k} \qquad (9)$$

and as a result:

$$COV(M)_{j,i} = \frac{\sum_{j=1}^{k}\left[M_{j,i} - (\frac{n\bar{A}_i}{k} + \frac{m\bar{B}_i}{k})\right]^2}{k} \qquad (10)$$

Now as M is composed of two sub matrices we can derive:

$$COV(M)_{j,i} = \frac{\sum_{j=1}^{n}\left[A_{j,i} - (\frac{n\bar{A}_i}{k} + \frac{m\bar{B}_i}{k})\right]^2 + \sum_{j=1}^{m}\left[B_{j,i} - (\frac{n\bar{A}_i}{k} + \frac{m\bar{B}_i}{k})\right]^2}{k} \qquad (11)$$

Here we expand the equations and consider in account that $k=n+m$:

$$\frac{n}{n+m}COV(A)_{j,i}$$

$$+\frac{m}{n+m}COV(B)_{j,i} \tag{12}$$

$$=\frac{n}{k}\frac{\sum\limits_{j=1}^{n}\left(A_{j,i}-\bar{A}_i\right)^2}{n}$$

$$+\frac{m}{k}\frac{\sum\limits_{j=1}^{m}\left(B_{j,i}-\bar{B}_i\right)^2}{m}$$

Expanding the square functions of Equation 11 and Equation 12 and subtracting those (excluding equal components) yields:

$$(-2\bar{M}_i+-2\bar{A}_i)(\sum\limits_{j=1}^{n}A_{j,i})$$

$$+(-2\bar{M}_i+-2\bar{B}_i)(\sum\limits_{j=1}^{m}B_{j,i}) \tag{13}$$

$$+k\bar{M}_i^2-n\bar{A}_i^2-m\bar{B}_i^2$$

This equation is the result of subtracting covariance matrices of the traditional PCA and two class WPCA. This Equation can be zero if each feature in A has an equal mean and variance to corresponding feature in B. On the other hand, if the ith feature in A and B does not have equal means and variances, this equation will have a nonzero result and we can say that the weighted covariance matrix is different from traditional one. When this equation is zero, PCA and WPCA work similarly. Otherwise, covariance matrix of WPCA is different from covariance matrix of PCA. Apparently this study can be expanded to non-diagonal elements.

Going toward multi-class dataset these equations can be expand to datasets with more than two classes of instances. The calculation of covariance in this situation would be like the following:

$$COV_w(M) = \frac{n_1}{n}COV(M_1)$$
$$+ \quad ... \quad + \frac{n_c}{n}COV(M_c) \tag{14}$$

Where n is the total population of dataset, n_1 to n_c are the number of instances belonging to each class and M_1 to M_c are c sub-matrices of M.

Experimental Results

Next step is to analyze and evaluate the sampled dataset versus different scenarios. PCA theory is used for the analysis, dimension reduction and evaluation of the features. All the feature values are normalized (zero mean and unit variance). Then covariance matrix is calculated and it presents the relation of the features with one another. As it is described in previous section, PCA is calculated using the covariance matrix.

Data Preparation

In order to compare PCA and WPCA we use a subset of DARPA99 dataset (Mahoney & Chan, 2003). DARPA is a very large dataset for testing intrusion detection systems which developed in Lincoln Laboratory. DARPA is used as off-line evaluation dataset in many reported works on network intrusion detection. It is also used as a benchmark to evaluate participants in some well known competitions like KDD cups. In this dataset more than 290000 instances exist. Each sample has 41 features but 20th feature is excluded and just 40 basic features are used. Excluded feature has no variance and its value in all records of the dataset is zero. Some of the features in this dataset have symbolic values and it is necessary to convert them to numbers. Briefly we pass these steps for each feature in our dataset. For every symbolic feature a conversion has to be performed to replace it with an associated numerical value. This includes symbolic data like protocols and services. The mean and variance of each feature will be set to a value between zero and one to make them comparable. Table 1 shows a list of all original features and their types in DARPA99 dataset.

There are 38 classes in DARPA dataset listed in Table 2. Most of classes are too small to be used in the experiments and only 7 classes are used in this study. Obviously, class populations in DARPA dataset are not equal and it is ideal for this study since the proposed method is more suitable when population of classes make dataset unbalanced.

Table 1. Features and their types in DARPA 1999

	Feature	type		Feature	type
1	Duration	continuous.	22	is_guest_login	symbolic.
2	protocol_type	symbolic.	23	count	continuous.
3	Service	symbolic.	24	srv_count	continuous.
4	Flag	symbolic.	25	serror_rate	continuous.
5	src_bytes	continuous.	26	srv_serror_rate	continuous.
6	dst_bytes	continuous.	27	rerror_rate	continuous.
7	Land	symbolic.	28	srv_rerror_rate	continuous.
8	wrong_fragment	continuous.	29	same_srv_rate	continuous.
9	Urgent	continuous.	30	diff_srv_rate	continuous.
10	Hot	continuous.	31	srv_diff_host_rate	continuous.
11	num_failed_logins	continuous.	32	dst_host_count	continuous.
12	logged_in	symbolic.	33	dst_host_srv_count	continuous.
13	num_compromised	continuous.	34	dst_host_same_srv_rate	continuous.
14	root_shell	continuous.	35	dst_host_diff_srv_rate	continuous.
15	su_attempted	continuous.	36	dst_host_same_src_port_rate	continuous.
16	num_root	continuous.	37	dst_host_srv_diff_host_rate	continuous.
17	num_file_creations	continuous.	38	dst_host_serror_rate	continuous.
18	num_shells	continuous.	39	dst_host_srv_serror_rate	continuous.
19	num_access_files	continuous.	40	dst_host_rerror_rate	continuous.
20	num_outbound_cmds	continuous.	41	dst_host_srv_rerror_rate	continuous.
21	is_host_login	symbolic.			

Implementation

In this study, three different methods are examined. In the experiments KNN method is used for the classification and random sampling is used for dividing dataset to train and test datasets. First, KNN classifier is applied on all features without any feature reduction. Later on, KNN is applied on some of the most valuable features obtained by the traditional PCA. Finally, KNN is applied on some of the most valuable features obtained by WPCA. The resulted dataset will be called No-PCA, PCA and WPCA respectively in this paper. There are several tests for each method. Each test is different in case of the number of classes and the K parameter for the KNN algorithm used. All reported results represent 10 runs average. Each run is performed on a different train and test sets. Difference among the datasets in the

Table 2. Attack classes in DARPA 1999

attack	frequency	attack	frequency	attack	frequency	attack	frequency
apache2.	795	mail-bomb.	5000	portsweep.	354	sqlattack.	2
back.	1098	mscan.	1053	pro-cesstable.	642	teardrop.	12
buffer_over-flow.	22	multi-hop.	18	ps.	16	udpstorm.	2
ftp_write.	3	named.	17	rootkit.	13	warezmas-ter.	1602
guess_pass-wd.	4367	neptune.	41218	saint.	736	worm.	2
httptunnel.	158	nmap.	84	satan.	1633	xlock.	9
imap.	1	normal.	59526	sendmail.	17	xsnoop.	4
ipsweep.	306	perl.	2	smurf.	164091	xterm.	13
land.	9	phf.	2	snmpgetat-tack.	7058		
loadmodule.	2	pod.	87	snmpguess.	2406		

experiments is resulted due to the random sampling for generating test and train dataset from the main dataset.

Several works in domain of network intrusion detection used KNN classifier to detect attacks in DARPA dataset. The reason for choosing KNN is its simplicity and popularity in this area as reported in related works.

Balanced Dataset with 3 Classes

There are 3 classes in this test. Each class has 3000 samples and dataset is a balanced dataset with 9000 samples. Class samples are reduced from original dataset to a derived one using uniform selection on the original dataset records are sorted based on their values. Considering feature values as characters, sorting process is identical to sorting alphabetical strings. To select m samples among n samples from each class uniformly, first all the samples should be sorted based on their values. Later on, one sample from each n/m consequent samples is selected. For example, in order to select 1000 samples from 20000 sorted samples from dataset records, one sample from each 20 consequent samples are selected. This dataset is divided into two equal sets for train and test, each contains 4500 samples. No-PCA method uses all the 40 features. PCA and WPCA methods only use 3 most valuable extracted features obtained by traditional PCA and WPCA respectively.

Figure 1. Accuracy of three methods for 3 different values of k on balanced 3 class dataset

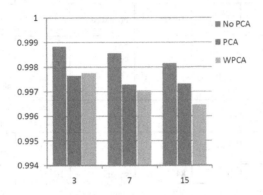

Each method is executed with 3 different values of K for KNN (3, 7, 15). The accuracy for the first experiment is more than the others. The graph in Figure 1 shows that in all the methods the accuracy decreases with increasing the K value. For K=3, the most accurate method is No-PCA while PCA and WPCA are relatively equal.

Unbalanced Dataset with 3 Classes

In the second test, there are 3 classes. Class populations are 1000, 3000 and 6000 samples and dataset is an unbalanced dataset with 10000 samples. Similar to the previous test, class samples are reduced from original dataset into a derived dataset using uniform selection on dataset records sorted based on their values. This dataset is divided into two equal sets one for training and the other one for test, each with 5000 samples. Each method is used for the training with all 5000 samples of the training dataset. No-PCA method used all 40 features. PCA and WPCA methods only used 3 most valuable of extracted features obtained by the traditional PCA and WPCA.

Each method is executed with 3 different values of K for KNN (3, 7, 15). As shown in Figure 2, the best accuracy achieved was for K=3. For K=3, the most accurate method is No-PCA with 99.88% accuracy while PCA and WPCA is relatively equal with 99.76% and 99.77% respectively.

Unbalanced Dataset with 5 Classes

There are 5 classes in this test. Class populations are 800, 1200, 5000, 1000 and 2000 samples and consequently dataset is an unbalanced dataset with 10000 samples. This

Figure 2. Accuracy of three methods for 3 different values of k on unbalanced 3 class dataset

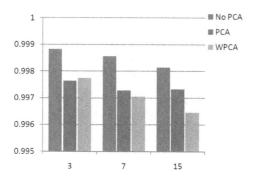

dataset is divided into two equal sets for train and test, each contains 5000 samples. Later on, each method is trained with all 5000 samples of the training dataset. Once No-PCA method is used all 40 features are extracted and when the two other two methods used only 3 most valuable features are extracted.

Each method is executed using 3 different values of K for KNN (3, 7, 15). As shown in Figure 3, the best accuracy achieved for K=3. For K=3, the most accurate method is No-PCA with 99.26% accuracy while PCA and WPCA is relatively equal with 98.83% and 98.73% respectively.

Unbalanced Dataset with 7 Classes

There are 7 classes in this test data. Class populations are 500, 1000, 4000, 1000, 1000, 3000 and 1500 samples and consequently dataset is an unbalanced dataset with 12000 samples. Two datasets contain 6000 samples are used as train and test set. All other test conditions are similar to previous tests.

Each method is run with 3 different values of K for KNN (3, 7, 15). The best accuracy is resulted for K=3. For K=3, the most accurate method is No-PCA with 99.34% accuracy while PCA and WPCA are 95.21% and 96.67% respectively. In this case, the difference between PCA and WPCA accuracy is 1.46% which shows significant improvement.

Unbalanced Dataset with 9 Classes

In this test, some sample from 9 more populated classes are used as train and test sets. Class populations are 500, 1000, 4000, 1000, 1000, 3000, 1500, 1000 and 200

Figure 3. Accuracy of the three methods for 3 different values of k on unbalanced 5 class dataset

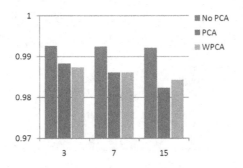

samples. The total dataset consists of 13200 samples in 9 unbalanced classes. Train and test sets have equal number of records, each one containing 6600 samples. All other test conditions are similar to previous test experiments.

The best accuracy is achieved for K=3. The accuracies are 99.12, 92.78 and 95.89 for No-PCA, PCA and WPCA respectively. In this case, WPCA outperforms PCA in accuracy by 3.11 percents.

Analysis of the Results

Experimental results show that WPCA and traditional PCA may lead to similar performance in most of the time but there are some conditions where WPCA outperforms traditional PCA. WPCA outperforms PCA when the number of classes is large. The complexity of a problem has a close relationship to number of classes, therefore, WPCA makes it possible to classify patterns more accurately than PCA once the classification problem is complex and the number of features is limited. The most difference between the accuracy of PCA and WPCA will occur on unbalanced dataset with 9 classes when only 3 extracted features are used. As shown in Figure 5, WPCA outperforms PCA by 3.11% more accuracy in this situation.

Comparing the eigenvectors of PCA and WPCA makes it understandable why WPCA can lead to better results. In order to compare these graphs, both of them are shown on a single graph in Figure 6. The graph of WPCA descends faster rather than traditional PCA. This is due to the fact that the first best extracted features in WPCA are more informative than the corresponding features in traditional PCA. In other words, using class labels in WPCA makes it possible to reduce the weights of features that traditional PCA specifies them as important.

Figure 4. Accuracy of three methods for 3 different values of k on 7 unbalanced class dataset

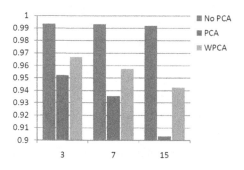

FUTURE RESEARCH DIRECTIONS

In proposed method, a weighting method was proposed to calculate more appropriate covariance matrix to create a better transform matrix. In this method, weights were calculated based on the population of classes in dataset but weighting methods are not limited to this. A good idea is to determine weights based on other parameters like the internal means and variances of classes.

WPCA is a supervised method and it is one of shortcoming of proposed methods. Supervised methods need labeled samples and unfortunately in many cases this information is not available. It limits the application of the WPCA. For example, WPCA is not applicable to clustering problems where class labels are not available. It seems a good idea to use cluster labels instead of class labels in situations which class labels are unavailable.

CONCLUSION

In this paper, an extended version of PCA named WPCA is used to develop a more efficient IDS. This approach pays more attention to the population of each class in the dataset. In order to achieve this goal weighted covariance matrix of dataset was calculated and the normal process of traditional PCA is followed using this special covariance matrix.

Experimental results show that WPCA and traditional PCA may lead to similar performance in most conditions. Increase in the number of classes has similar effect on accuracy of both methods and will decrease them. When the number of classes

Figure 5. Accuracy of three methods for 3 different values of k on 9 unbalanced class dataset

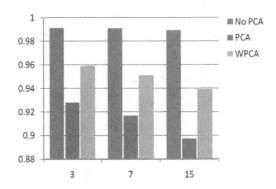

Figure 6. The sorted eigenvalues of WPCA and PCA

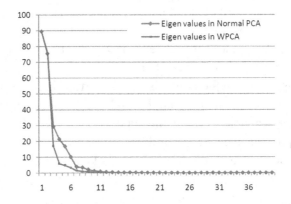

is 3, the best result is achieved by PCA method with 99.77% accuracy while these values for 5, 7 and 9 classes are 98.83%, 96.67% and 95.89%. Increment of K parameter in KNN will reduce the accuracy.

Experimental results show that WPCA and traditional PCA may lead to similar performance in most of situations but there are some situations where WPCA outperforms traditional PCA. WPCA outperforms PCA when the number of classes is large. The most difference between accuracy of PCA and WPCA results with unbalanced dataset with 7 classes when only 3 extracted features were used. As shown in Figure 4, WPCA outperform PCA by 1.46% more accuracy in this situation.

REFERENCES

Alzate, C., & Suykens, J. A. K. (2007). Image segmentation using a weighted kernel PCA approach to spectral clustering. In *Proceedings of the 2007 IEEE Symposium on Computational Intelligence in Image and Signal Processing* (pp. 208-213), Honolulu, USA.

Cheng, Q. (2006). *Spatial and spatially weighted principal component analysis for images processing.* International Geoscience and Remote Sensing Symposium (pp. 964 - 967).

Du, Y., Guo, Y., He, Y., & Cai, Y. (2008). A useful anomaly intrusion detection method using multiple-instance learning. *Journal of Computer Information Systems, 4*(1), 237–242.

Feng, Y., Zhong, J., Xiong, Z., Ye, C., & Wu, K. (2009). Enhanced swarm intelligence clustering algorithm based on RBFNN and its application in intrusion detection. *Journal of Computer Information Systems, 4*(1), 251–256.

Forbes, K., & Fiume, E. (2005). An efficient search algorithm for motion data using weighted PCA. In K. Anjyo, & P. Faloutsos (Eds.), *Proceedings of ACM SIGGRAPH/ Eurographics Symposium on Computer Animation* (pp. 67–76).

Golovko, V. A., Vaitsekhovich, L. U., Kochurko, P. A., & Rubanau, U. S. (2007). Dimensionality reduction and attack recognition using neural network approaches. *IJCNN, 2007,* 2734–2739.

Jackson, J. E. (1991). *A user's guide to principal components.* New York, NY: John Wiley & Sons.

Jolliffe, I. T. (2002). *Principal component analysis* (2nd ed.). New York, NY: Springer.

Kabiri, P., & Aghaei, M. (2011). Feature analysis for intrusion detection in mobile ad-hoc networks. Accepted for publication in. *International Journal of Network Security, 12*(1), 42–49.

Kabiri, P., & Zargar, G. R. (2009). Category-based selection of effective parameters for intrusion detection. *International Journal of Computer Science and Network Security, 9*(9).

Kim, D. S., Nguyen, H., Thein, T., & Park, J. S. (2005). An optimized intrusion detection system using PCA and BNN. In *Proceedings of the 6th Asia-Pacific Symposium on Information and Telecommunication Technologies, IEICE Communications Society* (pp. 356-359).

Koren, Y., & Carmel, L. (2004). Robust linear dimensionality reduction. *IEEE Transactions on Visualization and Computer Graphics, 10*, 459–470. doi:10.1109/TVCG.2004.17

Kuang, L., & Zulkernine, M. (2008a). *An intrusion-tolerant mechanism for intrusion detection systems.*The 3rd International Conference on Availability, Reliability and Security (pp. 319-326).

Kuang, L., & Zulkernine, M. (2008b). An anomaly intrusion detection method using the CSI-KNN algorithm. *SAC, 2008*, 921–926.

Li, Y., Lu, T., Guo, L., Tian, Z.-H., & Qi, L. (2009). Optimizing network anomaly detection scheme using instance selection mechanism.In *Proceedings of the Global Communications Conference* (pp. 1-7).

Liao, Y., & Vemuri, V. R. (2002). Use of K-nearest neighbor classifier for intrusion detection, *Computers and Security - COMPSEC, 21*(5), 439–448.

Mahoney, M. V., & Chan, P. K. (2003, September). An analysis of the 1999 DARPA/Lincoln laboratory evaluation data for network anomaly detection. In *Proceedings of the 6th International Symposium on Recent Advances in Intrusion Detection* (pp. 220-237), Pittsburgh, PA.

Middlemiss, M., & Dick, G. (2003). *Feature selection of intrusion detection data using a hybrid genetic algorithm/KNN approach: Design and application of hybrid intelligent systems* (pp. 519–527). Amsterdam, The Netherlands: IOS Press.

Nhat, V. D. M., & Lee, S. (2005). Two-dimensional weighted PCA algorithm for face recognition. In *Proceedings of the 2005 IEEE International Symposium on Computational Intelligence in Robotics and Automation*, Espoo, Finland (pp. 219 - 223).

Que, D., Chen, B., & Hu, J. (2008). A novel single training sample face recognition algorithm based on modular weighted (2D) PCA. *9th International Conference on Signal Processing, 2*(3), 1552-1555.

Sun, L., & Liu, G. (2010). *Visual object tracking based on incremental kernel PCA.* Paper presented at the 2010 International Workshop on Content-Based Multimedia Indexing (pp. 1-6).

Van de Plas, R., De Moor, B., & Waelkens, E. (2007). Imaging mass spectrometry based exploration of biochemical tissue composition using peak intensity weighted PCA, In *Proceedings of the 3rd IEEE/NIH BISTI Life Science Systems and Applications Workshop(LISA '07)* (pp. 209 - 212), Bethesda, Maryland.

Wang, H.-Y., & Wu, X.-J. (2005). Weighted PCA space and its application in face recognition. In *Proceedings of the 4th International Conference on Machine Learning and Cybernetics* (pp. 4522–4527), Guangzhou, China.

Wang, W., Zhang, X., Gombault, S., & Knapskog, S. J. (2009). *Attribute normalization in network intrusion detection*, 10th International Symposium on Pervasive Systems, Algorithms and Networks (ISPAN) (pp. 448-453).

Xiao, J., & Song, H. (2009). A novel intrusion detection method based on adaptive resonance theory and principal component analysis. In *Proceedings of the 2009 WRI International Conference on Communications and Mobile Computing (CMC '09)* (vol. 3, pp. 445-449). Washington, DC: IEEE Computer Society.

Xie, L., & Li, J. (2009). A novel feature extraction method assembled with PCA and ICA for network intrusion detection. In *Proceedings of the 2009 International Forum on Computer Science-Technology and Applications (IFCSTA '09)* (vol. 3, pp. 31-34).

Yang, D., & Qi, H. (2008, December). *A network intrusion detection method using independent component analysis*. Paper presented at the 19th International Conference on Pattern Recognition (ICPR '08) (pp. 1-4), Tampa, FL.

Zargar, G. R., & Kabiri, P. (2009). *Identification of effective network features to detect smurf attacks*, 2009 IEEE Student Conference on Research and Development (pp.49-52), Malaysia.

Zhang, L., & Zhang, Y. (2008). *Facial feature extraction with weighted modular two dimensional PCA*, the 2nd International Conference on Bioinformatics and Biomedical Engineering (ICBBE '08) (pp. 1992 – 1995).

Zhao, M., Li, P., & Liu, Z. (2008). Face recognition based on wavelet transform weighted modular PCA, In *Proceedings of the Congress on Image and Signal Processing (CISP '08)* (vol. 4, pp. 589-593).

ADDITIONAL READING

Kabiri, P., & Zargar, G. R. (2009). *Identification of Effective Network Features for Probing Attack Detection.* First International Conference on Networked Digital Technologies (pp. 405-410), VSB-Technical University of Ostrava, Czech Republic, July 29-31.

Li, Y., Lu, T., Guo, L., Tian, Zh., & Qi, L. (2009). *Optimizing Network Anomaly Detection Scheme Using Instance Selection Mechanism.* In Proceedings of the Global Communications Conference (pp. 1-7).

McHugh, J. (2000). Testing intrusion detection systems: a critique of the 1998 and 1999 DARPA intrusion detection system evaluations as performed by Lincoln Laboratory. *ACM Transactions on Information and System Security, 3*(4), 262–294. doi:10.1145/382912.382923

Tang, H., & Cao, Z. (2009). Machine Learning-based Intrusion Detection Algorithms. *Journal of Computer Information Systems, 5*(6), 1825–1831.

Yang, J., Zhang, J., Frangi, A. F., & Yang, J. Y. (2004). Two-dimensional PCA: a new approach to appearance based face representation and recognition. *IEEE Transactions on Pattern Analysis and Machine Intelligence, 26*(1), 131–137. doi:10.1109/TPAMI.2004.1261097

Zargar G. R., Kabiri, P. (2009). Identification of Effective Optimal Network Feature Set for Probing Attack Detection Using PCA Method. *Accepted for publication in the International Journal of Web Application, 2*(3), 164-174.

Zhou, Y. P., & Zhou, Y. P. (2009). Hybrid Model based on Artificial Immune System and PCA Neural Networks for Intrusion Detection. *In Proceeding of Asia-Pacific Conference on Information Processing,* 21-24. Mahoney M.V. & Chan P.K. (2003). *An analysis of the 1999 DARPA /Lincoln Laboratory evaluation data for network anomaly detection.* Technical Report CS-2003-02. Thomas C.& Balakrishnan N. (2008). *Usefulness of DARPA data set in Intrusion Detection System evaluation.* Proceedings of SPIE International Defense and Security Symposium, 6973-15.

KEY TERMS AND DEFINITIONS

Classification: The task of assigning unknown samples to known classes.

Clustering: The task of analyzing unknown samples and grouping them to a set of clusters.

K-Nearest Neighbor (KNN): KNN is a simple classifier which classifies new samples based on previously seen samples or training samples.

Network Intrusion Detection: The act of detecting intrusions in a computer network.

Principal Component Analysis (PCA): PCA is a classic technique in statistical data analysis, feature extraction and data compression.

Weighted Principal Component Analysis (WPCA): WPCA is a modified version of traditional PCA which calculates transformation matrix based on population of classes.

Compilation of References

Aggarwal, C. C., & Yu, P. S. (2005). An effective and efficient algorithm for high-dimensional outlier detection. *The VLDB Journal, 14*, 211–221. doi:10.1007/s00778-004-0125-5

Aggarwal, C. C., & Yu, P. S. (2001). *Outlier detection in high dimensional data.* SIGMOD Conference (pp. 37-46), Santa Barbara, California.

Aggarwal, C. C., Han, J., Wang, J., & Yu, P. S. (2004). A framework for projected clustering of high dimensional data streams. *International Conference on Very Large Data Base (VLDB)* (pp. 852-863), Toronto, Canada.

Ahson, A., & Ilyas, M. (2009). *SIP handbook* (pp. 3–173). New York: Taylor & Francis Group.

Akbar, M. A., Tariq, Z., & Farooq, M. (2009). *A comparative study of anomaly detection algorithms for detection of SIP flooding in IMS*, 2nd International Conference on Internet Multimedia Services Architecture and Applications (pp. 1-6).

Akujuobi, C. M., Ampah, N. K., & Sadiku, M. N. O. (2007). An intrusion detection technique based on change in hurst parameter with application to network security. *International Journal of Computer Science and Network Security, 5*(7), 55–64.

Akujuobi, C. M., & Ampah, N. K. (2007). Enterprise network intrusion detection and prevention system. *Society of photographic instrumentation engineers defense and security symposium* (vol. 6538, pp. 1-12).

Albari, M. Z. (2005). *A taxonomy of runtime software monitoring systems.* Retrieved August 9, 2008, from http://www.informatik.uni-kiel.de/~wg/Lehre/Seminar-SS05/Mohamed_Ziad_Abari/vortrag-handout4.pdf.

Almgren, M., Jonsson, E., & Lindqvist, U. (2007). A comparison of alternative audit sources for Web server attack detection. In *Proceedings of the 12th Nordic Workshop on Secure IT Systems (NordSec 2007)* (pp. 101–112), Reykjavik, Iceland.

Alzate, C., & Suykens, J. A. K. (2007). Image segmentation using a weighted kernel PCA approach to spectral clustering. In *Proceedings of the 2007 IEEE Symposium on Computational Intelligence in Image and Signal Processing* (pp. 208-213), Honolulu, USA.

Compilation of References

Amanullah, M. T. O., Kalam, A., & Zayegh, H. (2005). Network security vulnerabilities in SCADA and EMS. *Transmission and Distribution Conference and Exhibition: Asia and Pacific* (pp. 1-6).

Analoui, M., Mirzaei, A., & Kabiri, P. (2005). Intrusion detection using multivariate analysis of variance algorithm. In *IEEE 3ʳᵈ International Conference on Systems, Signals & Devices (SSD '05)* (vol. 3), Sousse, Tunisia.

Anderson, J. M., Berc, L. M., Dean, J., Ghemawat, S., Henzinger, M. R., Leung, S. A., & Weihl, W. E. (1997). Continuous profiling: Where have all the cycles gone? *ACM SIGOPS Operating Systems Review, 31*(5), 1–14. doi:10.1145/269005.266637

Anderson, J. P. (1980). *Computer security threat monitoring and surveillance (Tech. Rep.)*. Fort Washington, PA: James P. Anderson Company.

Anjum, F., Subhadrabandhu, D., Sarkar, S., & Shetty, R. (2004). *On optimal placement of intrusion detection modules in sensor networks* (pp. 690–699). BroadNets.

Anwar, M. M., Zafar, M. F., & Ahmed, Z. (2007). A proposed preventive Information Security System. *International Conference on Electrical Engineering* (pp. 1-6).

Apache mod_log_config. (2010). *Apache mod_log_config module*. Retrieved November 25, 2010, from http://httpd.apache.org/docs/2.2/mod/mod_log_config.html.

Aranya, A., Wright, C. P., & Zadok, E. (2004). Tracefs: A file system to trace them all. In *Proceedings of the 3ʳᵈ USENIX Conference on File and Storage Technoligies (FAST 2004)* (pp. 129–145). San Francisco, CA: USENIX Association.

Ariel, T., & Miller, B. P. (1999). Fine-grained dynamic instrumentation of commodity operating system kernels. In *Proceedings of the 3ʳᵈ Symposium on Operating Systems Design and Implementation (OSDI'99)* (pp. 117–130), New Orleans, LA.

Arvidson, M., & Carlbark, M. (2003). *Intrusion detection systems technologies, weaknesses and trends* (student thesis). Retrieved December 11, 2010, from http://liu.diva-portal.org/smash/record.jsf?pid=diva2:18938

Asgharian, Z., Asgharian, H., Akbari, A., & Raahemi, B. (2011). *A framework for SIP intrusion detection and response systems*, IEEE International Symposium on Computer Networks and Distributed Systems, Tehran, Iran.

Axelsson, S. (2000). *Instrusion detection systems: A survey and taxonomy* (Tech. Rep. 99-15). Göteborg, Sweden: Chalmers University of Technology.

Axelsson, S., Lindqvist, U., Gustafson, U., & Jonsson, E. (1998). An approach to UNIX security logging. In *Proceedings of the 21ˢᵗ National Information Systems Security Conference* (pp. 62–75), Arlington, VA.

Baeza-Yates, R. A., & Riberiro-Neto, B. A. (1999). *Modern information retrieval*. Boston, MA: ACM-Press / Addison-Wesley Longman Publishing Co., Inc.

Baker, M. G., Hartman, J. H., Kupfer, M. D., Shirriff, K. W., & Ousterhout, J. K. (1991). Measurements of a distributed file system. *ACM SIGOPS Operating Systems Review, 25*(5), 198–212. doi:10.1145/121133.121164

Barbara, D., Couto, J., Jajodia, S., & Wu, N. (2001a). Special section on data mining for intrusion detection and threat analysis: Adam: A testbed for exploring the use of data mining in intrusion detection. In *Association for Computer Machinery Special Internet Group on Management of Data. SIGMOD Record, 30*(4), 15–24.

Barbara, D., Wu, N., & Jajodia, S. (2001b). Detecting novel network intrusions using bayes estimators. In *Proceedings of the 1ˢᵗ SIAM International Conference on Data Mining (SDM 2001),* Chicago, USA.

Baxter, I. D. (2002). *Branch coverage for arbitrary languages made easy* (Tech. Rep.). Austin, TX: Semantic Designs. Retrieved November, 2010, from http://www.semdesigns.com/Company/Publications/TestCoverage.pdf

Beheshti, M., & Wasniowski, R. A. (2007). Data fusion support for intrusion detection and prevention. *International Conference on Information Technology* (p. 966).

Besson, J. L. (2003). *Next generation intrusion detection and prevention for complex environments* (Master Thesis in Computer Science). Retrieved December 11, 2010, from http://www.ifi.uzh.ch/archive/mastertheses/DA_Arbeiten_2003/Besson_Jean_Luc.pdf

Bhagwan, R., Savage, S., & Voelker, G. M. (2003). Understanding availability. *Peer-to-Peer Systems II* (LNCS 2735-2003).

Biermann, E., Cloete, E., & Venter, L. M. (2001). A comparison of intrusion detection systems. *Computers & Security, 8*(20), 676–683. doi:10.1016/S0167-4048(01)00806-9

Bignell, K. B. (2006). Authentication in the Internet banking environment; Towards developing a strategy for fraud detection. *International Conference on Internet Surveillance and Protection* (p. 23).

Bilodeau, M., & Brenner, D. (1999). *Theory of multivariate statistics.* New York, NY: Springer - Verlag, electronic edition at ebrary, Inc.

Bishop, M. (1987). Profiling under UNIX by patching. *Software, Practice & Experience, 17*(10), 729–739. doi:10.1002/spe.4380171006

Bishop, M. (1989). A model of security monitoring. In *Proceedings of the 5ᵗʰ Annual Computer Security Applications Conference* (pp. 46–52), Tucson, AZ, USA.

Bishop, M., Wee, C., & Frank, J. (1996). *Goal-oriented auditing and logging.* Retrieved November, 2010, from http://seclab.cs.ucdavis.edu/papers/tocs-96.pdf.

Bonachela, J. A., Hinrichsen, H., & Muñoz, M. A. (2008). Entropy estimates of small data sets, *Journal of Physics A. Mathematical and Theoretical, 41*(20), 11.

Compilation of References

Borg, A., Kessler, R. E., & Wall, D. W. (1990). Generation and analysis of very long address traces. In *Proceedings of the 17th Annual Symposium on Computer Architecture (ISCA-17)* (pp. 270–279), Seattle, WA, USA.

Botha, M., & von Solms, R. (2003). Utilising fuzzy logic and trend analysis for effective intrusion detection. *Journal of Computers & Security, 22*(5), 423–434. doi:10.1016/S0167-4048(03)00511-X

Boudjeloud, L., & Poulet, F. (2005). Visual interactive evolutionary algorithm for high dimensional data clustering and outlier detection. In *Proceedings of the 9th Pacific-Asia Conference on Advances in Knowledge Discovery and Data Mining (PAKDD)* (pp. 426-431), Hanoi, Vietnam.

Braden, R. T. (1988). A pseudo-machine for packet monitoring and statistics. *ACM SIGCOMM Computer Communication Review, 18*(4), 200–209. doi:10.1145/52325.52345

Brauckhoff, D., Tellenbach, B., Wagner, A., & May, M. (2006, October). *Impact of packet sampling on anomaly detection metrics.* Paper presented at the Internet Measurement Conference 2006, Rio de Janeiro, Brazil.

Breuning, M., Kriegel, H.-P., Ng, R., & Sander, J. (2000). *LOF: Identifying density-based local outliers.* SIGMOD Conference (pp. 93-104), Dallas, Texas.

Bridges, S. M., & Rayford, M. V. (2000). Fuzzy data mining and genetic algorithms applied to intrusion detection. In *Proceedings of the 23rd National Information Systems Security Conference.* Gathersburg, Maryland: National Institute of Standards and Technology.

Bridis, T., & Sullivan, E. (2007). US video shows hacker hit on power grid. *Associated Press Writers* Retrieved September, 27, 2007, from http://www.physorg.com/news110104929.html

Bringas, P. G. (2007). Intensive use of Bayesian Belief Network for the unified, flexible and adaptable analysis of misuses and anomalies in network intrusion detection and prevention systems. *International Conference on Database and Expert Systems Applications* (pp. 365-371).

Bruschi, D., Cavallaro, L., & Lanzi, A. (2007). An effective technique for preventing mimicry and impossible paths execution attacks. *International Conference on Performance, Computing, and Communications* (pp. 418-425).

Buck, B., & Hollingsworth, J. K. (2000). An API for runtime code patching. *Journal of High Performance Computing Applications, 14*(4), 317–329. doi:10.1177/109434200001400404

Bulatovic, D., & Velasevic, D. (1999). *A distributed intrusion detection system based on Bayesian alarm networks* (. *LNCS, 1740*, 219–228.

Cannady, J. (2009). Distributed detection of attacks in mobile ad hoc networks using learning vector quantization. *3rd International Conference on Network and System Security* (pp. 571–574).

Cantrill, B. M., Shapiro, M. W., & Leventhal, A. H. (2004). Dynamic instrumentation of production systems. In *Proceedings of the annual conference on USENIX Annual Technical Conference (ATEC '04)* (pp. 15–28). Boston, MA: USENIX Association.

Capuzzi, G., Spalazzi, L., & Pagliarecci, F. (2006). IRSS: Incident response support system. *International Symposium on Collaborative Technologies and Systems* (pp. 81-88).

Car, J., & Jakupovic, G. (2005). SCADA system security as a part of overall security of deregulated energy management system. *International Conference on Computer as a Tool* (pp. 338-341).

Chaboya, D. J., Raines, R. A., Baldwin, R. O., & Mullins, B. E. (2006). Network intrusion detection: Automated and manual methods prone to attacks and evasion. *Security and Privacy Magazine, 6*(4), 36–43. doi:10.1109/MSP.2006.159

Changxin, S., & Ke, M. (2009). Design of intrusion detection system based on data mining algorithm. *International Conference on Signal Processing Systems* (pp. 370–373).

Chen, A., Li, L., & Cao, J. (2009). Tracking cardinality distributions in network traffic. In *Proceedings of IEEE 28th Conference on Computer Comunications (INFOCOM 2009)* (pp. 819-827).

Chen, E. Y. (2006). *Detecting DoS attacks on SIP systems*, In 1st IEEE Workshop on VoIP Management and Security (pp. 53- 58).

Chen, Z., Chen, C., & Wang, Q. (2009). Delay-tolerant botnets. In *Proceedings of 18th International Conference on Computer Communications and Networks (ICCCN 2009)* (pp. 1-6).

Cheng, Q. (2006). *Spatial and spatially weighted principal component analysis for images processing*. International Geoscience and Remote Sensing Symposium (pp. 964 - 967).

Cho, S.-B. (2002). Incorporating soft computing techniques into a probabilistic intrusion detection system. *IEEE Transactions on Systems, Man and Cybernetics. Part C, Applications and Reviews, 32*(2), 154–160. doi:10.1109/TSMCC.2002.801356

Chu, J., Labonte, K., & Levine, B. N. (2002, July). Availability and locality measurements of peer-to-peer file systems. In *Proceedings of ITCom (Vol. 4868)*. Scalability and Traffic Control in IP Networks II Conferences. Proceedings of SPIE.

Chu, Y. h., Ganjam, A., Ng, T. S. E., Rao, S. G., Sripanidkulchai, K., & Zhan, J. & Zhang, H. (2003, December). *Early experience with an Internet broadcast system based on overlay multicast* (Tech. Rep. CMUCS-03-214). Pittsburgh, PA: Carnegie Mellon University.

Chunmei, Y., Mingchu, L., Jianbo, M., & Jizhou, S. (2004). Honeypot and scan detection in intrusion detection system. *Canadian Conference on Electrical and Computer Engineering* (pp. 1107–1110).

Chuvakin, A., & Peterson, G. (2010). *How to do application logging right*. Retrieved November 24, 2010, from http://www.computer.org/cms/Computer.org/ComputingNow/homepage/2010/1010/W_SP_ApplicationLogging.pdf.

Colon Osorio, F. C. (2007). Using Byzantine agreement in the design of IPS systems. *International Conference on Performance, Computing, and Communications* (pp. 528-537).

Compilation of References

Common Criteria. (2005). *Common criteria for Information Technology security evaluation: Part 2: Security functional requirements, Version 2.3.* Retrieved November 25, 2010, from http://www.commoncriteriaportal.org/files/ccfiles/ccpart2v2.3.pdf.

Computer Security Institute. (2009). *2009 computer crime and security survey.* Retrieved from http://www.gocsi.com/

Conway, J. H., & Guy, R. K. (1996). *The book of numbers* (pp. 143 & 258-262). New York, NY: Springer-Verlag.

Corrons, L. (PandaLabs). (2010). *Mariposa botnet.* Retrieved August 17, 2010 from http://pandalabs.pandasecurity.com/mariposa-botnet/

Crosbie, M., & Spafford, E. (1995). Defending a computer system using autonomous agents. In *Proceedings of the 18th National Information Systems Security Conference.*

Cui, H. (2002). *Online outlier detection over data streams.* Master thesis, Simon Fraser University, British Columbia, Canada.

Curry, T. W. (1994). Profiling and tracing dynamic library usage via interposition. In *Proceedings of the USENIX Summer 1994 Technical Conference (USTC'94)* (pp. 267–2780). Boston, MA, USA: USENIX Association.

Dagle, J. E., Windergren, S. E., & Johnson, J. M. (2002, January). *Enhancing the security of supervisory control and data acquisition (SCADA) systems: The lifeblood of modern energy infrastructure.* Paper presented at the Power Engineering Society Winter Meeting, New York, NY.

Dale, N., Weems, C., & Headington, M. (2002). *Programming and problem solving with C.* Sudbury, MA: Jones and Bartlett.

De Peppo, A. (2006). *Plab. Network tool for traffic traces.* Retrieved December 11, 2010, from http://www.grid.unina.it/software/Plab/

Debar, H., Dacier, M., & Wespi, A. (1999). *A revised taxonomy for intrusion-detection systems (Tech. Rep.).* Rüschlikon, Switzerland: IBM Zürich Research Laboratory.

Delgado, N., Gates, A. Q., & Roach, S. (2004). A taxonomy and catalog of runtime software-fault monitoring tools. *IEEE Transactions on Software Engineering, 30*(12), 859–872. doi:10.1109/TSE.2004.91

Dempster, A. P., Laird, N. M., & Rubin, D. B. (1977). Maximum likelihood from incomplete data via the em algorithm. *Journal of the Royal Statistical Society. Series B. Methodological, 39*(1), 1–38.

Denning, D. E. (1986). An intrusion-detection model. In *Proceedings of the 1986 IEEE Symposium on Security and Privacy* (pp. 118–131). Oakland, CA, USA: IEEE.

Dickerson, J. E., & Dickerson, J. A. (2000). Fuzzy network profiling for intrusion detection. In *Proceedings of NAFIPS 19th International Conference of the North American Fuzzy Information Processing Society* (pp. 301–306), Atlanta, GA.

Dongarra, J., London, K., Moore, S., Mucci, P., & Terpstra, D. (2001). *Using PAPI for hardware performance monitoring on Linux systems*. In Conference on Linux Clusters: The HPC Revolution, Urbana, IL.

Du, Y., Guo, Y., He, Y., & Cai, Y. (2008). A useful anomaly intrusion detection method using multiple-instance learning. *Journal of Computer Information Systems, 4*(1), 237–242.

Ehlert, S., Geneiatakis, D., & Magedanz, T. (2009). *Survey of network security systems to counter SIP-based denial-of-service attacks*. Amsterdam, The Netherlands: Elsevier.

Ehlert, S., Wang, C., Magedanz, T., & Sisalem, D. (2008). *Specification-based denial-of-service detection for SIP voice-over-IP networks*, 3rd International Conference on Internet Monitoring and Protection (pp. 59-66).

Esposito, M., Mazzariello, C., Oliviero, F., Peluso, L., Romano, S. P., & Sansone, C. (2008). Intrusion detection and reaction: An integrated approach to network security. *Intrusion Detection Systems* (pp. 171-210). Berlin, Germany: Springer Science+Business Media, LLC.

Etsion, Y., Tsafrir, D., Kirkpatrick, S., & Feitelson, D. (2007). Fine grained kernel logging with Klogger: Experience and insights. In *Proceedings of the 2nd ACM SIGOPS/EuroSys European Conference on Computer Systems 2007* (pp. 259–272). Lisbon, Portugal: ACM.

Eustace, A., & Srivastava, A. (1994). *ATOM: A flexible interface for building high performace program analysis tools (Tech. Rep.)*. Palo Alto, CA: DEC Western Research Laboratory.

Fadia, A. (2006). *Network security: A hacker's perspective*. Boston, MA: Thomson Course Technology.

Farris, J. J., & Nicol, D. M. (2004). *Evaluation of secure peer-to-peer overlay routing for survivable SCADA systems*. 2004 Winter Simulation Conference (pp. 308-317).

Federal Information Processing Standards Publication (FIPS PUB) 180-1. (1995, April). *Announcing the standard for secure hash standard*. Retrieved 2008 from http://www.itl.nist.gov/fipspubs/fip180-1.htm

Feng, Y., Zhong, J., Xiong, Z., Ye, C., & Wu, K. (2009). Enhanced swarm intelligence clustering algorithm based on RBFNN and its application in intrusion detection. *Journal of Computer Information Systems, 4*(1), 251–256.

Fessi, B. A., BenAbdallah, S., Hamdi, M., Rekhis, S., & Boudriga, N. (2010). Data collection for Information Security System. In *Proceedings of the 2nd International Conference on Engineering Systems Management and Applications (ICESMA 2010)*, Sharjah, United Arab Emirates.

Compilation of References

Fiedler, J., Kupka, T., Ehlert, S., Magedanz, T., & Sisalem, D. (2007). VoIP defender: Highly scalable SIP-based security architecture. In *Proceedings of the 1ˢᵗ International Conference on Principles, Systems and Applications of IP Telecommunications* (pp. 11-17).

Forbes, K., & Fiume, E. (2005). An efficient search algorithm for motion data using weighted PCA. In K. Anjyo, & P. Faloutsos (Eds.), *Proceedings of ACM SIGGRAPH/Eurographics Symposium on Computer Animation* (pp. 67–76).

Forrest, S., Hofmeyr, S. A., Somayaji, A., & Longstaff, T. A. (1996). A sense of self for Unix processes. In *Proceedings of the 1996 IEEE Symposium on Research in Security and Privacy* (pp. 120–128). Oakland, CA, USA: IEEE.

Ganame, A. K., Bourgeois, J., Bidou, R., & Spies, F. (2007). *A global security architecture for intrusion detection on computer networks.* IEEE International Parallel and Distributed Processing Symposium (IPDPS '07) (pp. 1-8).

Gans, M. (1996). *Development of a pole-mounted RTU for use on rural power lines.* Power System Control and Management Conference (pp. 103–107).

Garfinkel, S., & Spafford, G. (1996). *Practical UNIX and Internet security* (2nd ed.). Sebastopol, CA, USA: O'Reilly.

GDB. (2010). *GDB: The GNU project debugger.* Retrieved November 25, 2010, from http://www.gnu.org/software/gdb/gdb.html.

Geneiatakis, D., Vrakas, N., & Lambrinoudakis, C. (2009). Utilizing bloom filters for detecting flooding attacks against SIP based services. *Elsevier Journal on Computers and Security, 28*(7), 578–591.

Gnutella homepage. (2003). *Gnutella.* Retrieved August 16, 2010, from http://www.gnutella.org/

Golovko, V. A., Vaitsekhovich, L. U., Kochurko, P. A., & Rubanau, U. S. (2007). Dimensionality reduction and attack recognition using neural network approaches. *IJCNN, 2007,* 2734–2739.

Gomez, J., & Dasgupta, D. (2001). Evolving fuzzy classifiers for intrusion detection. In *Proceedings of the 2002 IEEE Workshop on the Information Assurance,* West Point, NY.

Graham, S. L., Kessler, P. B., & McKusick, M. K. (1984). GPROF: A call graph execution profiler. *ACM SIGPLAN Notices, 39*(4), 49–57. doi:10.1145/989393.989401

Gu, G. (2008). *Correlation-based botnet detection in enterprise networks* (Doctoral dissertation, Georgia Institute of Technology).

Gu, G., Perdisci, R., Zhang, J., & Lee, W. (2008). BotMiner: Clustering analysis of network traffic for protocol-and structure-independent botnet detection. In *Proceedings of the 17ᵗʰ Conference on Security symposium* (pp. 139-154). Berkeley, CA: USENIX Association.

Gu, G., Zhang, J., & Lee, W. (2008). BotSniffer: Detecting botnet command and control channels in network traffic. In *Proceedings of the 15th Network and Distributed System Security Symposium (NDSS)*, San Diego, CA.

Gu, Y., McCallum, A., & Towsley, D. (2005). *Detecting anomalies in network traffic using maximum entropy estimation*. Paper presented at the 5th ACM SIGCOMM Conference on Internet Measurement, Berkeley, CA.

Guan, J., Liu, D.-X., & Cui, B. G. (2004). *An intrusion learning approach for building intrusion detection models using genetic algorithms*. World Congress on Intelligent Control and Automation (pp. 4339–4342).

Guha, A., Krishnamurthi, S., & Jim, T. (2009). *Using static analysis for ajax intrusion detection. International World Wide Web Conferences* (pp. 561–570). Madrid, Spain: WWW.

Ha, D., Yan, G., Eidenbenz, S., & Ngo, H. (2009). On the effectiveness of structural detection and defense against p2p-based botnets. In *IEEE/IFIP International Conference on Dependable Systems & Networks (DSN '09)* (pp. 297-306).

Haji, F., Lindsay, L., & Song, S. (2005). *Practical security strategy for SCADA automation systems and networks*. Canadian Conference on Electrical and Computer Engineering (pp. 172-178).

Hall, M., Frank, E., Holmes, G., Pfahringer, B., Reutemann, P., & Witten, H. I. (2009). The weka data mining software: An update. *ACM SIGKDD Explorations Newsletter, 11*(1), 10–18. doi:10.1145/1656274.1656278

Harrington, D., Presuhn, R., & Wijnen, B. (2002). *RFC 3411: An architecture for describing simple network management protocol (SNMP) management frameworks* (STD 62).

Hedbom, H., Kvarnström, H., & Jonsson, E. (1999). Security implications of distributed intrusion detection architectures. In *Proceedings of the 4th Nordic Workshop on Secure IT Systems* (pp. 225–243), Kista, Sweden.

Hispasec Sistemas. (2010). *Virus Total*. Retrieved March 30, 2010, from http://www.virustotal.com/es/

Hosszú, G., & Czirkos, Z. (2007). Network-based intrusion detection. In Freire, M., & Pereira, M. (Eds.), *Encyclopedia of Internet technologies and applications* (pp. 353–359). Hershey, PA: Information Science Reference. doi:10.4018/978-1-59140-993-9.ch050

Howard, J. D., & Longstaff, T. A. (1998). *A common language for computer security incidents* (Tech. Rep. SAND98-8667). Albuquerque/Livermore, USA: Sandia National Laboratories.

Hu, P., & Heywood, M. I. (2003). Predicting intrusions with local linear model. In. *Proceedings of the IEEE International Joint Conference on Neural Networks, 3*, 1780–1785.

Hyvarinen, A., Krhunen, J., & Oja, E. (2001). *Independent component analysis*. Hoboken, NJ: Wiley Interscience, John Wiley & Sons Inc.doi:10.1002/0471221317

Compilation of References

IETF IDWG. (2006). *IETF Intrusion Detection Working Group* (IDWG). Retrieved January 4, 2006, from http://www.ietf.org/

Ihn-Han, B., & Olariu, S. (2009). *A weighted-dissimilarity-based anomaly detection method for mobile wireless networks*. International Conference on Computational Science and Engineering (pp. 29–34).

Intersect Alliance. (2003). *Guide to snare for Linux*. Retrieved November 25, 2010, from http://www.intersectalliance.com/resources/Documentation/Guide_to_Snare_for_Linux-3.2.pdf.

Invent, H. P. (2010). *SIPp*. Retrieved February 2011, from http://sipp.sourceforge.net/

Itzkowitz, M., Wylie, B. J. N., Aoki, C., & Kosche, N. (2003). Memory profiling using hardware counters. In *Proceedings of the 2003 ACM/IEEE Conference on Supercomputing (SC'03)* (pp. 17–29). Phoenix, AZ, USA: IEEE.

Jackson, J. E. (1991). *A user's guide to principal components*. New York, NY: John Wiley & Sons.

Jacobson, V., Leres, C., & McCanne, S. (2001). *Tcpdump/libpcap*. Retrieved December 11, 2010, from http://www.tcpdump.org

Janakiraman, R., Waldvogel, M., & Zhang, Q. (2003). *Indra: A peer-to-peer approach to network intrusion detection and prevention*. International Workshops on Enabling Technologies: Infrastructures for Collaborative Enterprises (pp. 226-231).

Jin, X., & Osborn, S. L. (2007). Architecture for data collection in database intrusion detection systems. In *Proceedings of the 4th VLDB Workshop on Secure Data Management (SDM 2007)*, Vienna, Austria.

Jing, Z. HouKuan, H., ShengFeng, T., & Xiang, Z. (2009). *Applications of HMM in protocol anomaly detection*. International Joint Conference on Computational Sciences and Optimization (pp. 347–349).

Jing-Wen, T., Mei-Juan, G., Ling-Fang, H., & Shi-Ru, Z. (2009). Community intrusion detection system based on wavelet neural network. *International Conference on Machine Learning and Cybernetics* (vol. 2, pp. 1026 – 1030).

Jolliffe, I. T. (2002). *Principal component analysis* (2nd ed.). New York, NY: Springer.

Jou, Y. F., Gong, F., Sargor, C., Wu, S., Wu, S. F., Chang, H. C., & Wang, F. (2000). Design and implementation of a scalable intrusion detection system for the protection of network infrastructure. *Defense Advanced Research Projects Agency Information Survivability Conference and Exposition* (vol. 2, pp. 69–83).

Kabiri, P., & Ghorbani, A. A. (2005). Research on intrusion detection and response: *A survey. International Journal of Network Security*, *1*(2), 82–104.

Kabiri, P., & Aghaei, M. (2011). Feature analysis for intrusion detection in mobile ad-hoc networks. Accepted for publication in. *International Journal of Network Security*, *12*(1), 42–49.

Kabiri, P., & Zargar, G. R. (2009). Category-based selection of effective parameters for intrusion detection. *International Journal of Computer Science and Network Security, 9*(9).

Kad (2010). *Handling interrupt descriptor table for fun and profit*. Retrieved November 25, 2010, from http://www.phrack.org/issues.html?issue=59&id=4#article.

Kang, J., Zhang, J.-Y., Li, Q., & Li, Z. (2009). Detecting new p2p botnet with multi-chart cusum. In *Proceedings of the International Conference on Networks Security, Wireless Communications and Trusted Computing (NSWCTC '09)* (vol. 1, pp. 688-691).

Kayacik, H. G., Zincir-Heywood, A. N., & Heywood, M. I. (2003). On the capability of an SOM based intrusion detection system. In. *Proceedings of the IEEE International Joint Conference on Neural Networks, 3*, 1808–1813.

Kayacik, H. G., Zincir-Heywood, A. N., & Heywood, M. I. (2004*). On dataset biases in a learning system with minimum A Priori information for intrusion detection*. Communication Networks and Services Research Conference (pp. 181–189).

Kent, K., & Souppaya, M. (2006). *Guide to computer security log management: Recommendations of the National Institute of Standards and Technology* (NIST) (special publication 800-92). Retrieved November 24, 2010, from http://csrc.nist.gov/publications/nistpubs/800-92/SP800-92.pdf.

Khoshgoftaar, T. M., & Abushadi, M. E. (2004). *Resource-sensitive intrusion detection models for network traffic*. High Assurance Systems Engineering Symposium (pp. 249–258).

Killourhy, K. S., Maxion, R. A., & Tan, K. M. C. (2004). A defense-centric taxonomy based on attack manifestations. In *Proceedings of the International Conference on Dependable Systems and Networks (DSN 2004)* (pp. 102–111). Florence, Italy: IEEE.

Kim, D. S., Nguyen, H., Thein, T., & Park, J. S. (2005). An optimized intrusion detection system using PCA and BNN. In *Proceedings of the 6th Asia-Pacific Symposium on Information and Telecommunication Technologies, IEICE Communications Society* (pp. 356-359).

Knorr, E. M., & Ng, R. T. (1998). *Algorithms for mining distance-based outliers in large dataset*. International Conference on Very Large Data Base (VLDB) (pp. 392-403), New York, NY.

Knorr, E. M., & Ng, R. T. (1999). *Finding intentional knowledge of distance-based outliers*. International Conference on Very Large Data Base (VLDB) (pp. 211-222), Edinburgh, Scotland.

Ko, C. (2003). System health and intrusion monitoring (SHIM): Project summary. *Defense Advanced Research Projects Agency Information Survivability Conference and Exposition* (vol. 2, pp. 202–207).

Kohler, E. (2009). *IPsumdump: A traffic tool*. Retrieved December 11, 2010, from http://www.cs.ucla.edu/~kohler/ipsumdump

Koren, Y., & Carmel, L. (2004). Robust linear dimensionality reduction. *IEEE Transactions on Visualization and Computer Graphics, 10*, 459–470. doi:10.1109/TVCG.2004.17

Compilation of References

Krizhanovsky, A., & Marasanov, A. (2007). *An approach for adaptive intrusion prevention based on the danger*. 2nd International Conference on Availability, Reliability and Security (pp. 1135-1142).

Kuang, L., & Zulkernine, M. (2008b). An anomaly intrusion detection method using the CSI-KNN algorithm. *SAC, 2008*, 921–926.

Kuang, L., & Zulkernine, M. (2008a). *An intrusion-tolerant mechanism for intrusion detection systems*. The 3rd International Conference on Availability, Reliability and Security (pp. 319-326).

Kui, Z. (2009). *A danger model based anomaly detection method for wireless sensor networks*. 2nd International Symposium on Knowledge Acquisition and Modeling (pp. 11–14).

Kuperman, B. A., & Spafford, E. (1999). *Generation of application level audit data via library interposition (Tech. Rep. CERIAS TR 99-11)*. West Lafayette, IN: COAST Laboratory, Purdue University.

Kuperman, B. A. (2004). *A categorization of computer security monitoring systems and the impact on the design of audit sources*. PhD thesis, Purdue University, West Lafayette, IN.

Labbe, K. G., Rowe, N. G., & Fulp, J. D. (2006). *A methodology for evaluation of Host-Based intrusion prevention systems and its application*. Information Assurance Workshop (pp. 378-379).

Lahmadi, A., & Festor, O. (2009). *SecSip: A stateful firewall for SIP-based networks*, 11th IFIP/IEEE International Symposium on Integrated Network Management (pp.172-179).

Lall, A., Sekar, V., Ogihara, M., Xu, J., & Zhangz, H. (2006). *Data streaming algorithms for estimating entropy of network traffic*. Paper presented in International Conference on Measurement and modeling of computer systems, Saint Malo, France.

Larson, U. E., Jonsson, E., & Lindskog, S. (2008a). A revised taxonomy of data collection mechanisms with a focus on intrusion detection. In *Proceedings of the 3rd IEEE International Conference on Availability, Security, and Reliability (ARES 2008)* (pp. 624–629). Barcelona, Spain: IEEE.

Larson, U. E., Lindskog, S., Nilsson, D. K., & Jonsson, E. (2008b). Operator-centric and adaptive intrusion detection. In *Proceedings of the 4th International Conference on Information Assurance and Security (IAS'08)* (pp. 161–166). Naples, Italy: IEEE.

Larus, J. R. (1993). Efficient program tracing. *Computer, 26*(5), 52–61. doi:10.1109/2.211900

Larus, J. R., & Ball, T. (1994). Rewriting executable files to measure program behavior. *Software, Practice & Experience, 24*(2), 197–218. doi:10.1002/spe.4380240204

LBNL. (2010). *TCPDUMP & LiBPCAP*. Retrieved March 30, 2010 from http://www.tcpdump.org/

Lee, W., Stolfo, S., & Chan, P. (1997). Learning patterns from Unix process execution traces for intrusion detection. In *AI approaches to fraud detection and risk management* (pp. 50–60). Providence, RI: AAAI Press.

Lee, W., Stolfo, S. J., & Mok, K. W. (2000). Adaptive intrusion detection: A data mining approach. *Journal of Artificial Intelligence Research, 14*(6), 533–567. doi:10.1023/A:1006624031083

Lee, W., & Xiang, D. (2001). Information-theoretic measures for anomaly detection. In *Proceedings of the 2001 Symposium on Research in Security and Privacy* (pp. 130–143), Oakland, CA.

Lee, W., & Xiang, D. (2001). Information-theoretic measures for anomaly detection. In *Proceedings of IEEE Symposium on Security and Privacy* (pp. 130-143).

Lee, W., Stolfo, S. J., & Mok, K. W. (1998). Mining audit data to build intrusion detection models. In *Proceedings of the 4th International Conference on Knowledge Discovery and Data Mining (KDD'98),* New York, NY.

Lei, J. Z., & Ghorbani, A. (2004). Network intrusion detection using an improved competitive learning neural network. In *Proceedings of the IEEE 2nd Annual Conference on Communication Networks and Services Research (CNSR '04)* (pp.190–197). Washington, DC: IEEE-Computer Society.

Leinwand, A., & Conroy, K. F. (1996). *Network management: A practical perspective.* New York, NY: Addison-Wesley.

Levon, J., & Elie, P. (2009). *Oprofile: A system-wide profiler for Linux systems.* Retrieved November 25, 2010, from http://oprofile.sourceforge.net/news/.

Li, Y., Lu, T., Guo, L., Tian, Z.-H., & Qi, L. (2009). Optimizing network anomaly detection scheme using instance selection mechanism.In *Proceedings of the Global Communications Conference* (pp. 1-7).

Li, Z., Goyal, A., & Chen, Y. (2007). Honeynet-based botnet scan traffic analysis. *Botnet Detection, 36,* 25–44. New York, NY: Springer.

Liao, Y., & Vemuri, V. R. (2002). Use of K-nearest neighbor classifier for intrusion detection, *Computers and Security - COMPSEC, 21*(5), 439–448.

Lincoln Laboratory. (1998-2000). *MIT. DARPA intrusion detection data.* Retrieved December 11, 2010, from http://www.ll.mit.edu/mission/communications/ist/corpora/ideval/data/index.html

Linux Audit Subsystem. (2004). *Linux audit subsystem design documentation for Kernel 2.6.* Retrieved November 25, 2010, from http://www.uniforum.chi.il.us/slides/HardeningLinux/LAuS-Design.pdf.

Liu, L., Chen, S., Yan, G., & Zhang, Z. (2008). Execution-based bot-like malware detection. *Information Security* (LNCS 5222, pp. 97-113). Berlin/Heidelberg, Germany: Springer-Verlag.

Lixia, X., Dan, Z., & Hongyu, Y. (2009). *Research on SVM based network intrusion detection classification.* 6th International Conference on Fuzzy Systems and Knowledge Discovery (pp. 362–366).

Love, R. (2005). *Linux kernel development* (2nd ed.). Utah, USA: Novell Press.

Ltrace. (2002). *ltrace – Default branch.* Retrieved November 25, 2010, from http://freshmeat.net/projects/ltrace/.

Compilation of References

Lu, W., Tavallaee, M., Rammidi, G., & Ghorbani, A. A. (2009). Botcop: An online botnet traffic classifier. In *7th Annual Communication Networks and Services Research Conference (CNSR '09)* (pp. 70-77).

Luk, C.-K., Cohn, R., Muth, R., Patil, H., Klauser, A., & Lowney, G. …Hazelwood, K. (2005). Pin: Building customized program analysis tools with dynamic instrumentation. In *Proceedings of the 2005 ACM SIGPLAN Conference on Programming Language Design and Implementation (PLDI'05)* (pp. 190–200). Chicago, IL, USA: ACM.

Lundin Barse, E. (2004). *Logging for intrusion and fraud detection.* PhD thesis, Chalmers University of Technology, Göteborg, Sweden.

Lundin Barse, E., & Jonsson, E. (2004). Extracting attack manifestations to determine log data requirements for intrusion detection. In *Proceedings of the 20th Annual Computer Security Applications Conference (ACSAC 2004)* (pp. 158–167). Tucson, AZ, USA: IEEE.

Luxenburger, R., & Schegner, P. (2004). A new intelligent auto-reclosing method considering the current transformer saturation. *8th International Conference on Developments in Power Systems Protection* (vol. 2, pp. 583-586).

Maggi, F., Robertson, W., Kruegel, C., & Vigna, G. (2009). Protecting a moving target: Addressing Web application concept drift. In *Proceedings of the 12th International Symposium on Recent Advances in Intrusion Detection (RAID 2009)*, Saint-Malo, Brittany, France.

Mahoney, M. V., & Chan, P. K. (2003, September). An analysis of the 1999 DARPA/Lincoln laboratory evaluation data for network anomaly detection. In *Proceedings of the 6th International Symposium on Recent Advances in Intrusion Detection* (pp. 220-237), Pittsburgh, PA.

Masud, M. M., Gao, J., Khan, L., Han, J., & Thuraisingham, B. (2008). A practical approach to classify evolving data streams: Training with limited amount of labeled data. In *8th IEEE International Conference on Data Mining (ICDM '08)* (pp. 929–934).

Mathew, S., Petropoulos, M., Ngo, H. Q., & Upadhyaya, S. (2010). A data-centric approach to insider attack detection in database systems. In *Proceedings of the 13th International Symposium on Recent Advances in Intrusion Detection (RAID 2010)*, Ottawa, Ontario, Canada.

Maymounkov, P., & Mazieres, D. (2002). A Peer-to-peer Information System based on the XOR Metric. In *Proceedings of IPTPS02*. Cambridge, USA: Kademlia.

Mazzariello, C. (2008). Irc traffic analysis for botnet detection. In *4th International Conference on Information Assurance and Security (ISIAS '08)* (pp. 318-323).

McCanne, S., & Jacobson, V. (1993). The BSD packet filter: A new architecture for user-level packet capture. In *Proceedings of the USENIX Winter 1993 Conference (USENIX'93)* (pp. 259–270). San Diego, CA, USA: USENIX Association.

McGregor, A., Hall, M., Lorier, P., & Brunskill, J. (2004). Flow clustering using machine learning techniques. In *Passive and Active Network Measurement* (LNCS, pp. 205-214). Berlin/Heidelberg, Germany: Springer-Verlag.

McKusick, M. K., Bostic, K., Karels, M. J., & Quarterman, J. S. (1996). *The design and implementation of the 4.4BSD operating system*. Boston, MA: Addison-Wesley.

McMillan, R. (2008). *CIA says hackers pulled plug on power grid. IDG News Service*, Retrieved January 19, 2008, from http://www.networkworld.com.

Middlemiss, M., & Dick, G. (2003). *Feature selection of intrusion detection data using a hybrid genetic algorithm/KNN approach: Design and application of hybrid intelligent systems* (pp. 519–527). Amsterdam, The Netherlands: IOS Press.

Mielke, C., & Chen, H. (2008). Botnets, and the cybercriminal underground. In *IEEE International Conference on Intelligence and Security Informatics (ISI 2008)* (pp. 206-211).

Mitrokotsa, A., Komninos, N., & Douligeris, C. (2007). *Intrusion detection with neural networks and watermarking techniques for MANET*. International Conference on Pervasive Services (p. 966).

Mogul, J. C., Rashid, R. F., & Acetta, M. J. (1987). The packet filter: An efficient mechanism for user-level network code. *ACM SIGOPS Operating Systems Review, 21*(5), 39–51. doi:10.1145/37499.37505

Momenzadeh, A., Javadi, H. H. S., & Dezfouli, M. A. (2009). *Design an efficient system for intrusion detection via evolutionary fuzzy system*. 11th International Conference on Computer Modeling and Simulation (pp. 89–94).

Moore, R. J. (2001). A universal dynamic trace for Linux and other operating systems. In *Proceedings of the FREENIX Track: 2001 USENIX Annual Technical Conference* (pp. 297–308). Boston, MA: USENIX Association.

Motta Pires, P. S., & Oliveira, L. A. H. G. (2006). *Security aspect of SCADA and corporate network interconnection: An overview*. International Conference on Dependability of Computer Systems (pp. 127-134).

Muthuprasanna, M., Ke, W., & Kothari, S. (2006). *Eliminating SQL injection attacks – A transport defense mechanism*. 8th International Symposium on Web Site Evolution (pp. 22-23).

Mutz, D., Vigna, G., & Kemmerer, R. (2003). An experience developing an IDS stimulator for the black-box testing of network intrusion detection systems. In *Annual Computer Security Applications Conference* (pp. 374-383), Las Vegas, NV.

Nadkarni, K., & Mishra, A. (2004). *A novel intrusion detection approach for wireless ad hoc networks*. Wireless Communications and Networking Conference (pp. 831–836).

Nassar, M., State, R., & Festor, O. (2007). *VoIP honeypot architecture*. International Symposium on Integrated Network Management (pp. 109-118).

National Computer Security Center. (1988). *A guide to understanding audit in trusted systems* (Tech. Rep. NCSC-TG-001). National Computer Security Center (NCSC).

Compilation of References

Nazario, J. (2006). *Botnet tracking: Tools, techniques, and lessons learned (Tech. Rep.)*. Chemsford, MA: Arbor Networks.

Nhat, V. D. M., & Lee, S. (2005). Two-dimensional weighted PCA algorithm for face recognition. In *Proceedings of the 2005 IEEE International Symposium on Computational Intelligence in Robotics and Automation*, Espoo, Finland (pp. 219 - 223).

Niccolini, S., Garroppo, R. G., Giordano, S., Risi, G., & Ventura, S. (2006). *SIP intrusion detection and prevention: Recommendation and prototype recommendation.* 1st Workshop on VoIP Management and Security (pp. 47-52).

Nilsson, D. K., & Larson, U. E. (2008a). Conducting forensic investigations of cyber attacks on automobile in-vehicle networks. In *Proceedings of the 1st ACM International Conference on Forensic Applications and Techniques in Telecommunications, Information and Multimedia (e-Forensics 2008)* (pp. 1–6). Adelaide, Australia: ACM.

Nilsson, D. K., & Larson, U. E. (2008b). Simulated attacks on CAN-buses: Vehicle virus. In *Proceedings of the 5th IASTED Asian Conference on Communication Systems and Networks (AsiaCSN 2008)* (pp.66–72). Langkawi, Malaysia: IASTED.

Ning, P., Cui, Y., & Reeves, D. S. (2002, November). Constructing attack scenarios through correlation of intrusion alerts. In *CCS'02* (pp. 245-254), Washington, DC.

NRG. (2011). *NRG Lab*. Retrieved February 2011, from http://nrg.iust.ac.ir/sip-security

Nucci, A., & Bannerman, S. (2007). Controlled chaos. *IEEE Spectrum, 44*(12), 42–48. doi:10.1109/MSPEC.2007.4390022

Nychis, G., Sekar, V., Andersen, D., Kim, H., & Zhang, H. (2008). *An empirical evaluation of entropy-based traffic anomaly detection*. Internet Measurement Conference, ACM-SIGCOMM (pp. 151-156).

Onut, I. V., & Ghorbani, A. A. (2007). A feature classification scheme for network intrusion detection. *International Journal of Network Security, 5*, 1–15.

Onut, I. V., & Ghorbani, A. A. (2006). *Toward a feature classification scheme for network intrusion detection.* 4th Annual Communication and Networks and Service Research Conference (p. 8).

Otrok, H., Debbabi, M., Assi, C., & Bhattacharya, P. (2007). *A cooperative approach for analyzing intrusion in mobile ad hoc networks.* 27th International Conference on Distributing Computing Systems Workshops (p. 86).

Ousterhout, J. K., Costa, H. D., Harrison, D., Kunze, J. A., Kupfer, M., & Thompson, J. G. (1985). A trace-driven analysis of the UNIX 4.2 BSD file system. *ACM SIGOPS Operating Systems Review, 19*(5), 15–24. doi:10.1145/323627.323631

Paez, R., & Torres, M. (2009). *Laocoonte: An agent based intrusion detection system*. International Symposium on Collaborative Technologies and System (pp. 217–224).

Palpanas, T., Papadopoulos, D., Kalogeraki, V., & Gunopulos, D. (2003). Distributed deviation detection in sensor networks. *SIGMOD Record, 32*(4), 77–82. doi:10.1145/959060.959074

Panchamukhi, P. S. (2004). *Kernel debugging with Kprobes*. Retrieved November 25, 2010, from http://www.ibm.com/developerworks/linux/library/l-kprobes.html.

Paninski, L. (2003). Estimation of entropy and mutual information. *Neural Computation, 15*, 1191–1253. doi:10.1162/089976603321780272

Paulson, L. D. (2002). Stopping intruders outside the gates. *Computer, 11*(35), 20–22. doi:10.1109/MC.2002.1046967

Peisert, S. P. (2007). *A model of forensic analysis using goal-oriented logging.* PhD thesis, University of California, San Diego, CA.

Piromsopa, K., & Enbody, R. J. (2006). *Arbitrary copy: Buffer-overflow protections.* International Conference on Electro/Information Technology (pp. 580-584).

Piromsopa, K., & Enbody, R. J. (2006). *Buffer-overflow protection: The theory.* International Conference on Electro/Information Technology (pp. 454-458).

Piscaglia, P., & Maccq, B. (1996). Multiresolution lossless compression scheme. *International Conference on Image Processing* (vol. 1, pp. 69-72).

Pokrajac, D., Lazarevic, A., & Latecki, L. (2007). Incremental local outlier detection for data streams, In *IEEE symposiums on computational Intelligence and Data Mining (CIDM'07)* (pp. 504-515), Honolulu, HI.

Pollet, J. (2002). *Developing a solid SCADA security strategy.* 2nd International Society of Automation Sensors for Industry Conference (pp. 148-156).

Price, K. E. (1997). *Host-based misuse detection and conventional operating systems' audit data collection.* Master's thesis, Purdue University, West Lafayette, IN.

Punti, G., Gil, M., Martorell, X., & Navarro, N. (2002). *Gtrace: Function call and memory access traces of dynamically linked programs in ia-32 and ia-64 Linux* (Tech. Rep. UPC-DAC-2002-51). Barcelona, Spain: Polytechnic University of Catalonia.

Que, D., Chen, B., & Hu, J. (2008). A novel single training sample face recognition algorithm based on modular weighted (2D) PCA. *9th International Conference on Signal Processing, 2*(3), 1552-1555.

Ramana, R. K., Singh, S., & Varghese, G. (2007). On scalable attack detection in the network. *Association for Computing Machinery Transactions on Networking, 1*(15), 31–44.

Ramaswamy, S., Rastogi, R., & Kyuseok, S. (2000). *Efficient algorithms for mining outliers from large data sets.* SIGMOD Conference (pp. 427-438), Dallas Texas.

Ransbottom, J. S., & Jacoby, G. A. (2006). *Monitoring mobile device vitals for effective reporting.* Military Communication Conference (pp. 1-7).

Compilation of References

RealSecure. (2006). *IBM Internet security systems: Ahead of the threat.* Retrieved January 5, 2006, from http://www.iss.net/

Rencher, A. C. (2002). Methods of multivariate analysis (2nd ed.). *Wiley series in probability and mathematical statistics.* Hoboken, NJ: John Wiley & Sons Inc.

Rhea, S., Geels, D., Roscoe, T., & Kubiatowicz, J. (2004, June). Handling churn in a DHT. In *Proceedings of USENIX Technical Conference.*

Risso, F., & Degioanni, L. (2001). An architecture for high performance network analysis. In *Proceedings of the 6th IEEE Symposium on Computers and Communications (ISCC'01).* Hammamet, Tunisia: IEEE.

Roesch, M. (1999). *Snort - Lightweight intrusion detection for networks.* Paper presented in 13th USENIX Conference on System Administration (pp. 229-238). Retrieved from http://www.snort.org/

Roesch, M. (1999). Snort-lightweight intrusion detection for networks. In *13th Systems Administration Conference (LISA '99)* (pp. 229-238).

Rosenberg, J., Schulzrinne, H., Camarillo, G., Johnston, A., Peterson, J., & Spark, R. ...Schooler, E. (2002). *RFC 3261, Session Initiation Protocol.* Retrieved from http://www.ietf.org/rfc/rfc3261.txt

Rubini, A., & Corbet, J. (2001). *Linux device drivers* (2nd ed.). Sebastopol, CA, USA: O'Reilly.

Russinovich, M. E., & Solomon, D. A. (2005). *Microsoft Windows internals* (4th ed.). USA: Microsoft Press.

Russinovich, M., & Cogswell, B. (2010). *Process monitor.* Retrieved November 25, 2010, from http://technet.micrsoft.com/en-us/sysinternals/bb896645.aspx.

Sampathkumar, V., Bose, S., Anand, K., & Kannan, A. (2007). *An intelligent agent based approach for intrusion detection and prevention in ad hoc networks.* International Conference on Signal Processing Communications and Networking (pp. 534-536).

SANS. 2006). *SANS consensus project Information System audit logging requirements.* Retrieved November 24, 2010, from http://www.sans.org/resources/policies/info_sys_audit.pdf.

Satti, M. M., & Garner, B. J. (2001). *Information security on Internet enterprise managed intrusion detection system (EMIDS).* International Multi-topic Conference (pp. 234-238).

Schmoyer, T. R., Lim, Y.-X., & Owen, H. L. (2004). *Wireless intrusion detection and response: A classic study using main-in-the-middle attack.* Wireless Communications and Networking Conference (pp. 883 – 888).

Schroeder, B. A. (1995). On-line monitoring: A tutorial. *Computer, 28*(6), 72–78. doi:10.1109/2.386988

Sekar, R., Gupta, A., Frullo, J., Shanbhag, T., Tiwari, A., Yang, H., & Zhou, S. (2002). Specification-based anomaly detection: A new approach for detecting network intrusions, In *Proceedings of the 9th ACM Conference on Computer and Communications Security* (pp. 265-274).

Shahrestani, A., Ramadass, S., & Feily, M. (2009). A survey of botnet and botnet detection. In *3rd International Conference on Emerging Security Information, Systems and Technologies (SECURWARE '09)* (pp. 268-273).

Shannon, C. (1948). A mathematical theory of communication. *Bell System Technical Journal, 27*, 379-423, & 623-656.

Shawn, O. (2010). *Tcptrace*. Retrieved March 30, 2010 from http://www.tcptrace.org/

Shepherd, A. D., Lane, S. E., & Steward, J. S. (1990). *A new microprocessor relay for overhead line SCADA application*. Distribution Switchgear Conference (pp. 100–103).

Sher, M., & Magedanz, T. (2007). *Protecting IP Multimedia Subsystem (IMS) server delivery platform from time independent attacks.* 3rd International Symposium on Information Assurance and Security (pp. 171-176).

Sisalem, D., Floroiu, J., Kuthan, J., Abend, U., & Schulzrinne, H. (2009). *SIP Security* (pp. 225–290). Hoboken, NJ: John Wiley & Sons. doi:10.1002/9780470516997.ch8

Smith, M. D. (1991). *Tracing with pixie* (Tech. Rep. CSL-TR-91-497). Palo Alto, CA: Stanford University.

Snort. (2002). *Snort - The de facto standard for intrusion detection/prevention.* Retrieved August 16, 2010, from http://www.snort.org/

SSAC. (2008). *Ssac advisory on fast flux hosting and dns* (Tech. Rep.). ICANN Security and Stability Advisory Committee. Retrieved on March, 2008 from http://www.icann.org/en/committees/security/ssac-documents.htm.

Stallings, W. (2003). *Cryptography and network security: Principles and practices.* India: Pearson Education, Inc.

Stinson, E., & Mitchell, J. (2008). Towards systematic evaluation of the evadability of bot/botnet detection methods. In *Proceedings of the 2nd Conference on USENIX Workshop on Offensive Technologies (WOOT '08)* (pp. 1-9). Berkeley, CA: USENIX Association.

Stoica, I., Morris, R., Karger, D., Kaashoek, M. F., & Balakrishnan, H. (2001, March). *Chord: A scalable peer-to-peer lookup service for Internet applications* (Tech. Rep. TR-819). Cambridge, MA: MIT.

Stone-Gross, B., Cova, M., Cavallaro, L., Gilbert, B., Szydlowski, M., & Kemmerer, R. ... Vigna, G. (2009). Your botnet is my botnet: Analysis of a botnet takeover. In *Proceedings of the 16th ACM Conference on Computer and Communications Security (CCS '09)* (pp. 635-647). New York, NY: ACM.

Compilation of References

Strace. (2010). *Strace – Default branch*. Retrieved November 25, 2010, from http://sourceforge. net/projects/strace.

Strayer, W., Lapsely, D., Walsh, R., & Livadas, C. (2007). Botnet detection based on network behavior. *Advances in Information Security, 36*, 1-24. New York, NY: Springer.

Sun, B., Xiao, Y., & Wang, R. (2007). Detection of fraudulent usage in wireless networks. *Transactions on Vehicular Technology, 6*(56), 3912–3923. doi:10.1109/TVT.2007.901875

Sun Microsystems. (1995). *SunSHIELD basic security module guide*. CA: Mountain View.

Sun Microsystems. (1988). SunOS Reference Manual: *The Network interface tap*.

Sun, L., & Liu, G. (2010). *Visual object tracking based on incremental kernel PCA*. Paper presented at the 2010 International Workshop on Content-Based Multimedia Indexing (pp. 1-6).

Syscalltrack. (2010). *Syscalltrack*. Retrieved November 25, 2010, from http://syscalltrack. sourceforge.net.

Tan, K. M. C., Killourhy, K. S., & Maxion, R. A. (2002). Undermining an anomaly-based intrusion detection system using common exploits. In *Proceedings of the 5th International Symposium on Recent Advances in Intrusion Detection* (pp. 54–73). Zurich, Switzerland: Springer-Verlag.

Tang, J., Chen, Z., Fu, A., & Cheung, D. W. (2002). *Enhancing effectiveness of outlier detections for low density patterns*. Pacific-Asia Conference on Knowledge Discovery and Data Mining (PAKDD), Taipei, Taiwan.

TCPDUMP. (2010). TCPDUMP & LibCAP. Retrieved February 2011, from http://www.tcp-dump.org/

The Freenet Project. (2004). *Freenet: The free network*. Retrieved August 16, 2010, from http:// freenetproject.org/

The giFT project. (2006). *Open-source implementation of the FastTrack protocol*. Retrieved August 16, 2010, from http://developer.berlios.de/projects/gift-fasttrack/

Thottan, M., & Ji, C. (2003). Anomaly detection in IP networks. *IEEE Transactions on Signal Processing, 51*(8), 2191–2204. doi:10.1109/TSP.2003.814797

Trac Project. (2003). *Libtrace*. Retrieved December 11, 2010, from http://www.wand.net.nz/ trac/libtrace

Tront, J. G., & Marchany, R. C. (2004). *Internet security: Intrusion detection and prevention*. 37th Annual Hawaii International Conference on System Sciences (p. 188).

Tsang, C.-H., & Kwong, S. (2005). *Multi-agent detection system in industrial network using ant colony clustering approach and unsupervised feature extraction*. International Conference on Industrial Technology (ICIT '05) (pp. 51–56).

Tukey, J. W. (1977). *Exploratory data analysis*. Addison-Wesley Series in Behavioral Science.

Van de Plas, R., De Moor, B., & Waelkens, E. (2007). Imaging mass spectrometry based exploration of biochemical tissue composition using peak intensity weighted PCA, In *Proceedings of the 3rd IEEE/NIH BISTI Life Science Systems and Applications Workshop(LISA '07)* (pp. 209 - 212), Bethesda, Maryland.

Velarde-Alvarado, P., Vargas-Rosales, C., Torres-Román, D., & Martinez-Herrera, A. (2008). Entropy-based profiles for intrusion detection in LAN traffic. *Advances in Artificial Intelligence: Algorithms and Applications. Research in Computing Science, 40*, 119–130.

Velarde-Alvarado, P., Vargas-Rosales, C., Torres-Roman, D., & Martinez-Herrera, A. (2009). Detecting anomalies in network traffic using the method of remaining elements. *IEEE Communications Letters, 13*(6), 462–464. doi:10.1109/LCOMM.2009.090689

Velarde-Alvarado, P., Vargas-Rosales, C., Torres-Roman, D., & Martinez-Herrera, A. (in press). IP traffic anomaly exposure, an information theoretic-based approach. *Journal of Applied Research and Technology*.

Velarde-Alvarado, P., Vargas-Rosales, C., Torres-Román, D., & Muñoz-Rodríguez, D. (2008). Entropy based analysis of worm attacks in a local network. *Research in Computing Science, 34*, 225–235.

Villamarin-Salomon, R., & Brustoloni, J. (2008). Identifying botnets using anomaly detection techniques applied to dns traffic. In *Proceedings of the 5th IEEE Consumer Communications and Networking Conference (CCNC 2008)* (pp. 476–481).

Vlachos, V., & Spinellis, D. (2007). A PROactive malware identification system based on the computer hygiene principles. *Information Management & Computer Security, 15*(4), 295–312. doi:10.1108/09685220710817815

Vogels, W. (2000). File system usage in Windows NT 4.0. *ACM SIGOPS Operating Systems Review, 34*(2), 17–18. doi:10.1145/346152.346177

Vokorokos, L., Kleinova, A., & Latka, O. (2006). *Network security on the intrusion detection system level.* International Conference on Intelligent Engineering Systems (pp. 534-536).

Wagner, A., & Plattner, B. (2005). Entropy based worm and anomaly detection in fast IP networks. In *Proceedimgs of the 14th IEEE International WorksShop on Enabling Tech.: Infrastructure for Collaborative Enterprise* (pp. 172 – 177).

Wagner, D., & Soto, P. (2002). Mimicry attacks on host-based intrusion detection systems. In *9th ACM Conference on Computer and Communications Security* (pp. 255–264). Washington, DC: ACM.

Wall, D. W. (1989). *Link-time code modification (Tech. Rep.-Res. Rep. 89/17)*. Palo Alto, CA: DEC Western Research Laboratory.

Wang, Y. (2009). *Statistical techniques for network security. Modern statistically-based intrusion detection and protection*. Hershey, PA: IGI Global.

Compilation of References

Wang, H.-Y., & Wu, X.-J. (2005). Weighted PCA space and its application in face recognition. In *Proceedings of the 4th International Conference on Machine Learning and Cybernetics* (pp. 4522–4527), Guangzhou, China.

Wang, K., & Stolfo, S. (2004). Anomalous payload-based network intrusion detection. In E. Jonsson, A. Valdes, & M. Almgren (Eds.), *Recent Advances in Intrusion Detection* [REMOVED HYPERLINK FIELD](LNCS 3224, pp. 203–222). Berlin/Heidelberg, Germany: Springer-Verlag.

Wang, W., Zhang, X., Gombault, S., & Knapskog, S. J. (2009). *Attribute normalization in network intrusion detection*, 10th International Symposium on Pervasive Systems, Algorithms and Networks (ISPAN) (pp. 448-453).

Weaver, N., Paxson, V., & Sommer, R. (2007). *Work in progress: Bro-LAN Pervasive network inspection and control for LAN traffic* (pp. 1–2). Securecomm and Workshops.

Weber, W. (1999). *Firewall basics*. 4th International Conference on Telecommunications in Modern Satellite, Cable and Broadcasting Services (vol. 1, pp. 300-305).

Wei, W., Xiangliang, Z., Gombault, S., & Knapskog, S. J. (2009). *Attribute normalization in network intrusion detection*. 10th International Symposium on Pervasive Systems, Algorithms, and Networks (pp. 448–453).

Weinberg, Y., Tzur-David, S., Dolev, D., & Anker, T. (2006). *High performance string matching algorithm for a network intrusion prevention system*. Workshop on High Performance Switching and Routing (p. 7).

Wetmore, B. R. (1993). *Paradigms for the reduction of audit trails.* Master's thesis, University of California Davis, Davis, CA.

Wilson, C. (2007). *Botnets, cybercrime, and cyberterrorism: Vulnerabilities and policy issues for congress* (Tech. Rep.). Washington, DC: Library of Congress Congressional Research Service.

Wireshark. (2010). *Wireshark: The world's foremost network protocol analyzer*. Retrieved March 30, 2010, from http://www.wireshark.org/

Wu, J. M. (1995). *Maximum likelihood estimation in the random coefficient regression model via the EM algorithm*. Phd Thesis, Texas Tech University, Lubbock.

Wu, Y.-S., Bagchi, S., Garg, S., Singh, N., & Tsai, T. (2004). *SCIDIVE: A stateful and cross protocol intrusion detection architecture for voice-over-IP environments*, International Conference on Dependable Systems and Networks (pp. 433- 442).

Xiao, J., & Song, H. (2009). A novel intrusion detection method based on adaptive resonance theory and principal component analysis. In *Proceedings of the 2009 WRI International Conference on Communications and Mobile Computing (CMC '09)* (vol. 3, pp. 445-449). Washington, DC: IEEE Computer Society.

Xie, L., & Li, J. (2009). A novel feature extraction method assembled with PCA and ICA for network intrusion detection. In *Proceedings of the 2009 International Forum on Computer Science-Technology and Applications (IFCSTA '09)* (vol. 3, pp. 31-34).

Xinidis, K., Charitakis, I., Antonatos, S., Anagnostakis, K. G., & Markatos, E. P. (2006). An active splitter architecture for intrusion detection and prevention. *Transactions on Dependable and Secure Computing, 1*(3), 31–44. doi:10.1109/TDSC.2006.6

Xu, K., Zhang, Z., & Bhattacharyya, S. (2008). Internet traffic behavior profiling for network security monitoring. *Transactions on Networking, IEEE/ACM, 16*(3), 1241 – 1252.

Yaghmour, K., & Dagenais, M. R. (2000). Measuring and characterizing system behavior using kernel-level event logging. In *Proceedings of the USENIX Annual Technical Conference (ATEC '00)*. San Diego, CA, USA: USENIX Association.

Yang, D., & Qi, H. (2008, December). *A network intrusion detection method using independent component analysis*. Paper presented at the 19th International Conference on Pattern Recognition (ICPR '08) (pp. 1-4), Tampa, FL.

Yau, S. S., & Zhang, X. (1999). *Computer networks intrusion detection, assessment and prevention based on security dependency relation*. Computer Software and Applications Conference (pp. 86–91).

Ye, N., Newman, C., & Farley, T. (2006). A system-fault-risk framework for cyber attack classification. *Information Knowledge System Management, 2*(5), 135–151.

Yee, C. G., Rao, G. V. S., & Radha, K. (2006). *A hybrid approach to intrusion detection and prevention business intelligent applications*. International Symposium on Communications and Information Technologies (pp. 847-850).

Yegneswaran, V., Saidi, H., Porras, P., Sharif, M., Mark, W., & President, V. (2008). *Eureka: A framework for enabling static analysis on malware* (Tech. Rep.). Atlanta, Gerogia: Georgia Institute of Technology.

Yen, S.-J., & Lee, Y. (2009). Cluster-based under-sampling approaches for imbalanced data distributions (LNCS). *Expert Systems with Applications, 36*, 5718–5727. doi:10.1016/j.eswa.2008.06.108

Yoshida, K. (2003). Entropy based intrusion detection. In *Proceedings of IEEE Pacific Rim Conference on Communications, Computers and signal Processing (PACRIM '03)* (vol. 2, pp. 840–843). IEEE Explore.

Yung-Da, W., & Paulik, M. J. (1996). A discrete wavelet model for target recognition. *39th Midwest Symposium on Circuit and Systems* (vol. 2, pp. 835-838).

Zamboni, D. (2001). *Using internal sensors for computer intrusion detection*. PhD thesis, Purdue University, West Lafayette, IN.

Compilation of References

Zanero, S., & Savaresi, S. M. (2004). Unsupervised learning techniques for an intrusion detection system. In *Proceedings of the 2004 ACM symposium on Applied computing* (pp. 412–419). Nicosia, Cyprus: ACM Press.

Zargar, G. R., & Kabiri, P. (2009). *Identification of effective network features to detect smurf attacks*, 2009 IEEE Student Conference on Research and Development (pp.49-52), Malaysia.

Zhang, J., & Wang, H. (2006). Detecting outlying subspaces for high-dimensional data: The new task, algorithms and performance. [KAIS]. *Knowledge and Information Systems*, 333–355. doi:10.1007/s10115-006-0020-z

Zhang, H., Gu, Z., Liu, C., & Jie, T. (2009). *Detecting VoIP-specific denial-of-service using change-point method*, 11ᵗʰ International Conference on Advanced Communication Technology (vol. 2, pp.1059-1064).

Zhang, J., Gao, Q., & Wang, H. (2006).*A novel method for detecting outlying subspaces in high-dimensional databases using genetic algorithm*. IEEE International Conference on Data Mining (pp.731-740), Hong Kong, China.

Zhang, J., Gao, Q., Wang, H., Liu, Q., & Xu, X. (2009). Detecting projected outliers in high-dimensional data streams. *International Conference on Database and Expert Systems Applications* (pp. 629-644).

Zhang, J., Gao, Q., Wang, H., & Wang, H. (2010). Detecting anomalies from high-dimensional wireless net- work data streams: A case study. *Soft Computing - A Fusion of Foundations, Methodologies and Applications - Special Issue on Recent Advances on Machine Learning and Cybernetics, 15*(6).

Zhang, L. (2009). A *sublexical unit based hash model approach for SPAM detection*. PhD Thesis, the University of Texas at San Antonio.

Zhang, L., & Zhang, Y. (2008). *Facial feature extraction with weighted modular two dimensional PCA*, the 2ⁿᵈ International Conference on Bioinformatics and Biomedical Engineering (ICBBE '08) (pp. 1992 – 1995).

Zhang, X., Wang, Z., Gloy, N., Chen, J. B., & Smith, M. D. (1997). System support for automatic profiling and optimization. In *Proceedings of the 16ᵗʰ ACM Symposium on Operating Systems Principles (SOSP '97)* (pp. 15–26). New York, NY, USA: ACM.

Zhao, M., Li, P., & Liu, Z. (2008). Face recognition based on wavelet transform weighted modular PCA, In *Proceedings of the Congress on Image and Signal Processing (CISP '08)* (vol. 4, pp. 589-593).

Zhaoyu, L., & Uppala, R. (2006). *A dynamic countermeasure method for large-scale network attacks*. International Symposium on Dependable, Autonomic and Secure Computing (pp. 163-170).

Zheng-De, Z., Zhi-Guo, L., Dong, Z., & Fei-Teng, J. (2006). *Study on joint prevention technique of information security in SUN*. International Conference on Machine Learning and Cybernetics (pp. 2823-2827).

Zhong, S., Khoshgoftaar, T. M., & Nath, S. V. (2005). A clustering approach to wireless network intrusion detection. *IEEE International Conference on Tools with Artificial Intelligence (ICTAI)* (pp. 190-196).

Zhou, S., Costa, H. D., & Smith, A. J. (1985). *A file system tracing package for Berkeley UNIX (Tech. Rep.).* Berkeley, CA: University of California at Berkeley.

Zhou, C., Liu, Y., & Zhang, H. (2006). *A pattern matching based Network Intrusion Detection System.* 9th International Conference on Control, Automation, Robotics and Vision (pp. 1-4).

Zhou, F., Zhuang, L., Zhao, B. Y., Huang, L., Joseph, A. D., & Kubiatowicz, J. (2003). Approximate object location and spam filtering on peer-to-peer systems. In *ACM Middleware.*

Zhu, C. Kitagawa. H., & Faloutsos, C. (2005). *Example-based robust outlier detection in high dimensional datasets.* IEEE International Conference on Data Mining (pp. 829-832).

Zhu, C., Kitagawa, H., Papadimitriou, S., & Faloutsos, C. (2004). OBE: Outlier by example. *Pacific-Asia Conference on Knowledge Discovery and Data Mining (PAKDD)* (pp. 222-234).

Zhu, Z., Lu, G., Chen, Y., Fu, Z., Roberts, P., & Han, K. (2008). Botnet research survey. In *32nd Annual IEEE International Computer Software and Applications (COMPSAC '08)* (pp. 967-972).

Ziviani, A., Gomes, A., & Monsores, M. (2007). Network anomaly detection using nonextensive entropy. *IEEE Communications Letters, 11*(12), 1034–1036. doi:10.1109/LCOMM.2007.070761

About the Contributors

Peyman Kabiri received his PhD in Computing and MSc in Real time Systems from the Nottingham Trent University, Nottingham-UK in years 2000 and 1996 respectively. He received his BEng in Computer Hardware Engineering from Iran's University of Science and Technology, Tehran-Iran in 1992. He was with the Faculty of Computer Science/University of New Brunswick as project coordinator from early September 2004 till the end of September 2005. His previous academic positions were as follows: Assistant Professor in School of Computer Engineering Iran University of Science and Technology where he is currently an Assistant Professor and Director of the Intelligent Automation Laboratory. He teaches courses in under graduate, post graduate levels and supervises BEng, MSc, and PhD students. He has published a number of journals and conference papers and he was Reviewer for several conferences and journals. His research interests include network intrusion detection, machine learning, remote sensing and robotics.

* * *

Ahmad Akbari received his PhD in Electrical Engineering from the University of Rennes, Rennes, France, in 1995. Dr. Akbari is currently an Associate Professor at Iran University of Science and Technology, Iran. Dr. Akbari works on Speech Processing related research topics (especially speech enhancement) for more than 20 years. His current research interests include Intrusion Detection and Response Systems, VoIP Communications, Next Generation Networks, VoIP and SIP Security and also Data Communications Networks. Dr. Akbari's work has appeared in several peer-reviewed journals and conference proceedings.

Cajetan M. Akujuobi received the BS degree from Southern University, Baton Rouge, LA, in 1980, the MS degree from Tuskegee University, AL, in 1983, and the PhD degree from George Mason University, Fairfax, VA, in 1995, all in electrical engineering, and the MBA degree from Hampton University, Hampton, VA, in 1987. He is a Professor and Dean of the College of Science, Mathematics,

Technology & Engineering at Alabama State University, Montgomery, Alabama. He was a Professor in the Department of Electrical Engineering and was the Founding Director of Analog and Mixed Signal, DSP Solutions and High Speed (Broadband) Communication Programs at Prairie View A & M University, Prairie View, TX. He was also the Founding Director of the Center of Excellence for Communication System Technology Research. His research interests include signal/image processing and communication systems (broadband telecommunications) using such tools as wavelet and fractal transforms. His other research interests are in the areas of digital signal processor solutions, analog mixed-signal systems, and control system-based communications. He was a Participant and collaborative Member of ANSI TIE1.4 Working Group that had the technical responsibility of developing T1.413, Issue 2 ADSL standard. He has been published extensively and has also written many technical reports. He was selected as one of the U.S. representatives for engineering's educational and consultation mission to Asia in 1989. Prof. Akujuobi is a Senior Member of ISA, ASEE, SPIE, and Sigma Xi, the Scientific Research Society. He is one of the founding corporate members of the IEEE Standards Association (IEEE-SA), Industry Advisory Committee (IAC).

Nana K. Ampah is currently working with Jacobs Engineering Group, Houston, Texas, as an Electrical Engineer. He graduated from Prairie View A&M University, Prairie View, Texas, with a PhDEE in Telecommunications and Signal Processing in December, 2008. He is a member of IEEE and belongs to organizations such as Ghana Institute of Engineers - GhIE (Associate Member) and Ghana Institute of Management and Public Administration (GIMPA) Alumni Association (Member). Nana K. Ampah also graduated from Prairie View A&M University with an MSEE in Telecommunications and Signal Processing in May, 2004. He also graduated from Kiev Polytechnic Institute (KPI) in Kiev, Ukraine, in June, 1993, with an MSEE specializing in Power Systems and Networks. He was also awarded a Post-graduate Certificate in Urban Management by GIMPA in June, 2001. He worked with the Electricity Company of Ghana for 8 years and has over 6 years experience in the design, construction, commissioning and management of urban and rural electrification projects. He was a Project Engineer under a World Bank funded urban/rural electrification project from 1996 to 2002. He also worked with Skanska Jensen International as a Materials Coordinator (Consultant) on a World Bank funded rural electrification project in 1997. He is currently doing research work in the network security area involving the development of Intrusion Detection and Prevention Systems (IDS/IPS) for Homeland Security and Enterprise Networks.

Hassan Asgharian received his MSc in Computer Engineering from Amirkabir University of Technology (AUT) in 2009 and he also has got his BSc from Computer

Engineering Department of Iran University of Science and Technology (IUST) in 2006. Currently he is a PhD candidate in computer engineering in IUST and working as a Research Assistant in the Network Research Group (NRG) of the Research Center of Information Technology (RCIT) of Computer Engineering Department in Iran University of Science and Technology.

Zoha Asgharian received her MSc in Computer Engineering from Iran University of Science and Technology, Iran, in 2011 and she also has got her BSc from the Computer Engineering Department of Iran University of Science and Technology in 2008. She worked as a Research Assistant in the Network Research Group (NRG) of the Research Center of Information Technology (RCIT) Lab in Computer Engineering Department in Iran University of Science and Technology.

Marcelo Campo received a PhD degree in Computer Science from the Universidade Federal do Rio Grande do Sul, Porto Alegre, Brazil, in 1997 and the Systems Engineer degree from the UNICEN, in 1988. He is an Associate Professor at UNICEN and Head of the ISISTAN Research Institute. He is also a Research Fellow of the CONICET. His research interests include intelligent aided software engineering, software architecture and frameworks, agent technology and software visualization.

Zoltán Czirkos is a PhD candidate and Assistant Lecturer at the Budapest University of Technology and Economics, Department of Electron Devices. His main fields of interest are programming languages, operating system security and peer to peer communication. In 2005, he participated the Proceedings of the Conference of Scientific Circle of Students, with the paper 'Development of P2P Based Security Software', and received the second award. He published several technical papers and wrote chapters as co-author in the field of the collaborative security.

Mehran Garmehi received his BS degree in computer engineering in Shahid Beheshti Tehran University Tehran and the MS degree in computer architecture from Sharif University of Technology, Tehran. He is currently a PHD student in Iran University of Science and Technology under supervision of Dr. Analoui. His main research interests include content distribution and delivery, caching and replication in computer networks.

Ali A. Ghorbani currently serves as Dean of the Faculty of Computer Science. His current research focus is Web intelligence, network & information security, complex adaptive systems, and critical infrastructure protection. He authored more than 240 reports and research papers in journals and conference proceedings and has edited eight volumes. He served as General Chair and Program Chair/co-Chair for eight International Conferences and 10 International Workshops. He is the co-inventor of three patents in the area of Web intelligence and network security. He has supervised more than 120 research associates, postdoctoral fellows, and undergraduate and graduate students. Dr. Ghorbani is the Founding Director of Information Security Centre of Excellence at UNB. He is also the coordinator of the Privacy, Security and Trust (PST) network and PST annual conferences. Dr. Ghorbani is the co-Editor-In-Chief of *Computational Intelligence*, an international journal, and Associate Editor of the *International Journal of Information Technology* and *Web Engineering* and the *ISC Journal of Information Security.*

Gábor Hosszú received the MSc degree from Technical University of Budapest in electrical engineering and the Academic degree of Technical Sciences (PhD) in 1992. After graduation he received a three-year grant of the Hungarian Academy of Sciences. Currently he is a full-time Associate Professor at the Budapest University of Technology and Economics. He published several technical papers, chapters and books. In 2001 he received the three-year Bolyai János Research Grant of the Hungarian Academy of Sciences. He leads a number of research projects. His main interests are the Internet-based media-communication, multicast and P2P communication, network intrusion detection systems, character encoding and VHDL based system design.

Erland Jonsson (1946) is Professor of Computer Security and past head of the Department of Computer Engineering at Chalmers University of Technology, Göteborg, Sweden. Prior to taking up his present post, he worked for the ERICSSON Company for almost 20 years with among other things hardware and software design as well as quality assurance for telecommunications and space applications. His present research interests include intrusion detection, security modeling and security metrics. He has supervised over 10 PhD students in these areas. He is or was a member of a number of scientific advisory boards, and is/has been a member of the program or steering committee of a large number of conferences. One example is the International Symposium on Recent Advances in Intrusion Detection (RAID), and he chaired its program committee in 2004. He is a major promoter of the security area in the Nordic countries. Among other things he started NordSec, a Nordic conference and forum for security research and development. Further, he was one of the initiators of SWITS, the Swedish IT Security network for PhD students. Lately he has been active in establishing a Security Arena in Lindholmen Science Park, in close cooperation with industry.

Ulf E. Larson (1975) holds a PhD in Computer Security from Chalmers University of Technology, Göteborg, Sweden. Ulf works as an IT-security consultant focusing on secure application development. His research interests include data collection and data mining, intrusion detection, digital forensics, and secure application development.

Stefan Lindskog (1967) received his Licentiate and PhD degree in Computer Engineering from Chalmers University of Technology, Göteborg, Sweden in 2000 and 2005, respectively. In 2008, he received the Docent degree in Computer Science at Karlstad University, Karlstad, Sweden. He joined the Department of Computer Science at Karlstad University, Sweden, in 1990, where he is currently a full Professor. His research focus is on the design of tunable and adaptable security services as well as on security and performance analysis of security services and protocols. He has authored/coauthored one textbook, five book chapters, and over 45 journal and conference papers.

Alberto Martínez-Herrera received the bachelor's degree in Telecommunications from the Universidad Autónoma del Estado de Hidalgo, Hidalgo, Mexico. His research interests are focused on areas related to cryptology, especially on elliptic curve cryptography and cryptanalysis of symmetric ciphers. He also has been working on network security systems, mainly related to the DNS protocol and developing methods of intrusion detection. He was granted with an ISOC fellowship to attend at the 68th IETF meeting, held in Prague, Czech Republic, at March 2007. Nowadays he is pursuing a PhD in Information Technologies and Communications at the Instituto Tecnológico y de Estudios Superiores de Monterrey (ITESM), Campus Monterrey, Mexico.

Mohsen Moshky received a BS degree in computer engineering in 2005. He received MS degree in artificial intelligence in 2008 from Iran University of Science and Technology. He is currently pursuing the PhD degree from Iran University of Science and Technology, Tehran, Iran. He is a member of intelligent Automation Lab. since 2008. His areas of concentration are pattern recognition and data analysis.

Bijan Raahemi received his PhD in Electrical and Computer Engineering from the University of Waterloo, Canada, in 1997. He then held several research positions in telecommunications industry, including Nortel Networks and Alcatel-Lucent, focusing on Computer Networks Architectures and Services, Dynamics of Internet Traffic, and Performance Analysis of Data Networks. Dr. Raahemi is currently an Associate Professor at University of Ottawa, Canada. His current research interests include data mining, Information Systems, and data communications networks. Dr. Raahemi's work has appeared in several peer-reviewed journals and conference proceedings. He also holds eight patents in Data Communications. He is a Senior

Member of the Institute of Electrical and Electronics Engineering (IEEE), and a Member of the Association for Computing Machinery (ACM).

César Vargas Rosales received a PhD in electrical engineering from Louisiana State University in 1996. Thereafter, he joined the Center for Electronics and Telecommunications at Instituto Tecnológico y de Estudios Superiores de Monterrey (ITESM), Campus Monterrey, Mexico. He is currently the Telecommunications and Microelectronics program Director at ITESM. Dr. Vargas has been a Member of the Sistema Nacional de Investigadores (SNI) since 1997, and is the coauthor of the book Position Location Techniques and Applications. He has carried out research in the area of personal communication systems on CDMA, smart antennas, adaptive resource sharing, location information processing, and multimedia services. His research interests are personal communications networks, position location, mobility and traffic modeling, intrusion detection, and routing in reconfigurable networks. Dr. Vargas is the IEEE Communications Society Monterrey Chapter Head and has been a Senior Member of the IEEE since 2001.

García Sebastián received a System Engineer degree from the UTN FRBA(Universidad Tecnológica Nacional, Facultad Regional Buenos Aires) in 2004. He is Assistant Professor at UNICEN (Universidad Nacional del Centro), Adjunct Professor at UFASTA University, and a Research Fellow of the CONICET (The National Scientific and Technical Research Council). His research interests are botnet detection methods and anomaly detection methods.

Deni Torres-Roman received a PhD degree in telecommunication from Technical University Dresden, Germany in 1986. He was Professor at the University of Oriente, Cuba. Co-author of a book about Data Transmission. He was awarded the Telecommunication Research Prize in 1993 from AHCIET Association and was recipient of the 1995 Best Paper Award from AHCIET Review, Spain. Since 1996 he has been an Associate Professor at Center for Investigation and Advanced Studies (CINVESTAV-IPN). His research interests include hardware and software designs for applications in the telecommunication area. He is a member of the IEEE.

Pablo Velarde-Alvarado is currently a Researcher and full-time Professor at the Area of Basic Sciences and Engineering of the University Autonomous of Nayarit. He received the BTech degree in Electronics Engineering from the University Autonomous of Guadalajara (UAG), in 1993, and the MSc and PhD degrees in Electrical Engineering from the Center for Research and Advanced Studies (CINVESTAV-IPN) at Guadalajara City, in 2001 and 2009, respectively. He is currently a SNI Candidate in the National System of Researchers. His research interests include

IP-Traffic Modeling and design of concise behavior models for Entropy-based Intrusion Detection Systems.

Ji Zhang is currently a Lecturer (Assistant Professor) in the Department of Mathematics and Computing, and the Principal Advisor for Research in Division of ICT Services, University of Southern Queensland (USQ), Australia. His research interests are knowledge discovery and data mining (KDD), databases, information privacy and security. He was a Post-doctoral Research Fellow in CSIRO ICT Center at Hobart, Australia from 2008-2009. He received his degree of PhD from the Faculty of Computer Science at Dalhousie University, Canada in 2008, degree of MSc from Department of Computer Science at National University of Singapore in 2002 and degree of BE from Department of Information Management and Information Systems at the Southeast University, China in 2000. He has published over 50 papers in major peer-reviewed papers in major international journals and conferences.

Alejandro Zunino received a PhD degree in Computer Science from the UNICEN (Universidad Nacional del Centro), in 2003, his MSc in Systems Engineering in 2000 and the Systems Engineer degree in 1998. He is an Adjunct Professor at UNICEN, a Member of ISISTAN Research Institute, and a Research Fellow of the CONICET (The National Scientific and Technical Research Council). He has over 50 papers published in conferences and journals about distributed systems. His research interests are grid computing, service oriented computing, Web services and botnet detection methods.

Index